Netflix and the Re-inventio

Mareike Jenner

Netflix and the Re-invention of Television

Second Edition

Mareike Jenner
Anglia Ruskin University
Cambridge, UK

ISBN 978-3-031-39236-8 ISBN 978-3-031-39237-5 (eBook)
https://doi.org/10.1007/978-3-031-39237-5

Cover image: Jane_Kelly/Getty Images
Cover design by Tom Howey

This Palgrave Macmillan imprint is published by the registered company Springer Nature Switzerland AG
The registered company address is: Gewerbestrasse 11, 6330 Cham, Switzerland

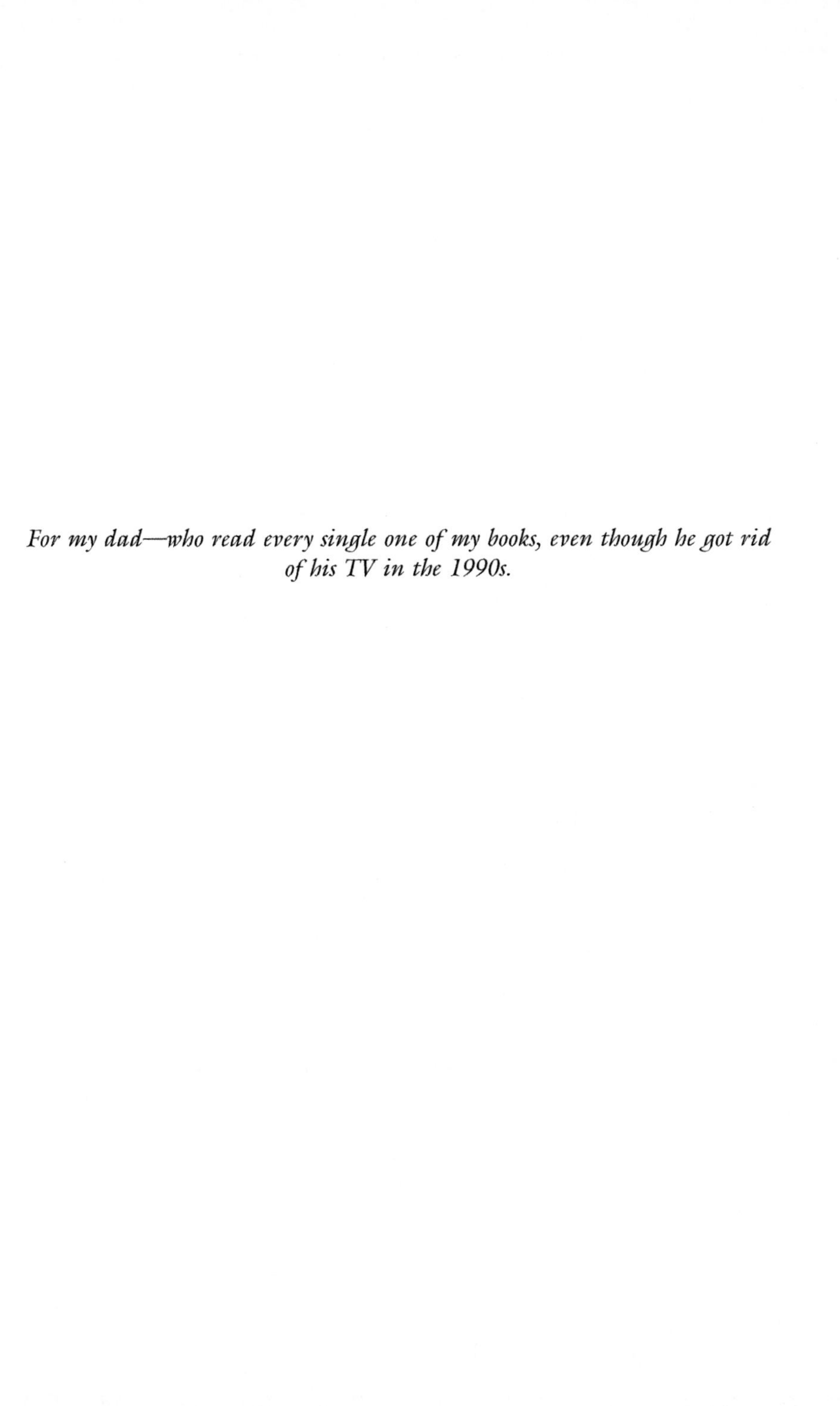

For my dad—who read every single one of my books, even though he got rid of his TV in the 1990s.

Acknowledgements

I really want to thank my editor, Lina Aboujieb, for suggesting this second edition and providing encouragement along the way.

Many thanks to my colleagues at Anglia Ruskin University who have offered much help and advice as I have reorganised my work life over the last few years. I owe many thanks to other friends and colleagues for their consistent support. I specifically want to thank Bärbel Göbel-Stolz and Tanya Horeck for giving me so many helpful pointers and generously sharing research. I also want to thank all participants in the Binge-Watching workshop that took place at ARU in 2018–2019 for offering me so many different ways to think about streaming.

There are more people doing research on streaming and algorithmic culture than I can possibly do justice to in a bibliography, but I want to thank all those who do.

With a lot of thanks and appreciation to my family, for their support as well as Laura, Christina, Judith and Sandra.

Contents

CHAPTER 1

Introduction to the Second Edition: Netflix and the Streaming Wars

Things move fast in contemporary television. The medium is, and has always been, in a perpetual state of change, but the accelerated pace of shifts in online culture and the cultural centrality of streaming makes these particularly visible. Additionally, the tech industry, in particular, tends to package things as 'new' that, at the same time, are perfectly consistent with existing media behaviours and habits (see Gitelman 2006). Disney+ and other streamers rely on media infrastructures built by Netflix, which are consistent with linear television. Netflix' shifting economic prospects throughout 2022 and forward are testament to increased competition, and the reasons for this are varied and multiple as several journalistic articles highlight (see, for example Adalian 2022). While Netflix may recover from its current crisis, what is clear is that its influence in the transnational streaming landscape has diminished. In a post for the *CST* blog (Jenner 2022), I have argued that, among the different streaming platforms, Netflix constitutes the 'normal' of streaming, as the 'baseline' of the shape streaming takes for viewers, a habit, even usual. This position reflects its seniority, but also success in building the existing infrastructures of transnational streaming. Thus, no matter what the future holds for Netflix, its influence on how streaming is organised, not only on an industrial level, but also in the way streaming looks and feels for viewers, remains visible and immense. Thus, its influence on current (and, likely, future) television cannot be underestimated. In this second edition

M. Jenner, *Netflix and the Re-invention of Television*,
https://doi.org/10.1007/978-3-031-39237-5_1

of *Netflix and the Re-invention of Television*, I want to focus on highlighting this influence, which persists independently from the companies' economic short-term position.

I am predominantly interested in theorising what streaming *is* and how it can be understood via the continuities and differences to linear television. Earlier in its company history, Netflix established itself mostly via continuities to linear television, as explored throughout this book. Media reporting often focussed on the way Netflix shapes the current television landscape, for example through its use of binge-watching or its use of algorithms. I am interested here in the histories and perceptions of what we understand as 'television' and how Netflix and its contents and interface shape these ideas. I have previously highlighted how Netflix ties into a broader tradition of what we understand as 'television'. These continuities are explored in this book, for example in the conceptualisation of TV IV in the Introduction, the broader move towards self-scheduling in TV history explored in Part I, the relationship between scheduling and self-scheduling and different meanings of binge-watching explored in Part II, or its engagement with transnational TV in Part III. As this book explores, my interest lies specifically with how the concept of *control* shapes what Netflix, and television more broadly, is. These continuities mean that our idea of what steaming is and can be is shaped by factors beyond industry or technology, but also its social function. Perhaps, what can be added in this Introduction to the Second Edition is also the way Netflix exercises control on how the current television landscape is shaped.

This Introduction to the Second Edition offers an overview of how Netflix operates in the current TV landscape, not on an industry level, but as an influential part of television culture. While I recognise the importance of industry studies for this field, my interest lies more on the conceptual and the way meanings are constructed via the platform and its texts. I also emphasise in what ways, specifically, Netflix influences how transnational streamers operate. To this purpose, this Introduction starts out by outlining Netflix' position in the so-called 'streaming wars', especially the way it can be theorised as 'normality' or a 'baseline' for how streaming is structured. Secondly, I focus on binge-watching, Netflix and the way it influences interfaces and textual structures on different streaming platforms. A particular focus lies with the way public discourse around binge-watching vs. weekly release creates an artificial binary that is not actually visible in narrative structures or production of the eponymous '8-hour-movie' so often talked about in marketing. Importantly, this artificial binary also serves to create two different sides in this supposed war, though most streamers use a mixture of both models. As a third point, this Introduction discusses the way Netflix and other local and transnational streamers shape the way fictional drama on linear television is structured, especially as linear television is a stakeholder usually ignored in the analogy of the streaming wars that captures much of the supposed 'territory' (i.e. subscribers) streamers fight for.

Much has changed in the five years since *Netflix and the Re-invention of Television* came out. Yet, the ways the history of control via ancillary technology and its own emphasis on binge-watching shapes contemporary television, as well as the way it influences the shape and structure of transnational streaming, remains relevant.

Netflix in the Streaming Wars

In March 2020, when national lockdowns were introduced to manage the Covid-19 pandemic in large parts of the world following a model established in Wuhan/China in late 2019, streaming services achieved a new relevance. Netflix series *Tiger King* (Netflix, 2020–21), released just as lockdowns in the US and large parts of Western Europe came into effect, immediately achieved hit status.[1] We cannot know how things would have worked out for the series if it had not had such 'fortunate' (or unfortunate for people stuck in lockdowns) timing. However, as it is, *Tiger King*'s success is at least as much shaped by this context as its contents. But Netflix was not the only streamer that benefitted. With schools closed and children at home while parents worked remotely, we can easily imagine how some families opted for a Disney+ subscription. Disney+ also builds on entire diegetic universes, like the Marvel and Star Wars universes, allowing for an extensive immersion in content for adult viewers and families (see Hunting and Gray 2023). Further, film distributors moved releases online in the face of long-term cinema closures, and Amazon continues to offer 'Blockbuster Releases' on its platform, indicating that the release windows for cinema and streaming releases have

[1] Statista.com provides an overview of Netflix subscribers (https://www.statista.com/statistics/250934/quarterly-number-of-netflix-streaming-subscribers-worldwide/) while Catherine Johnson (2020) has tracked changes in television viewing in the UK.

permanently shifted. The term streaming wars became popular in the run-up to the launch of Disney+ in 2019 to describe competition between different streaming companies but remains prevalent to describe transnational as well as local competition between streamers. The transnational streaming services that make up the cohort that supposedly 'fights' the 'war' are Netflix, Amazon, AppleTV and Disney+, at least at the time of writing. Yet, they remain in competition with various local streamers like Hulu in the US or Britbox in the UK, as well as Sky TV's aggregator app NOW TV (in some areas WOW TV). NOW covers many transnational markets and serves to disseminate, among other series, HBO content in the absence of an HBO Max service in many markets. Yet, NOW also shows live TV, making it incredibly localised. This is in addition to linear television, which remains the preferred way of watching TV and, as medium that commonly broadcasts live, proved an essential tool of political and scientific communications in times of a public health crisis.[2] The focus here is on transnational streamers, though the actors in the streaming wars vary from country to country. Meanwhile, it is often Amazon, AppleTV and Disney+ that stand in direct competition to Netflix in a different way than local streamers and linear television.

As Amanda Lotz (2022, 123) and Karen Petruska (2023) argue, streamers often follow different goals. In her analysis of Amazon Prime, Petruska points out that Amazon tries to tie customers more closely to Amazon products (Kindle, Amazon Music, Audible, etc.), following Jeff Bezos' logic that the more time customers spend on the platform, the more likely they are to buy something: "All of Amazon's Prime benefits serve one end: to situate customers within its corporate ecosystem more fully, firmly, and inescapably" (Petruska 2023, 430).[3] As Neil Landau put it: "while Netflix and Hulu [in the US market] are media companies, Amazon is, first and foremost, a *retail* company" (2015, 17, italics in the original). Meanwhile, Kyra Hunting and Jonathan Gray (2023)

[2] Data on linear viewing in different countries is shared by statista.com. UK-specific, Ofcom produces annual reports on linear TV-watching versus streaming.

[3] Journalist Brad Stone argues this logic is flawed, though I would argue the picture is more complicated as Amazon may publish subscriber numbers to Prime or, in the case of very successful series, viewing figures, but not necessarily how many viewers of *Lord of the Rings: The Rings of Power* (Amazon, 2022-) moved on to also purchase a Kindle, or Kindle books, an audible subscription, or other Amazon products.

point to the various ways Disney+ uses the already existing intertextualities between Disney children's texts that serve to tie viewers from a young age to the brand. Netflix, with much less content at its disposal and no products to sell, follows the models of linear television more closely, and in some markets even experiments with linear TV scheduling. Thus, the way competition is structured differs heavily from linear television, but also makes the metaphor of a streaming 'war' difficult to apply:

> The metaphor of war is highly problematic for all sorts of reasons, not least of which is its failure to acknowledge oligopolistic collaboration, but it also posits all streamers as somehow equivalent armies 'fighting' over the same territory equipped with a similar arsenal. (Hunting and Gray 2023, 650)

Of course, the reality is not only that streamers want different things and, thus, employ different strategies, but also that the 'territory' fought for (subscribers), is not a zero-sum game. Many viewers will hold subscriptions to more than one service. Further, some streamers are more interested to build a positive brand experience for customers than to 'win' the 'war'. Simply put, for a company like Amazon, selling more products and drawing people into its 'consumption universe' of Kindle and Audible books, for example, is ultimately more important than viewing figures. Apple functions in similar ways. This makes it difficult to develop a measure by which to compare the 'success' of platforms. Of course, viewing figures matter as an indicator of the cultural relevance of a text or platform, but considering the limited information available on viewers and the different purposes this serves, the competition between streaming services is complex.

If Netflix is the 'normal' of streaming in this varied field, which is dominated by so many different strategies and interests, then it is useful to understand how it establishes that role. The first aspect of this is the interface and how Netflix 'orders' its texts for viewers. Unlike the early 2010s, when Netflix positioned itself in the market, control is no longer a selling point for streaming, but an expected feature. As explored in this book, control over the schedule is an important aspect of television history. This control is control *without* power, as described and conceptualised in Part I. Viewers exercise control over their immediate environment, but not necessarily over accessibility or availability of programmes. Rather than a feature uniquely tied to Netflix, every streamer now offers control over what to watch when and on which device. The study of interfaces remains an important aspect of studying TV. As Catherine Johnson points out, interfaces:

> … also shape our expectations of online TV more broadly. The layout of an online TV interface and the menus, tabs and buttons that help users navigate within that service offer and encourage certain behavioural choices (to watch, search, browse and so on). (2019, 111)

I argue here that the Netflix interface has significantly impacted transnational streaming and the way it 'orders' texts and structures viewing and privileges and shapes behaviours.

Secondly, Netflix' content in many respects emulates the more 'middlebrow' fare that continues to dominate linear TV. Licensing rights in each territory and long-term availability of older series vary worldwide, but Netflix has also developed its own slate of sitcoms. At the time I was writing the first edition, only a few were available (as discussed in Chapter 9), often mirroring some of the characteristics of so-called 'quality' television and developing visual distinctiveness, at least through opening credits. While its newer sitcoms do not follow this pattern, it reveals a desire to emulate the televisuality of its successful licensed sitcoms *The Office* (NBC, 2005–13) or *Friends* (NBC, 1994–2004). Other offerings span a bandwidth of decidedly televisual programmes from reality TV (*Queer Eye* [Netflix, 2018–], *Selling Sunset* [Netflix, 2019–]), both self-produced and licensed; to true crime documentaries (*Bad Vegan* [Netflix, 2022], *Jimmy Saville: A British Horror Story* [Netflix, 2022]); to crime and action series (*Queen Sono* [Netflix, 2020], *Anatomy of a Scandal* [Netflix, 2022]); soaps and telenovelas (*Virgin River* [Netflix, 2019–], *Monarca* [Netflix 2019–21], *La Venganza de Las Juanas* [Netflix, 2021–]); animation (*BoJack Horseman* [Netflix, 2014–20], *Tuca & Bertie* [Netflix, 2019, Adult Swim, 2021]); kids programming (*Anne with an E* [Netflix, 2017–19]); to television that more easily fits into the category of American 'quality' television (*Maid* [Netflix, 2021], *Dahmer* [Netflix, 2022]); or 'blockbuster' TV (*Stranger Things* [Netflix, 2016–], *Bridgerton* [Netflix, 2019-]). There is, however, a visible emphasis on 'middlebrow' television, which reinforces an idea of 'normality' or 'normal' TV—or at least streaming that comes close to more traditional ideas of television. Importantly, these ideas are formulated around an American notion of what middlebrow TV is. Victoria E.

Johnson (2008) positions this via the ideology of the American Heartland, a geographical and cultural 'middle' in the US. It seems impossible to apply such a geographically bound concept to a transnational streamer, in a, as argued in PART III, decentred media system (see Couldry 2012). However, Netflix generally orients itself on American linear television hierarchies of popular taste (as discussed in Chapter 9), as well as in other areas like ideological concepts of diversity (as discussed in Chapter 10). Further, as Johnson explains, the geographical 'middle' of the US, the Heartland, is more ideological myth than a real place, signifying a certain culture of taste and values, an idea of political 'neutrality'. In the way Netflix employs it even captures the ahistorical transnationalism of its 'grammar of transnationalism' (see Chapters 10 and 12). As an ideological myth, it can be applied to a decentred media system that, in many respects, orients itself on the US. As Johnson outlines, linear television in the US has often tried to position itself in relation to this supposed Heartland. For Netflix, such a focus becomes particularly visible in its early sitcom *The Ranch* (Netflix, 2016–20) which is literally set in the American mid-west and embodies the ideology of the Heartland. Thus, on the one hand, the focus on the cultural middle positions Netflix as 'normal' through its programming. On the other hand, the application itself, the logo and the wider interface are familiar by now, perhaps overly so. Marketing phrases like 'Netflix and chill' have taken on their own cultural meaning. While Netflix remains cagey on viewer numbers, what we can tell from looking at national or international Top 10 the company provides is that these regularly include less 'spectacular' titles like *Virgin River* and *Queer Eye*. Further, we do not actually know, yet, how streaming deals with familiarity. Netflix may very well become a case study in this in the long term, but has itself only produced original programming since 2013.

As the examples of *Friends* and *The Office* show, the idea of rewatching has become central to streamers. In this volume, I argue that the term binge-watching captures a range of practices and, as part of autonomous scheduling, also repeat viewings, the history of which is also explored in Part I. This is tied to broader structures of television, especially in the US, where reruns are common. Netflix' use of these network TV sitcoms shows the continued relevance of reruns in whatever form, even in times when viewers have more ('new' and 'old') content at their disposal than ever before. Further, in a landscape where autonomous scheduling is central, not only do viewers default to reruns, but their structuring to fit models of binge-watching remains central. Importantly, both, *Friends* and *The Office* use narrative structures where a broader narrative is propelled further in episodes, which sets them apart from earlier sitcoms which ended on the reinstatement of the status quo (see Feuer 1986). On linear TV, reruns of both sitcoms remain popular, and it is relevant that both were produced (at least later seasons) around the same time technologies that make self-scheduling easier became available, such as DVDs, DVRs or catch-up services. On streaming, the ongoing narratives make it easy to integrate both sitcoms into structures of binge-watching. By licensing these series in many territories, Netflix managed to draw on network TV's status quo: sitcoms, which are designed to appeal to a mass audience. Further, both have done extremely well on the international licensing market, even though a number of local adaptations of *The Office* exist. As such, both series not only exemplify a status quo of US TV, but also of transnational TV. But Netflix also managed to integrate both into its new 'format' that privileges binge-watching by highlighting already existing narrative structures through its interface. The series, thus, serve to highlight Netflix' associations with linear TV (as explored below), its use of middlebrow culture and its binge-structure.

The way Netflix becomes part of everyday life is, as Roger Silverstone (1994) argues in relation to linear television, via integration of the TV schedule into the practices and habits of viewers. Lothar Mikos and Deborah Castro explore this in their audience research on how binge-watching (often through Netflix) is integrated into everyday life. They tie this specifically to the domestic realm and argue:

> All in all, there is a clear intersection point between the different modes of media use and the rhythms of everyday life. People are not able to overcome the dialectical system, the global structure of quotidian life, meaning that watching television and using streaming services mainly takes place in the evenings during times of recreation, allowing escape attempts from everyday pressures. (2021, 117)

Their transnational research on Dutch and German audiences took place before the lockdowns, but this already shows that binge-watching, often on Netflix, becomes habit for viewers. We can see here, though, how interfaces structure viewing habits to the extent that other streamers have adopted Netflix' system.

Netflix, Binge-Watching and the Streaming Wars

What cannot be denied is Netflix' enormous and lasting influence on viewing patterns, which impacts how content is released. In other words, its use of binge-watching, which developed to become almost synonymous with Netflix. Even though streamers like Disney+ and AppleTV as well as some series on Amazon *(Lord of The Rings: Rings of Power* [Amazon, 2022–], *The Boys* [Amazon, 2019-]), rely on weekly release models, marketing language actually highlights factors about series that makes it 'bingeable': the 8-hour movie, which directors often use to describe their series, would, presumably be meant to be watched sequentially and with little interruption. Release models differ for different streaming services, though interfaces on all platforms encourage sequential viewing by using features such as auto-play.

An important case study here is Amazon. When Netflix first entered the market of what Petruska and Woods call self-produced originals (2019), its main competition (as transnational streamer) was AmazonVideo. Amazon tried to avoid too obviously following into Netflix' footsteps (see Landau 2015, 16–23) and, thus, at first avoided the binge model as release strategy. In parts, this was linked to a conception of AmazonVideo as 'free' bonus when customers signed up to Prime, which offered two-day shipping at no additional cost other than the subscription fee (where possible). As recalled in the journalistic *Amazon Unbound* (Stone, 2021), Jeff Bezos believed that getting customers to sign up to Prime would get them to spend more money on the site more widely. Jonathan Carr writes in 2013 about Amazon's first original series, *Alpha House* (Amazon, 2013–14) in *The New York Times*:

> For Amazon, programming is an add-on, a benefit of being a member of Amazon Prime. In addition to free two-day shipping, the company's 11 million Prime members have access to Amazon Prime Instant Video, with more than 40,000 movies and television episodes, and beginning next week, "Alpha House." The first three episodes will be available on Nov. 15, free to all Amazon customers, and additional episodes will then be available to subscribers of Amazon Prime every week. (Carr 2013)

Carr emphasises the experiment with release models at play here: on the one hand, the strategy bets on 'bingeability' as viewers are meant to sign up to Prime because they want to consume the rest of the series, which usually ends episodes on cliff-hangers. Yet, it also bets on slower release through weekly publication. The series now is available in full to binge. Importantly, AmazonVideo's interface, at the time, meant that the next episode would not play automatically, but viewers had to navigate back to the main page for the series and click on the next episode. As such, it did not nudge, or at least, privilege, binge-watching to the same extent the Netflix interface did. Of course, this was later changed, but also evidences how conflicted Amazon was. In 2013, Netflix absolutely dominated conversation about online TV and established its brand as more or less synonymous with binge-watching (as explored in Part II), which, naturally, made using the term less attractive to other streamers. What has emerged for many platforms is a kind of double-think when it comes to binge-watching that makes visible to what extent Netflix has become associated with the term. On the one hand, fellow streamers rarely use the term binge-watching in a positive manner, as, presumably, they do not want to be associated with a terminology synonymous with its competitor. Thus, the language of weekly release is used as binary opposite to binge-watching. At the same time, texts are structured for sequential viewing and interfaces are structured to encourage binge-watching, including auto-play, a 'skip intro' option as well as a reminder on the main page to 'continue watching' (or equivalents). Importantly, Disney+'s reliance on expansive narrative universes also highlights the viewer responsibility to find a path through linearly structured texts and intertextual networks.

Following patterns of HBO series of the first decade of the 2000s, the narrative unit of most streaming series is less the individual episode, but the season, as Brian G. Rose points out about *The Wire* (HBO, 2004–8):

> Instead of the individual episode, the basic structural unit would be the series as a whole, permitting vast twelve- or thirteen-part story arcs (with some plot strands buried for weeks at a time), kaleidoscopic character groupings (with a shifting cast of more than thirty players), and a quirky belief that viewers needed to work hard to keep up and make thematic connections that were rarely italicized or foregrounded. (Rose 2008, 83)

I have recounted the ways Netflix often employs the narrative structures of complex television before (see Jenner 2020). What is important, though, is the way other streaming services do, too, no matter the release model. What is remarkable is the way that this structural unit also dominates more televisual genres like sitcoms and reality TV. Again, Netflix hardly invented this structure and, in fact, profits from the way sitcoms like *The Office* and *Friends* employ it, but also has reformulated this into a publishing model. Hence, sitcoms like *The Upshaws* (Netflix, 2021-) are distributed in seasons of eight to ten episodes, also with ongoing narratives. The storylines are rarely as complex as in its drama series and storylines only reach across a few episodes, but the expectation of sequential viewing, as discussed below, is visible.

Thus, as much as the release models binge-watching vs. weekly release tend to be presented as binary, they function more as marketing terms than how series are presented. As the example of Amazon shows, the advances of AppleTV and Disney+ into weekly release are hardly unprecedented, even in the world of transnational streaming platforms. They mostly seem to serve as a way to set the streamers apart from Netflix. The artificial binary between release models serves to create and reinforce the narrative of a 'war' between streamers setting the different sides clearly apart from each other. This narrative serves to position Netflix as the 'norm' other streamers react against. Simply put, the release model serves as marketing tool to create 'buzz', but series are still produced for binge-watching. This is different than weekly release of episodes on broadcast television, as the organisational logic of the schedule serves different purposes (as explored in Chapter 8).

Netflix and Linear Television

In order to conceptualise the relationship between Netflix and linear television, it is also useful to contextualise it with other streamers. As Derek Johnson (2018 and 2023) argues, different streamers can be understood as akin to channels. His collection focusses largely on the US, though it also deals with some transnational streamers. However, the big transnational streaming services discussed here are decidedly different from linear television in their economics and their broader functions. As argued above, the streaming wars draw into focus how many streamers are different from linear television as they follow different economic and cultural goals. Yet, what several transnational streaming services have in common is that they function akin to television itself, at least to the consumer. Each of the platforms offers a breadth of content that is equivalent to 'television', even building its own universes, as Disney+ shows, but also the transnational streaming franchises discussed in Chapter 13. Thus, the platforms, from a viewer perspective, are each a channel, but also a complete 'television' on its own. The streaming services exist in parallel and on our TV screens, we can access each like a channel. Even if we access TV via apps on a laptop, tablet or phone screen, they still occur to us as a choice similar to the way we choose channels. Amazon and Apple offer the option to subscribe to different channels while Disney+ offers a variety of collections in addition to programmes ordered as different channels. Thus, the streaming services function both, as channels, and as a whole TV at the same time. It remains difficult to grasp what streaming actually is: is it television itself or is it a group of platforms that are each 'television' by itself? Obviously, this leads back to a question that I grappled with in the Introduction to the First Edition: what is television? 'Television' remains a malleable term defined by complex discursive shifts that currently accommodates a variety of developments in streaming, both similar and different to linear TV. What most transnational streamers have in common is a desire to replace television altogether, which probably leads to the metaphor of war as this is also often understood to have a clearly identifiable 'winner'. This supposed winner then walks away with the largest territory.

Sequential viewing may be the most obvious way the TV III focus on narrative complexity and Netflix' focus on binge-watching have influenced contemporary television, both linear television and local and transnational streaming services (see also Dunleavy 2017). The American television of TV II was often produced to allow for reruns to be inserted into schedules (see Kompare 2005). An example of this are the two endings filmed for the *Magnum, P.I.* (CBS, 1980–8) episode 'Novel Connection' (07/08) in a crossover episode with *Murder, She Wrote* (CBS, 1984–96; 'Magnum on Ice', 03/08) in 1988 (see Kjelstrup 2007). One ending leads directly into the *Murder, She Wrote* episode, which was shown later the same week upon original broadcast. The second ending, however, offers narrative closure at the end of the *Magnum, P.I.* episode, allowing it to be inserted into schedules as rerun, even without the *Murder, She Wrote* episode to offer resolution. Streaming, however, automatically privileges viewing episodes in sequence, even if they were produced differently. Of course, viewing out-of-sequence is perfectly possible and some streamers even have a feature that automatically toggles episodes, but the default option is that, once a series is chosen, the next episode is played automatically. Meanwhile, the default for reruns on broadcast television is markedly different.

Elsewhere, in an analysis of CBS' re-booting of various action series, I argue that series like *MacGyver* (CBS, 2016–21) or *Magnum, P.I.* (CBS,

2018–22, NBC, 2022–3) try to avoid narrative structures that are too complex (Jenner, forthcoming). In an almost defiant, nostalgic move, these series offer more definitive endings to episodes than streaming series. And yet, they cannot escape that, unlike the original versions of these series, they are produced for an aftermarket where sequential viewing is dominant, rather than reruns. This is visible in the way character arcs are developed over the length of seasons. For US network TV, in this case CBS, this is a way streaming influences the way both series are structured. The reaction is both against and to the binge structures: on the one hand promising audiences less complexity and need to pay close attention, on the other hand producing series for sequential viewing. This is important as it points to the way streaming (not just Netflix) influences the structures of all TV. Of course, this development was present before when DVD box sets became an important aftermarket for TV in the early 2000s. The change from out-of-sequence to sequential viewing, which is implicit in the various behaviours and narrative structures captured by the term binge-watching, may be one of the most significant ways in which it has changed the current TV landscape.

As this suggests, TV history remains important here. Much of what sets streamers apart is the historical content streamers make available (from *Friends* to *Scrubs* [NBC, 2001–8, ABC 2009–10] to *Adventures of the Gummi Bears* [NBC, 1985–88, ABC, 1989–90, Syndicated 1990–1] to *The Dick Van Dyke Show* [CBS, 1961–6]). Yet, as hardly all television from TV history is available on platforms, the version of TV history told here is also a heavily curated one (see also Alexander 2016). The adage that history is told by the winners is relevant here, as many series featured were usually ratings successes in the US and elsewhere. Yet, lists circulated on social media also often highlight the successful series of the past that are not available on streaming, usually due to licensing and copyright difficulties. Further, for TV series from outside of the US or series that went directly into syndication, the situation may be even more dire. Individual streamers insert, construct and understand themselves as part of TV history, especially for a legacy production company like Disney. Disney+ makes much of this history, from films and children's TV to all seasons of *The Simpsons* (Fox, 1989–), ordered via different collections. Yet, the removal of racist episodes of TV series (such as an episode involving Blackface from *Golden Girls* [NBC, 1985–92]) or entire films like *Song of the South* [Foster and Jackson, 1946]), show the companies' reluctance to further reflections on its history or the history of film and TV. Netflix does not have the same history but, especially in the US, has removed episodes from series like *Community* (NBC, 2009–15) as well. As such, Netflix is a platform that, at once, aims to insert itself into television history, but like its fellow streamers, tries to eliminate friction with contemporary social values. As much as Disney aiming to deny its historical roots may serve the company, no such gains are visible for Netflix and its curation of content. Its history does not reach that far back and many of its properties (including *Community*) are licensed, not self-produced. Yet, Netflix and other streamers play a vital role in the way TV history is currently understood and constructed, making more content available than ever before, but carefully constructing a version of TV history that not only centralises the US, but also consciously excludes (some) controversial parts of that history.

Changes to the Second Edition

Things have changed, both in the streaming landscape and television studies. The material in the book has been updated throughout to reflect more recent research, as new literature amassed shortly after the First Edition of the book came out with titles like Catherine Johnson's *Online TV* (2019) and Roman Lobato's *Netflix Nations* (2019). New work has been produced in journal articles, as referenced throughout. Additional research, especially in crucial fields like transnational industry studies and audience research, has also been produced. Further, some of the vocabularies and terminologies have become established, such as Petruska and Woods' use of the term self-produced Originals to describe what I have previously termed in-house productions. They also describe false Originals, content Netflix has licensed, but maintains exclusive broadcaster in a market where it sells the programme as Original. I edited the collection *Binge-Watching and Contemporary Television Studies* (2021) which also includes a variety of new insights into the way Netflix influences wider television. Part II on binge-watching has been updated, especially in view of Netflix' perspective on diversity. This, possibly, has been the feature public discourse has most struggled to get to terms with, as the platform, which has been and remains associated with inclusion of LGBTQIA+ characters and hired Ryan Murphy to produce content, has also given voice to transphobic comedy. Further, a platform heavily associated with racial diversity, often produced very recently (*Orange is the New Black* [Netflix 2013–19], *Dear White People* [Netflix, 2017–22]), has also fired many staff of colour and cancelled projects with a focus on diversity as its economic fortunes shifted. Thus, considerations on diversity, the colour-blind casting used especially in costume drama, and visibility politics, have been added in Chapter 10. Part III on transnationalism and Netflix has been updated to consider transnational streaming franchises and the way Netflix reformulates the franchise model and creates networks of meanings with franchises like *Criminal* and *Money Heist*. These are similar to the intertextual networks Hunting and Gray (2023) identify on Disney+ but have their own dynamics. A new chapter has been added to consider this shift in more detail. In this, I also consider Netflix's series in comparison with Amazon and its strategies for *LOL: Last One Laughing*. Aside from differences in genre, this comparison serves to highlight the way different streamers use and structure these franchises in more detail.

Conclusion

The system of 'television' has certainly become more complex since the First Edition of this book came out. Popular discourse often aims to capture this via the use of binaries (binge model vs. weekly release) and binaristic metaphors (such as a 'war' with clearly identifiable antagonists), though these often serve to reduce complicated issues to simplistic ideas about the various interdependencies that govern television. These relationships become even more complex when transnational platforms are considered as part of local economies and television systems. And yet, the theorisations and arguments put forth in this book have hardly become outdated. The economic forces that govern Netflix may shift and change and maybe, eventually, even diminish or completely eradicate the company. No matter what Netflix' role in transnational streaming is in the future, its impact on television will likely be felt for a long time. Thus, even though Netflix' position in the market and viewer perceptions have changed, this book remains relevant. Some of the content here has been revised to reflect changes within the streaming environment and more up-to-date literature has been added. However, the theorisations this book offers remain relevant to the way we can think about Netflix, but also other streaming services in the so-called streaming wars.

This book focusses a lot on the continuities streaming has with television history. The last few years have brought differences more into focus. Yet, both need to be acknowledged to get a clearer view of television history and to develop a more complex way of thinking about streaming services. As I have shown here, the binary thinking that is produced by the streamers and reproduced in popular media is not helpful in understanding what streaming is beyond economic entities. At the time of writing, the world faces price rises for fuel and energy on a massive scale and the resulting global cost-of-living crisis will affect streamers in significant ways. This may very easily shift what the so-called streaming wars are and how different platforms are positioned in the broader system of television. Yet, some aspects will likely stay the same: the importance of viewer control, the relevance of bingeability (no matter the release model) and sequential viewing, or the way streaming platforms understand and implement transnationality. These are not necessarily how individual streamers can set themselves apart to the same degree Netflix set itself apart from linear television a decade ago. Yet, they remain important to streaming, even as this system grows to be increasingly complex.

Bibliography

Adalian, J. 2022. "Netflix's Bad Habits Have Caught up with it." In *Vulture*. https://www.vulture.com/2022/04/netflix-bad-decisions-have-caught-up-with-it.html. Accessed: 01.03.2023

Alexander, N. 2016. "Catered to Your Future Self: Netflix's "Predictive Personalization" and the Mathematization of Taste." In K. McDonald and D. Smith-Rowsey (eds.), *The Netflix Effect: Technology and Entertainment in the 21st Century*, pp. 81–97.

Carr, D. 2013. "With 'Alpha House,' Amazon Makes Bid for Living Room Screens and Beyond." In *The New York Times*. https://www.nytimes.com/2013/11/04/business/media/with-alpha-house-amazon-makes-bid-for-living-room.html?smid=tw-nytmedia&seid=auto&_r=2&pagewanted=all. Accessed: 08.03.2023.

Couldry, N. 2012. *Media, Society, World: Social Theory and Digital Media practice*. Cambridge: Polity, Cambridge.

Dunleavy, T. 2017. *Complex Serial Drama and Multiplatform Television*, 1st ed. Milton: Taylor & Francis Group.

Feuer, J. 1986. "Narrative Form in American Network Television." In C. McCabe (ed.), *High Theory/Low Culture*, 101–114. Manchester: Manchester University Press.

Gitelman, Lisa. 2006. *Always Already New: Media, History, and the Data of Culture*. Cambridge, MA, USA: MIT Press.

Hunting, K. & Gray, J. 2023. "Disney+. Imagining Industrial Intertextuality." In D. Johnson (ed.), *From Networks to Netflix. A Guide to Changing Channels. Second Edition*, Routledge, New York, pp. 650–67.

Jenner, M. forthcoming. *Recycling Middlebrow Culture: Action TV Re-Boots*. Edinburgh University Press, Edinburgh.

Jenner, M. 2022. *'Normality', Netflix and TV*. https://cstonline.net/normality-netflix-and-tv-by-mareike-jenner/. Accessed: 01.03.2023.

Jenner, M. (ed.). 2021. *Binge-Watching and Contemporary Television Studies*. Edinburgh: Edinburgh University Press.

Jenner, M. 2020. "Researching Binge-Watching." *Critical Studies in Television* 25 (3): 267–279.

Johnson, C. 2020. "How Coronavirus Might have Changed TV Viewing Habits for Good—New Research." In *The Conversation*. https://theconversation.com/how-coronavirus-might-have-changed-tv-viewing-habits-for-good-new-research-146040. Accessed: 01.03.2023.

Johnson, C. 2019. *Online TV*. London: Routledge.

Johnson, D. (ed.). 2023. *From Networks to Netflix. A Guide to Changing Channels*, 2nd edn. New York: Routledge.

Johnson, D. 2023. "Introduction." In D. Johnson (ed.), *From Networks to Netflix. A Guide to Changing Channels*. 2nd edn, Routledge, New York, pp. 14–50.

Johnson, D. 2018. "Introduction." In D. Johnson (ed.), *From Networks to Netflix: A Guide to Changing Channels*, 1st edn, pp. 1–22.

Johnson, V.E. 2008. *Heartland TV: Prime Time Television and the Struggle for U.S. Identity*. New York University Press, New York.

Kjelstrup, R.J. 2007. "Challenging Narratives: Crossovers in Prime Time." *Journal of Film and Video* 59 (1): 32–45.

Kompare, D. 2005. *Rerun Nation: How Repeats Invented American Television*, New York, N.Y : Routledge, New York, N.Y.

Landau, N. 2015. *TV Outside the Box*, 1st ed. Routledge.

Lobato, R. 2019. *Netflix Nations: The Geography of Digital Distribution*. New York: New York University Press.

Lotz, A. 2022. *Netflix and Streaming Video. The Business of Subscriber-Funded Video on Demand*. Cambridge: Polity.

Mikos, L., and D. Castro. 2021. "Binge-Watching and the Organisation of Everyday Life." In M. Jenner (ed.), *Binge-Watching and Contemporary Television Studies*, 112–130. Edinburgh: Edinburgh University Press.

Petruska, K. 2023. "Amazon Prime Video. Scale, Complexity, and Television as Widget." In D. Johnson (ed.), *From Networks to Netflix: A Guide to Changing Channels*. 2nd edn. New York: Routledge, pp. 425–45.

Petruska, K. & Woods, F. 2019. "Traveling Without a Passport: 'Original' Streaming Content in the Transatlantic Distribution Ecosystem." In H, M. Hilmes & R.E. Pearson (eds.), *Transatlantic Television Drama: Industries, Programs, & Fans*, Oxford University Press, Oxford, pp. 49–67.

Rose, B.G. 2008. "The Wire." In G.R. Edgerton & J.P. Jones (eds.), *The Essential HBO Reader*, pp. 81–92.
Silverstone, R. 1994. *Television and Everyday Life*. London: Routledge, London.
Stone, B. 2021. *Amazon Unbound: Jeff Bezos and the Invention of a Global Empire*. New York: Simon & Schuster.

Television

Adventures of the Gummi Bears (1985–91), USA: ABC, Syndicated.
Alpha House (2013–14), USA: Amazon.
Anatomy of a Scandal (2022), UK: Netflix.
Anne with an E (2017–19), USA: Netflix.
Bad Vegan (2022), USA: Netflix.
BoJack Hoseman (2014–20), USA: Netflix.
Boys, The (2019–), USA: Amazon.
Bridgerton (2020–), USA: Netflix.
Community (2009–15), USA: NBC.
Dahmer (2022), USA: Netflix.
Dear White People (2017–22), USA: Netflix.
Dick Van Dyke Show, The (1961–6), USA: CBS
Friends (1994–2004), USA: NBC.
Golden Girls (1985–92), USA: NBC.
Saville, Jimmy. 2022. *A British Horror Story*. USA: Netflix.
Lord of the Rings: Rings of Power, (2022–), USA: Amazon.
Maid (2021), USA: Netflix.
Magnum, P.I. (1980–8), USA: CBS.
Magnum, P.I. (2018–23), USA: CBS, NBC.
MacGyver (2016–21), USA: CBS.
Monarca (2019–21), MX: Netflix.
Murder, She Wrote (1984–96), USA: CBS.
Office, The (2005–13), USA: NBC.
Orange is the New Black (2013–19), USA: Netflix.
Queen Sono (2020), SA: Netflix.
Queer Eye (2018–), USA: Netflix.
Ranch, The (2016–20), USA: Netflix.
Scrubs (2001–10), USA: NBC, ABC.
Simpsons, The (1989–), USA: Fox.
Selling Sunset (2019–), USA: Netflix.
Stranger Things (2016–), USA: Netflix.
Tiger King, (2020–1), USA: Netflix.
Tuca & Bertie (2019–21), USA: Netflix, Adult Swim.
Upshaws, The (2021–), USA: Netflix.

Venganza de las Juanas, La (2021–), MX: Netflix.
Virgin River (2019–), USA: Netflix.
Wire, The (2004–8), USA: HBO.

Film

Foster, H., and W. Jackson. 1946. *Song of the South*. USA: Disney.

CHAPTER 2

Introduction: Netflix and the Re-invention of Television

At the 2009 Emmy awards, host Neil Patrick Harris reprised his role as Dr. Horrible from the three-part-musical *Dr. Horrible's Sing-Along-Blog* (iTunes, 2008). This had been written and directed by Joss Whedon during the 2007–2008 Hollywood writer's strike and distributed via iTunes as a webseries, bypassing traditional broadcasting systems. In the Emmy sketch, Dr. Horrible threatens that online series will take over television, effectively replacing the industry present at the event. Dr. Horrible's nemesis Captain Hammer (Nathan Fillion), however, states: "Don't worry, America. I've mastered this internet and I'm here to tell you: it's nothing but a fad! TV is here to stay! […] People will always need big, glossy, shiny, gloss-covered entertainment. And Hollywood will be there to provide it. Like the Ottoman empire, the music industry and Zima, we're here to stay. Musical villains, piano-playing cats, they're a flash in the pan!". Much like *Dr. Horrible's Sing-Along Blog* itself can be read as a deliberate protest against the television industry in times of bitter conflict, the sketch points to the threats online video services pose to traditional industry structures. Even though it pokes fun at online video's frequent need for buffering, Captain Hammer's short-sighted view of the internet is a jibe against the television industry's unpreparedness for the competition through online streaming services. Only four years later, the Emmy awards included three nominations for *House of Cards* (Netflix,

M. Jenner, *Netflix and the Re-invention of Television*,
https://doi.org/10.1007/978-3-031-39237-5_2

2013–18) and one nomination for the Netflix-produced season 4 of *Arrested Development* (Fox, 2003–6, Netflix, 2013–19).

2007, the year before *Dr Horrible's Sing-Along Blog* was released on iTunes, was the year the BBC iPlayer was launched in the UK, a major signal that television would soon move online. It is also the point Michael Curtin pinpoints as a moment when some of the enormous shifts that currently dominate television first occurred: in the US, Nielsen introduced ratings for advertisements in light of widespread DVR use. There was also growing competition from the videogame industry, culminating in the 2007–2008 Hollywood writer's strike, which compromised US television schedules significantly:

> Interestingly, intermedia rights were the key point of disagreement between the networks and the writers during the strike, with the latter arguing for a share in revenues earned via new delivery systems. (Curtin 2009, 10)

Though this kind of conflict is not unprecedented, it suggests how important the different publication platforms and formats had already become. These shifts signalled television's move onto other screens, publication models and industry structures. Discussing online-distributed television in the US, Amanda Lotz pinpoints the moment of change in 2010, arguing that "this year marks a significant turning point because of developments that year that made internet distribution technology more useable" (2017, location 302). The specific moment could also be located in late 2012, when Netflix started to publish 'Netflix Originals', acquiring exclusive international licensing rights to *Lilyhammer* (NRK, 2012–14) which had previously only been shown in Norway, and getting involved in the production as co-producer of the series. The following year would see Netflix publish its first self-produced Originals, *House of Cards*, *Hemlock Grove* (Netflix, 2013–15), *Orange is the New Black* (Netflix, 2013–19), and Season 4 of *Arrested Development*. This set the scene for what the industry calls OTT (Over The Top) broadcasting. As with any era, it may be difficult—even impossible—to locate an exact moment of change. Yet, we can notice that the media industry, and what we define as television, has changed with the increased possibilities of online streaming. It is also impossible to pinpoint a specific organisation that drove this change: YouTube, the BBC, Hulu, iTunes, Netflix, as well as others, played a part, but none of them is more 'responsible' for shifts in our understanding of television than the others. Furthermore, these changes all take place at different paces with different emphases in varying national media systems. The US television industry was hardly as ill-prepared for the coming shifts as the *Dr. Horrible* sketch at the Emmys suggests. At the time, it was working to implement some changes itself. Particularly the American Hulu, a catch-up service which unites programmes from Fox, NBC and ABC can be viewed as tying different changes together. It later also proved well equipped to offer its own original content, from *Farmed and Dangerous* (Hulu, 2013), its earliest production, to the critical and commercial hit *The Handmaid's Tale* (Hulu, 2017-). In the UK, the BBC iPlayer offered viewers the option to self-schedule television online, the position of the BBC as Public Service Broadcasting (PSB) allowing for ad free programming. The BBC certainly managed to set a standard for other PSBs in Europe, which soon followed to build their own online presences.

The competition ultimately posed by Netflix, once it started producing its own original programming, was difficult to foresee. This is not to argue that the OTT broadcasting industry is the cause for all of television's troubles, as Lotz (2014) describes in some detail. But the advent of Netflix and Amazon original programming certainly poses a challenge to existing media conglomerates that hoped to be able to dictate changes. As it is, Netflix, previously an online DVD-rental service and unconnected to the large media conglomerates that dominate media worldwide, became a powerful player in the reorganisation of what television *is*. Other companies quickly followed its example by providing original 'quality' TV as well as licensed programming without ad breaks in exchange for monthly or (in the case of Amazon, at least initially) annual subscriptions. Netflix also quickly expanded globally, to some extent challenging the power of international conglomerates even more.

Netflix and the Re-invention of Television focusses on Netflix as a dominant challenger to linear television, viewing practices, nationalised media systems and established concepts of what television *is*. Many media companies have met the challenges posed by Netflix and formulated responses: they have produced revivals of 'cult' TV, such as new seasons of *The X-Files* (Fox, 1993–2003, 2016–18) or *Twin Peaks: The Return* (Showtime, 2017) they have built their own sophisticated streaming systems; or they have adjusted licensing and publication models, so that viewers outside of the US can access new episodes quickly after they have aired. Yet, Netflix has been at the forefront of all these developments: it revived *Arrested Development* in 2013, it constructed a sophisticated algorithm to nudge viewers towards specific choices; and it published content online on the same time in all countries where it is available. It quickly recognised binge-watching as a way to promote itself and its original content, it understood that television content is no longer inherently tied to the television set, and it established itself as transnational broadcaster. Netflix is a driving force in changing how television is organised and will be organised in the future. It has proven truly remarkable in the way it has re-organised what television is and how television viewing is structured. Still, it can be argued that many of these developments are changes that television was undergoing anyway, as signalled by technological and industrial developments as well as changes in viewer behaviour (see Lotz 2014). Yet, Netflix accelerated many developments. It also managed to pose a challenge to established media conglomerates while positioning streaming not as an alternative to television, but *as* television. This is not to say that it overhauled how power within this industry is organised, but that it managed to position itself alongside other powerful players. Even in the so-called 'streaming wars' Netflix maintains a central position, facing off against some of the most powerful media companies in the world (Apple, Amazon, Disney). Further, it has arguably shaped fellow transnational streamers' structures and strategies. This book analyses Netflix critically, but also looks at the processes that allowed its shaping of contemporary streaming as television cultures.

Netflix and the Re-invention of Television

Considering its mode of delivery via broadband internet and the fact that Netflix is often received via laptops or other devices, it is worth questioning whether Netflix can be considered television at all. Netflix is clearly not broadcast television. The 'liveness' of television has often been argued to be a central characteristic of the medium, particularly in its early years. Network television in a post-network era and its linear equivalents outside of the US have continuously emphasised its 'liveness' with popular competition shows and reality TV formats. Netflix cannot deliver this, largely due to its reliance of autonomous scheduling through viewers. Its experiments with formats that rely on the illusion of liveness, such as late-night comedy, have not worked out. Another distinction is that Netflix is not tied to existing channel brands of television, such as the BBC or HBO, or media conglomerates like Disney. Instead, it has built its own brand. Not only is it not linked to television's branding structures, but, at least so far, it is also not part of the large media conglomerates, such as Viacom, Time Warner or NewsCorp, that dominate international television industries. Crucially, Netflix has also abandoned the idea of the linear television schedule: Netflix puts all episodes of one series online at once, resembling more models of book, or, more accurately, DVD publishing (see Lotz 2014 and 2017). DVD box sets of TV series, after all, were a key technology to allow not just time-shifting, but self-scheduling independent from television schedules. These distinctions are more than just semantics, as broadcasting suggests a linear, synchronised (and communal) experience, whereas with publishing, commodities can be consumed as scheduled by users. Binge-watching as viewing practice pre-figures OTT, particularly with the rising popularity of DVD box sets in the early 2000s (Lotz 2014, location 1780). Nevertheless, Netflix' active promotion of the term and its significance to Netflix suggests its centrality to the brand. Overturning these significant, even central, aspects, might position Netflix as an alternative to television (like DVDs), but not as the medium itself.

And yet, in popular and academic discourse, Netflix is often perceived *as* television. First and foremost, this is linked to the way Netflix defines, and consequently markets, itself: in a GQ profile of Netflix founder and CEO Reed Hastings in January 2013, he states that the goal "is to become HBO faster than HBO can become us" (Hass 2013). This needs to be read as an explicit challenge to HBO, leader of the so-called 'quality revolution' of the late 1990s and early 2000s. Much like HBO, several US cable channels (such as AMC, Showtime, FX) have built their brand identity around high-quality original drama. HBO remains central to contemporary ideas of 'quality' TV. Netflix' *House of Cards*, with its first episode directed by David Fincher, starring Academy Award winners Kevin Spacey and Robin Wright, an adaptation of the BBC series of the same title, was a highly ambitious project that imitated HBO's branding strategy (see Johnson 2012, 37–59). By positioning itself as competitor to HBO, Netflix implicitly defined itself as television, rather than an online broadcaster like YouTube. There lies some irony in the fact that Netflix challenged HBO, a channel that marketed itself for years as being 'not TV'. HBO is received via cable broadcasting systems and submits to the 'rules' of the television schedule where one episode is aired every week. Despite its marketing, which aimed to highlight the difference of its output from other television content, HBO *is* TV. Second,

Netflix positioned itself as television through its productions: its first 'Netflix Original', *Lilyhammer* was first licensed and later co-produced with Norwegian Public Service Broadcaster NRK.[1] An early original series was Season 4 of *Arrested Development*, which had been shown on broadcast television before it was cancelled in 2006. Netflix, thus, linked itself with 'traditional' television. Third, Sam Ward notes that:

> In the run-up to its launch in Britain, Netflix joined major British broadcasters Sky, the BBC, and Channel 4 at Los Angeles Screenings, where deals for the international distribution of American content are negotiated. (2016, 226)

Ward argues that, with this appearance, Netflix positioned itself as television channel and exporter of American content to other territories, joining other industry figures at an important sales event. In his rather polemic book *Television is the New Television*, journalist Michael Wolff argues:

> It is not Netflix bringing digital to television, but, quite obviously, Netflix bringing television programming and values and behaviour [...] to heretofore interactive and computing-related text. (2015, location 958)

Wolff's argument is that digital media is adopting the business model of television, particularly in relation to advertising. Furthermore, Ward points to promotion materials used by Netflix to introduce itself to the UK market, which explicitly feature people watching Netflix on a television set. In fact, in the UK, Netflix became available as an app on TV screens for Virgin Media subscribers in 2013 via DVR set-top boxes. As a fifth point, it can be argued that television had recently undergone a transformation that already allowed viewers to watch texts uninterrupted by advertising at the pace they wanted. In its legal version, this was linked to the rise of the DVD box set that allowed viewers to watch TV series

[1] Most aspects of the production of *Lilyhammer* are Norwegian, including most of the cast, only the financing comes from Netflix and the main character is played by American actor Steven Van Zandt, known from *The Sopranos* (HBO, 1999–2007) (see Mikos and Gamula 2014, 90–4).

on laptops.[2] As a DVD-rental company, Netflix was well aware of the frequency with which US viewers rented discs and how long it took to return them. Based on this, Netflix concluded that television content and the television set are no longer understood to be inherently linked, and the concept of television is permeable. This leads back to the first point on this list: by stating that Netflix is television, Netflix can become television.

Television has never been a stable object easily defined, but discursively constructed via social practices, spaces, content, industry or technological discourses. Often, the shifts in how we understand or interact with television *feel* less radical than they actually are, which is why a discursive construction of television can accommodate shifts in technology and habits. As Lisa Gitelman explains:

> The introduction of new media [...] is never entirely revolutionary: new media are less points of epistemic rupture than they are socially embedded sites for the ongoing negotiation of meaning as such. Comparing and contrasting new media thus stand to offer a view of negotiability in itself—a view, that is, of the contested relations of force that determine the pathways by which new media may eventually become old hat. (2006, 6)

As B. G.-Stolz makes a similar point when she argues:

> each innovation restarts what I term a cycle of de-habituation and re-habituation in viewer engagement and consumption practices; in other words, our falling out of use with "classic" television and all that is today deemed televisual and new. [...] Instead, if looked at closely, they are only perceived as altered, as the elements changed are in effect miniscule and reframe rather than re-invent engagement practices. (2021, 145)

Much of this can be explained via existing and changing media habits. Wendy Hui Kyong Chun argues:

> Habit frames change as persistence, as it habituates: it is a reaction to change—to an outside sensation or action—that remains beyond that change within the organism. (2016, location 336)

[2] In its illegal version, DVD box sets were frequently ripped and put online for the purposes of illegal downloads. This also enabled binge-watching via PCs or laptops if viewers did not wish to go through the extra effort (and expense) of burning DVDs.

It may be a technology's ability to connect directly to our existing media habits that make these shifts unnoticeable. When they acquired VCRs, some viewers may have already been used to channel-surfing on cable TV, thus already being involved in a practice of modifying the schedule based on their own desires and needs. DVDs build on the practices and habits of the VCR, and Netflix' use of binge-watching builds onto the popularity of DVD box sets, as the company rhetoric never grows tired of reminding us (see, for example, Jurgensen 2013). Television as discourse has proven remarkably flexible in accommodating technologies, industrial changes, or changes in the social practices, or spaces in the history of the medium. In *Video Revolutions*, Michael Z. Newman forwards a cultural view of video as a medium:

> From this perspective, a medium is understood relationally, according to how it is constituted through its complementarity or distinction to other media within a wider ecology of technologies, representations, and meanings. A medium is, furthermore, understood in terms not only of its materiality, affordances, and conventions of usage, but also of everyday, commonsense ideas about its cultural status in a given context. (2014, 3)

Newman identifies shifts in the technologies and cultural uses of the term video. Similarly, the term television has been used to describe different technologies, has been invested with varying degrees of cultural significance and 'value', and, thus, has meant different things at different times and in different social contexts.

Though this book maintains that Netflix' role in shaping a contemporary global media landscape is central, it also insists that Netflix never exists in a vacuum. Critics like Wheeler Winston Dixon (2013) suggest that Netflix has the power to do away with physical forms like DVD or even make parts of film history 'disappear', simply by not including them in its library. After Netflix has expanded massively across the world between 2014 and 2016, it can be observed that such an argument ignores that Netflix' libraries look very different from country to country. Furthermore,—and this could also not have been predicted by Dixon in 2013—Netflix has dropped large amounts of licensed content over the course of 2016 in favour of its own in-house productions or Netflix Originals, suggesting that it increasingly needs to be viewed as one online channel among many, as also suggested by Derek Johnson (2018 and 2022) and explored further in the Introduction to the Second Edition.

This book makes a distinction between Netflix in-house productions and Netflix Originals—despite the fact that Netflix does not. For the Second Edition, I have adopted Petruska and Woods' terminology of self-produced Original and false Original (2019). It distinguishes between programmes produced and broadcast by linear broadcasters and licensed by Netflix elsewhere and programmes produced or commissioned by Netflix, which is the original broadcaster worldwide (such as *House of Cards*, *Orange is the New Black*, *Club de Cuervos* [Netflix, 2015–19], *Love* [Netflix, 2016–18], etc.). These programmes are not literally produced in-house, but Netflix functions as producer and original (and exclusive) broadcaster. As Netflix Chief Content Officer Ted Sarandos explains in an interview with Neil Landau:

> We use the word 'original' to indicate the territory, where it originates. 'Netflix Originals' is used in the US, because you can't see them anywhere else. For us, the word 'exclusive' doesn't ring true to people. And 'created by' doesn't either. (Landau 2016, 12)

Not all content labelled Netflix Originals can be separated into a binary of self-produced and false Originals. *Lilyhammer* was produced by Norwegian channel NRK first, but Netflix bought it after only its pilot was produced and is sharing in its production costs. In its dealings with Marvel Studios, both production companies are heavily invested (this was before the Marvel catalogue moved to Disney+). Yet, it is considered important, here, to acknowledge that much of the content branded 'Netflix Original' is only considered original due to the companies' rather liberal usage of the word. Looking at Netflix as global company, it is only prudent to acknowledge that different content can be featured under this term.

There are two main themes to this book: the first one is to consider how Netflix changes ideas of what television is. The second theme that runs through this book is a consideration of the nexus of concepts of control and choice, and their relationship with power and subversion. Netflix builds on the marketing language of previous ancillary technology of television by emphasising that it offers both, more control and more choice, to viewers. Yet, much as with previous technologies, as outlined in Part I, this control does not translate to substantial shifts in power. Though Netflix disrupts the way media systems are organised, particularly in the US, it hardly offers a subversion that leads to sustainable changes to the organisation of power—at least not in the relationship between audiences and industry. Yet, control can be exercised by many actors and means something different in each context. Different ancillary technologies allow for different kinds of control, but national media systems, in a globalised world, also offer different forms of control to broadcasters. Overall, the central argument is that, even though Netflix changes conceptions of television, it does not substantially overturn relations of power between audience, industry and the nation-state within neoliberal capitalist systems. Nevertheless, it impacts on these regimes of control and power by restructuring how they are organised.

Netflix as TV IV

Derek Kompare notes in *Rerun Nation* (2005) that the different technological innovations to television need to be understood not merely as technological innovation, but "*reconceptions*, profoundly altering our relationship with dominant media institutions, and with media culture in general" (2005, 199, emphasis in the original). Each phase or stage of television is a reconception of the medium, a point in time when the technologies that define what television is change radically, changing the way viewers interact with the medium and the paradigms under which content is produced, structured and presented. Yet, because reconceptions do not occur suddenly, but are discursive shifts, they are always already prefigured by previous stages. The technological shifts of the 1980s are all preceded by public debates and technological developments of previous versions of television. The shifts in 'quality' in the late 1990s and early 2000s are preceded by a range of 'quality' TV series from *M*A*S*H* (CBS, 1972–83) to *Hill Street Blues* (NBC, 1981–7) to *Twin Peaks* (ABC, 1990–1) to *Buffy the Vampire Slayer* (WB, 1997–2001, UPN, 2001–3). The digital technologies of this period all tie in with behaviours and habits familiar from previous eras and build on publication strategies and behaviours associated with these. The way media change and turn into something else has been dealt with in different ways and explored from different perspectives. Bolter and Grusin (1999) use the concept of *remediation*, though their use of the term refers to the way content moves from one medium to another. Thus, remediation deals more with content rather than media technologies. A central concept in this broad historical approach is the division of television history into three different periods. Roberta Pearson summarises these as follows:

> In the United States, TVI, dating from the mid-1950s to the early 1980s, is the era of channel scarcity, the mass audience, and three-network hegemony. TVII, dating from roughly the early 1980s to the late 1990s, is the era of channel/network expansion, quality television, and network branding strategies. TVIII, dating from the late 1990s to the present, is the era of proliferating digital distribution platforms, further audience fragmentation, and, as Rogers, Epstein and Reeves [2002] suggest, a shift from second-order to first-order commodity relations. (Pearson 2011, location 1262-6)

Pearson argues herself that these 'periodisations' simplify complex discourses of television history. She also makes clear that this description is specific to the United States. Though other Western markets tend to be a few years behind on most of these developments, they roughly match the 'periods' of US television. While countries may regulate their markets differently, particularly in relation to PSB, a major factor in the shifts from each period to the next is technology. The shifts from TV I to TV II can be linked to the development of technologies like the VCR, affordable remote controls, cable systems or satellite technology. TV III is largely defined through a shift towards the digital. The availability of these technologies means that these major shifts happen around the same time, though they may take different forms in terms of content or industry. This history becomes messier when we look towards the former USSR, some Asian markets, such as China or North Korea, or some African markets where the availability and history of mass communication technology is different from the USA or Western Europe. Nevertheless, periodisations, albeit simplifications, are a good way to offer a broad idea of television history. At the very least, they highlight that speaking of television at different times means speaking of different *kinds* of television. These different eras or periods tie together a number of technological, socio-cultural, industrial or aesthetic discourses. In and of themselves, these discourses are complicated and complex and not always as neatly aligned as might be suggested by this terminology.

John Ellis, discussing largely the British television industry, divides television's eras into an era of 'scarcity', an era of 'availability' and an era of 'plenty'. These terms relate to the number of channels and, linked to that, the availability of an increasing amount of content:

> The first era is characterized by a few channels broadcasting for part of the day only. It was the era of scarcity, which lasted for most countries

> until the late 1970s or early 1980s. As broadcasting developed, the era of scarcity gradually gave way to an era of availability, where several channels continuously jostled for attention, often with more competition from cable and satellite services. The third era, the era of plenty, is confidently predicted by the television industry itself. It is foreseen as an era in which television programmes (or, as they will be known, 'content' or 'product') will be accessible through a variety of technologies, the sum of which will give consumers the new phenomenon of 'television on demand' as well as 'interactive television'. The era of plenty is predicted even as most nations and individuals are still coming to terms with the transition to the era of availability. (2000, 39)

Ellis' division into eras and the model of TV I, II, and III overlap in many respects. But though these 'periods' of television work well as a broad—if simplified—conceptualisation of television history, it is not the only way to look at it. In *Video Revolutions* (2014), Newman maps different meanings of the term video. He divides the history of the term into three different phases:

> In the first phase, the era of broadcasting's development and penetration into the mass market, video was another word for television. The two were not distinct from each other. In the second, TV was already established as a dominant mass medium. Videotape and related new technologies and practices marked video in distinction to television as an alternative and solution to some of TV's widely recognized problems. It was also distinguished from film as a lesser medium visually and experientially, though at the same time it was positioned as a medium of privileged access to reality. In the third phase, video as digital moving image media has grown to encompass television and film to function as the medium of the moving image. These phases are defined in terms of their dominant technologies (transmission, analog recording and playback, digital recording and playback) but more importantly by ideas about these technologies and their uses and users. (2014, 2)

The first phase covers television's early years (at least in the US) and, thus, was often associated with television's 'liveness'. The second phase covers the use of magnetic tape, which enabled American broadcasters to account for the USA's different time zones by time-delaying broadcasts recorded in New York for West Coast audiences. As Newman points out, film and video were viewed as distinct media, with video functioning more as an extension of live broadcasting. This property also speaks to video's later conceptualisation as time-shifting technology in the form of Betamax in the 1970s. Covering the term and cultural use of video rather than focussing on Betamax or VCR technologies, Newman also points to video's use in art, where video was used to formulate ideas that run counter to mass communication's ideological outlook(s). The third category sees the meaning of the term widened to essentially mean recorded moving images. These three phases can also be viewed as phases that determine the technologies television is associated with. In the first stage, when video and television are virtually interchangeable, the medium is defined through 'liveness' and towards the end of the phase, a degree of viewer independence is introduced through the remote control. The second phase could be termed the age of the VCR and cable, offering vast amounts of choice, the ability to time-shift and autonomously schedule (predominantly films). The third stage describes the shift towards the digital.

All these 'phases', 'stages' or eras seem to refer to the same phenomena. Although all are simplifications of complex, nationally specific discourses,—always determined and necessitated by the approaches taken to analyse them—what cannot be denied is that they are led by and linked to technological shifts. TV I is marked by the (increasingly) affordable television set itself, TV II by more affordable and accurate remote controls, cable and satellite technology as well as the VCR, and TV III by DVD and the DVR and digital broadcasting technologies. While each period is marked by its own technological innovations, this is linked with industrial shifts, changes in content (particularly aesthetics and narrative forms), associated viewing habits and shifts in the social connotations of television. However, these eras are not neatly contained phases or stages. Key aspects may be the same (technology, industry, content), but historical moments can never be directly pinpointed. Partly, this may be an issue of perspective (national context, focus on specific aspects of a discourse), but these developments are also relatively slow-moving. For each successful technology, a range of other technologies fail. Some industry practices may have been developed outside of the TV industry or outside of the industrial structures of conglomeration. Thus, these 'phases' need to be viewed as rough conceptualizations with messy, often blurry, outlines. Newman starts *Video Revolutions* by stating:

> At different times video has been different things for different people, and its history is more than just a progression of material formats: cameras, transmitters and receivers, tapes and discs, decks that record and play them, digital files, apps and interfaces. It is also a history of ideas about technology and culture, and relations and distinctions among various types of media and the and the social needs giving rise to their uses. (2014, 1)

This can easily be applied to other technologies, such as television, as well. Thus, the title of this book, *Netflix and the Re-invention of Television*, needs to be taken as something less radical than may be expected. Netflix did not completely re-invent what television is, but it is part of a reconception that was already prefigured by the habits linked to DVDs or DVRs, objects that are made obsolete or in need of technological adjustment.

Looking at these phases as technological shifts, changes to content and marketing strategies that target increasingly smaller audience segments (from mass medium to niche medium) justify a categorization of contemporary shifts as TV IV. The category of TV III, with an emphasis on technological change (the digital) and content ('quality' TV) is inadequate to contain the significant changes streaming providers Netflix, Amazon and Hulu, and more recently, Disney+ and AppleTV, make to television itself. Netflix is at the forefront of these developments and not only challenges traditional systems of broadcasting and scheduling. Having expanded massively over the last few years, Netflix also shifts established models of release schedules, on the one hand by making entire seasons of content available at once, and on the other hand, maybe more importantly, also making original content available on the same time internationally.

Confronted with a vast, almost unlimited, amount of national, social, industrial and technological discourses, it seems tempting to view television as a stable object in the physical manifestation of the television set. Alternatively, it can be viewed as a medium delineated by specific forms of programming (the serial form, a mode of address, 'liveness', game show or news formats), or as a technology with a linear history. Yet, individual periods of television are marked by lively debate of what television is, what its cultural meanings and ideological dangers are and what its implications and potentials for the future are. Television studies analyses from different eras are quite instructive in the way television has often been perceived and conceptualised as complex and unstable medium. For example, in

Television. Technology and Cultural Form, originally published in 1974, Raymond Williams tries to get to terms with the relationship between television and (presumably British, or at least Western) society. Williams argues that technological developments respond to the 'needs' of audiences. He argues that, despite its technological shortcomings (which, in the medium's early stages, were vast), the medium responds to a 'need' to combine existing media forms, such as radio, newspaper, theatre and cinema, into one:

> But it remains true that, after a great deal of intensive research and development, the domestic television set is in a number of ways an inefficient medium of visual broadcasting. Its visual inefficiency by comparison with the cinema is especially striking, whereas in the case of radio there was by the 1930s a highly efficient sound broadcasting receiver, without any real competitors in its own line. Within the limits of the television home-set emphasis it has so far not been possible to make more than minor qualitative improvements. Higher-definition systems, and colour, have still only brought the domestic television set, as a machine, to the standard of a very inferior kind of cinema. Yet most people have adapted to this inferior visual medium, in an unusual kind of preference for an inferior immediate technology, because of the social complex—and especially that of the privatised home—within which broadcasting, as a system, is operative. (Williams 1974, 28)

Williams views television as a powerful 'alternative' to both, radio and cinema, offering a broad palette of programming. There is, of course a tension in his own argument, which positions television as both, variety medium and 'inferior cinema'. Writing in 1974, this may seem as a useful way to think of television, though it needs to be highlighted that Williams discusses TV I.[3] The conceptualisation of television as uniting a variety of other media is something that still characterises the discourse of television. It may be exactly this aspect that makes it so permeable to developments that change its technologies, associated habits or reach. In 1990, Charlotte Brunsdon argues that 'good' television (as opposed to 'bad', commercial television) is:

[3] At the time of Williams' writing, TV I was on the cusp of TV II, though many technologies were not yet affordable for a mass audience, yet.

> ...constructed across a range of oppositions which condense colonial histories, the organising and financing of broadcasting institutions, and the relegitimation of already legitimate artistic practices. That is to say, the dominant and conventional way of answering the question 'What is good television?' is to slip television, unnoticeably, transparently, into already existing aesthetic and social hierarchies. (1990, 60)

As Brunsdon goes on to argue, this kind of judgement leaves out the majority of television content. The existing aesthetic and social hierarchies are usually established by other media, something that is particularly reflected in the use of the term 'cinematic' to describe 'good' television aesthetics. Applying aesthetic judgements from other media to television ignores the standards and techniques the medium creates for itself (Creeber 2013, 7). And, yet, it is difficult to avoid these comparisons to other media, even now, as the discursive construction of television has grown to include 'quality' television drama, accomplished aesthetics and many different kinds of screens. Much of this has to do with industry discourses: actors, writers, directors or other creative talent switch comfortably between media forms. Though the numbers of cinema talent that have gravitated towards television may have increased since the late 1990s, it is hardly a new phenomenon. *Alfred Hitchcock Presents...* (CBS, 1955–60, NBC, 1960–62) is one of the most prominent and earliest examples (on US TV), *Columbo* (NBC, 1971–2003) featured stars like Peter Falk, Vera Miles or John Cassavettes and individual episodes were directed by Robert Butler, who would later establish the visual style of *Hill Street Blues*, or Steven Spielberg.[4] In the 1980s and 1990s, US television attracted Michael Mann or David Lynch. In India, *Kaun Banega Crorepati?* (KBC, 2000–12), the Indian version of *Who Wants to be a Millionaire* (ITV, 1998–2014), has been hosted by some of the most acclaimed Bollywood stars. In most Western countries, particularly European countries with relatively small film and television industries, actors routinely switch between theatre, television and film with acting schools teaching the different acting styles associated with each medium.[5]

[4] Yet, Spielberg's involvement with *Columbo* pre-dates his film debut *Jaws* (Spielberg, 1975).

[5] As much as this is true for actors and different parts of the crew, not all staff, such as directors, share in this.

As such, television has always been staffed by people who easily transition between media. The conglomeration of the media industries in the 1990s also contributed to this kind of convergence of various media. As Williams shows, this perception of television as not one medium, but many, has accompanied constructions of television early on. In more recent years, the term 'convergence' encapsulates the concept, highlighting how different media forms are united online through a variety of texts and practices. Such a 'meshing' of media makes it impossible to always judge television by its own standards. Thus, terms like 'cinematic', usually describing the aesthetic style of serialised 'quality' TV, do imply a comparison with the medium of cinema and associated cultural hierarchies, but this comparison is inherent in television's role as convergence medium. This does not mean that television is not a medium in its own right but serves more as an example of the vast complexity of the discursive, unstable construction of what television is now and has been in its past. John Hartley argues that television:

> ...needs not to be seen in *categorical* terms as, for instance, an instrument of capitalist exploitative expansionism, class struggle, gender supremacism, colonial oppression, ideological hegemony, psycho-sexual repression, nationalist power, cultural control, always doing something to someone, always negatively, and usually in a combination of two or more of the above, but in *historical* and 'evolutionary' terms – how TV can be understood as a product, a part and a promoter of historical changes of very long duration in the previously strictly reserved areas of culture and politics. Meanwhile, the habits, changes and histories of analytical, theoretical and critical discourses about television, media and culture need to be seen increasingly as part of the historical milieu which needs explaining, rather than as some safe haven of scientific truth for academics to use as that mythical 'effective standpoint from which to criticize society'. (Hartley 1999, 25; italics in the original)

Though Hartley particularly criticises ideological approaches to television, his criticism also highlights the complexity of the medium itself and the means to study it. Anna McCarthy describes a major cultural and theoretical problem in grasping television when she points out that:

> [Television] is both a thing and a conduit for electronic signals, both a furniture in a room and a window to an imaged elsewhere, both a commodity and a way of looking at commodities (2001, 93)

Thus, the complexity of the medium means that no one approach can grasp it and any attempts to define what television is in its entirety will inevitably be limited. Thus, this book cannot hope to grasp the medium in its full complexity. It highlights some important discourses that constitute what television is and what it has been in the past. In this, it draws attention to the discursive nature of the medium without claiming to be able to do justice to the 'whole' of the medium. Because of this, it uses Netflix as a spectre to theorise a range of shifts in the discursive construction of television.

This book thinks about Netflix as part of a reconception of television that is still ongoing. This reconception is a process that unites a variety of discourses, of which Netflix is only one. As Johnson outlines in the introduction of his edited collection *From Networks to Netflix*:

> It is thus worth considering the contemporary television industries as a struggle between legacy channels adapting to new conditions, on the one side, and the new portals that threaten to replace them, on the other. (2018, 8)

His industry studies perspectives inform a very specific view of TV IV, but pointing to the concept of a struggle between various forces is highly significant in understanding the discursive construction of television. These struggles are not limited to industry, but are also cultural, generational, technological, economic and so on. They affect how content is created and where, as well as what kind of content. They shape how viewers understand themselves within media systems and how they put different technologies to use. Additionally, as with all discourses, the discourse of television does not end. This poses a number of problems for research, as, not only is the current reconception ongoing, but it is also contemporary. As already mentioned, though Netflix is currently not part of a larger conglomerate, this does not mean that it may not become one. Its presence in 190 countries is, at this point, largely theoretical as established media systems, language barriers or availability of broadband connections may prohibit large-scale adoption. The three parts of this book explore different aspects of this reconception from different perspectives: its positioning within existing media habits and technologies, its use of binge-watching to structure and market itself and its transnationalism and integration into existing national media systems. Sheila Murphy notes in the introduction to her book on television as central to new media developments:

> The problem about studying the present— or even the recent past— is that it is never over, and one is very much entangled and enmeshed within the discourse of the day. Critical distance, that much-lauded academic quality that allows one to understand the social, economic, historically inflected context of a cultural production, is elusive when that medium and its attendant technologies are right there in front of us, part of our regularly self-scheduled programs and processes. (2011, 12)

While writing this book, Netflix has not only introduced a vast array of new programmes and translation languages, it has also performed updates to its interface, some to comply with national media policies. Discourses about the 'threat' Netflix poses to American or other national media systems have become less frenzied over the past few years. Yet, the initial social discourses of cultural legitimation via 'quality' TV, though still persistent, have also been countered by moral outrage, even moral panic, over depictions of teen suicide in *13 Reasons Why* (2017–20) or violence in *Squid Game* (Netflix, 2021–), as discussed in Chapter 12. The pace with which Netflix has managed to establish itself in the US and in transnational markets is remarkable, but the discourse surrounding it tends to shift with it. New critical perspectives are also bound to emerge. This book is written with these problems in mind and, partly because of this, there is an effort to tie Netflix to television history throughout this book. Grounding Netflix in the history of a medium makes it a less 'slippery' object of analysis.

Gitelman (2006) warns of treating media as a singular entity with agency, or, on the other side of the spectrum, valorising the individual inventor. This book frequently uses phrases along the lines of 'Netflix does...'. Netflix is understood here as a company and its language and marketing tie it to the medium (and industry) of television. Netflix as a company consists of complex hierarchies and its achievements and failures are the result of complicated collective processes. Though CEO Reed Hastings and Chief Content Officer Ted Sarandos have emerged as public faces and spokespersons for Netflix, their main function is to explain and, ideally, sell Netflix to customers and investors. As such, they develop narratives that suggest a consistency of processes within the company and the discourse of television that rarely exists. Things become even more complicated when discussing the medium of television itself. The technology itself is about transmitting and receiving broadcasting signals, while those who broadcast those signals (whether through traditional TV signals, cable, satellite or Wi-Fi) abide a specific set of rules and norms. Yet, these might differ significantly depending on the broadcast technology used: in the US, regulation of cable television is significantly different from regulations for free-to-air television (Santo 2008). The EU laws governing streaming are different than those regulating 'traditional' broadcasting. The technology of the television set mediates some of these norms, but the narrative and aesthetic norms of television also contain much of what television *is*. This book tries to pin down some of the constantly shifting discourses regarding television. In cases where the medium is invested with agency, this needs to be understood as a complicated, constantly shifting, socially constructed network of meaning.

TV IV is understood here as a process. This process brings together discourses of technology, audience behaviour, industry, policy, national media systems, etc. Netflix is currently an important part of TV IV, but it is hardly the only one, as shown in the so-called streaming wars. Nevertheless, Netflix' usage of binge-watching and its specific location in discourses of transnational broadcasting are a significant part of this process. *Netflix and the Re-invention of Television* explores Netflix' position in the process of TV IV.

The Structure of This Book

Netflix and the Re-invention of Television is divided into three distinct parts that all consist of three chapters (with a new chapter in Part III for the Second Edition) and follow their own internal logic and their own theoretical frameworks. What unites these three parts is the concept of control and its relationship with discursive constructions of television. Part I deals with the way control is exercised by the individual over television and the way the medium reconceptualises in accordance with this kind of control. This is embedded in neoliberal processes that place labour in the form of self-discipline onto the individual. In other words, different technologies give viewers (supposedly) increased ability to make choices as these choices are vastly extended. The 'right' choices can lead to a 'better' individual (see Salecl 2010). This history also influences the way Netflix employs concepts of control, as discussed in Part II. Meanwhile, Part III looks at the negotiation of power and control between Netflix as transnational broadcaster and the way national media systems have traditionally employed television. A number of critics, such as Gilles Deleuze (1992) have analysed and outlined the (bio-)politics of these 'control societies'. Others have focussed on how these processes structure societies in relation to contemporary digital technologies (Chun 2006, Franklin 2015). Jonathan Cohn argues that recommendation algorithms function as "a primary technology of this control society" (2019, 7), focussing specifically on the way recommendation system marginalise communities and further neoliberal capitalism. While I do not deny the validity and importance of this argument, the focus here is to look at the various forms of control that emerge in relation to television and how these need to be placed in broader historical discourses. The emphasis is less on how television controls the viewer through ideological messages or technology, including algorithmic recommendation systems (as often feared), but more on the way viewers exercise control over the medium. As outlined in Part I, this control is not to be mistaken for power, though it may be linked to negotiations of power. As Seb Franklin outlines, control functions as a way labour is embedded into the private sphere as part of neoliberal societies (2015, 3–39). Control works in a specific way in relation to television and, more specifically, Netflix. The promise of control over the schedule is embedded in Netflix' structure, but this is framed here as part of a specific history of the negotiation of power and control in relation to television.

Part I of *Netflix and the Re-invention of Television* positions Netflix within a discourse of television's ancillary technologies. As Bret Maxwell Dawson (2008) argues, many of these ancillary technologies were introduced as supposedly 'repairing' television's flaws and weaknesses. This theory gives some insights into why the term 'television' can be extended so easily to include other technologies: they are used to 'repair' the restrictions and limitations of the medium. Generally, this 'repairing' has been marketed and conceptualised as giving viewers more 'control' over the schedule. This highlights the function of this discourse within a neoliberal discourse where control is synonymous with 'self-improvement' and in which the individual is responsible for 'repairing' the medium. Perhaps the ultimate technology of control is the remote control or RCD (Remote Control Device). First remote controls for television became available as early as 1948 in the US, but with only few available channels and at a high cost, they remained relatively marginal products. The early 1980s brought significant changes to television as a medium and to uses of RCDs. On the one hand, new cable systems extended the number of available channels. On the other hand, infrared technology made the remote control more accurate and cheaper to produce, leading manufacturers to include them with new television sets or VCRs (see Benson-Allott 2015, 81). Remote controls are often neglected in today's discussions of the period, perhaps because they have become so ingrained in our media habits it has become impossible to imagine TV without them. Nevertheless, remote controls have become central technologies to manage television as it grew to contain more channels and new options of what viewers could do with their television set, from watching VHS tapes to playing video games. Thus, Chapter 4 explores some of the discourses of control surrounding RCDs in the 1980s, how it was perceived in the US market and how television content changed in response. It also explores the social function of RCDs in contradictory, broader cultural discourses as it became both, a symbol of power and control, and subjugation. Considering its position as 'invisible' technology (see Bellamy and Walker 1996, 10), it is remarkable how prominently it featured in gender discourses or as object to encapsulate anxieties surrounding young people and the working class in the 1980s and 1990s. Chapter 5 focusses on another ancillary technology of the period, the VCR and possibilities for subversion of established media practices. This chapter looks at the VCR as an ancillary technology that has influenced how the television set has become something that viewers can essentially program themselves either by renting video tapes or recording television content. The flexibility provided by the VCR makes it clear how the television became a technology that could easily be controlled by viewers. Yet, the VCR is also one of several technologies of the era that transforms the television set into a 'hub' of media convergence, a technology that serves to display media forms other than television. The chapter, thus, emphasises links between the VCR, time-shifting and media convergence by extending both, choice and control for audiences. Chapter 6 conceptualises control in a TV III era where digital technologies allow viewers to time-shift television via a number of different technologies. This is also a period where television increasingly moves away from the television set and online via YouTube as well as various online technologies. Though this period extends on possibilities for viewers to control television, the various methods industry uses to monitor and control viewer behaviour are also extended on. DVD extended the possibilities for viewing TV through DVD box sets, but ultimately could be included in similar business models that sell-through

VHS tapes and the VHS rental business already provided. Meanwhile, the DVR extended the possibilities for recording and time-shifting television flow and could even 'skip' advertising. Yet, both technologies also offered possibilities for industry to control and police the various uses of television more closely. Meanwhile, YouTube develops as an alternative to television viewing by extending viewer control as far as functioning as producers of online videos. The TV industry's responses in the form of BBC iPlayer and Hulu contain television in the form of specific brand infrastructures. Allowing viewers more freedom to schedule their own viewing, while still contingent on the release structures of the linear television schedules, also highlights how more control is given to viewers. As the various discussions of control in Part I show, control does not extend to power in these scenarios. In fact, industry power remains relatively stable, despite increasing control given to viewers. This is even observable where, for example RCDs, are treated as symbols to discuss different forms of power and control in other social discourses. Thus, discussions of power and control in Part I serve to frame an understanding of television's cultural positioning, which is carried on into a TV IV era.

Part II explores the centrality of binge-watching to Netflix' positioning within discourses of TV IV and control. Binge-watching, as a viewing practice, reaches further back than Netflix. It became a particularly common terminology in relation to DVD box sets. As Brunsdon (2010) points out, this development ran in parallel with what Newman and Levine later call the 'legitimation' of television (2012). Thus, there is a strong discursive linkage between the concept of 'quality' television and binge-watching. In line with this, it is hardly surprising that Netflix, with its aspiration to 'become HBO' promoted the concept as viewing practice, and even publishing model, for its own content. Though still a relatively marginalised practice in 2013, marketing campaigns for *House of Cards* and Season 4 of *Arrested Development* highlighted the term 'binge' and sometimes even went as far as to suggest *how* to binge-watch. Jenji Kohan, creator of *Orange is the New Black*, has often joined similar calls, which function as a way to explain binge-watching to viewers and to distance it from its etymological roots in binge-drinking or binge-eating. This distance makes it more 'acceptable' or 'legitimate'. But binge-watching is used by Netflix not merely as a way to align it with 'quality'. Maybe more importantly, it is used *in lieu* of a schedule. Perhaps due to its roots as a DVD-rental company, most Netflix content is published in seasons (with few exceptions published in weekly episodes). This organisation already promotes binge-watching. This is supported by the 'post-play' or 'auto-play' function, which gives viewers only a short time to decide if they want to watch the next episode. The 'front page' of the interface reminds viewers of what they have not completed watching and allows them to pick up where they left off, even when switching devices. When a series is finished, Netflix suggests other, usually also serialised, options. Netflix may not offer a schedule, but it nudges viewers to consider specific viewing options. Lisa Glebatis Perks (2015) argues that media marathoning consists of an 'entrance flow' and an 'insulated' flow. To apply this to Netflix, suggestions provided through Netflix' recommendation algorithm are meant to establish an entrance flow and the insulated flow describes the flow of binge-watching. Both serve to organise and structure the viewing experience.

Chapter 8 considers the relationship between the television schedule and binge-watching as organising structure of Netflix and its recommendation algorithm. This chapter deals with television studies debates surrounding the schedule, such as segmentation and flow, but also the function of genre in television schedules and as a significant aspect of Netflix' recommendation algorithm. Taking Perks' concepts of insulated flow and entrance flow further, this chapter offers a detailed analysis of Netflix' organising structure, looking at its algorithm as well as the way it defines and manages viewer control. As discussed in Part I, debates surrounding control and ancillary technologies to television often relate to the broadcast schedule. Thus, Netflix' organisation of content becomes highly relevant to issues of power and control in the television discourse. Chapter 9 explores the development of a Netflix brand via its negotiation of cultural value in the form of 'quality' TV and more popular genres. By exploring the comedy strand on Netflix, with a specific view on the 'quality' comedy formats in the form of *Master of None* (Netflix, 2015–21), *Grace and Frankie* (Netflix, 2015–22) or *G.L.O.W* (Netflix, 2017–19) and its sitcom strand with series like *Fuller House* (Netflix, 2015–20), or *The Ranch* (Netflix, 2016–20). The analysis focusses on how Netflix, initially branding itself as purveyor of 'quality' television, is exploring more 'popular' genres and how binge-watching and its own branding often poses problems in this. In more recent years, Netflix has turned more and more towards popular fare, solidifying an idea of Netflix as 'normal' or 'default', as explored in the Introduction to the Second Edition in relation to the so-called streaming wars. Chapter 9 looks at the marketing of Netflix with an emphasis on binge-watching. In 2013, marketing campaigns often exploited a linkage between 'quality' television and binge-watching. Marketing campaigns that accompanied early Netflix in-house productions *House of Cards* and season 4 of *Arrested Development* highlighted and explained binge-watching by addressing an audience familiar with figures like Kevin Spacey (at least before his firing due to allegations of sexual harassment and assault) or *auteur* figure Mitch Hurwitz. In 2013, Netflix' publication model for these series and the publicity accompanying them spawned a lively debate about the sustainability of such a model, bringing the term binge-watching (or binge viewing or, more simply, bingeing) into mainstream debates of watching television. Around 2015, and at least partially owing to the successful linkage of terms like 'quality' television, binge-watching and Netflix, the company has recalibrated its brand to emphasise diversity, often with America serving as 'baseline' for what diversity looks like. Its emphasis now lies on the concept of diversity, aiming for a broad spectrum of experiences to be represented via Netflix texts. However, more recently, this has been contested by loud protests following the publication of transphobic comedy specials by Dave Chapelle, and, less vocally protested, Ricky Gervais. For the Second Edition, this leads to a reconfiguration of how diversity functions on Netflix, especially within the framing of Netflix as 'normal' and 'familiar'.

Part III considers Netflix as transnational television and the systems of national power and control it disrupts. At least partially, this is in response to existing research on Netflix, which is largely America-centric. This is understandable: the service has been available in the US for the longest time, where it is also more embedded in cultural discourses surrounding television than in many other countries. The American market is also its strongest subscriber base (see statista.com). As an American company, its in-house productions are largely American. The American television industry also looms large in global television markets. Therefore, Netflix is often understood largely as competition to US broadcasters rather than as competition to established channels in other markets, such as Canal + in France or MTV as transnational broadcaster. Additionally, American and British media studies remain dominant in international academic discourses. Yet, as Netflix' transnational scope becomes more visible it also becomes an important aspect to consider. For example, Netflix' decision to commission four Adam Sandler films in 2014 (extended in early 2017 to include four more films) was largely based on the star's global appeal, rather than his American box office value. Netflix has also added a large amount of non-English-language self-produced Originals. Additionally, it launched the Hermes project in 2017 to radically speed up translation of Netflix' in-house productions. In August 2017, only a few months after Hermes' launch, new dubbing languages, such as Russian, Italian, Czech or German became available for self-produced Originals. This effort to hurry translation is a visible sign that Netflix is invested in a project to not only become available, but also widely accessible to audiences within transnational markets. Considering how well Netflix is doing in countries like the UK and the US, traditionally early adopter markets where necessary technology and infrastructure (broadband) are readily available, it can be easy to forget the needs and demands other markets place. Yet, Netflix needs to be conceptualised as a global actor, not 'just' another American media conglomerate operating on a global scale. Thus, Part III deals with the transnational nature of Netflix and the way it addresses a transnational audience. Netflix is currently available in 190 countries with more than 100 million subscribers. Though 'actual' availability may vary across the globe depending on language barriers, access to electricity, broadband or computers or other technology, it cannot be denied that the company has expanded at an impressive speed. Even if some markets may turn out to be less profitable than others, either due to viewer's preference for national television or due to other factors, Netflix addresses an audience of a large number of national or cultural backgrounds. Furthermore, Netflix has to integrate and assimilate into a large number of national media systems. Part III theorises these tensions by positioning Netflix as transnational.

Chapter 12 looks at textual strategies employed by Netflix' in-house productions to address a transnational audience. National television works to establish an ideology of 'the nation' and Netflix has to position itself as transnational broadcaster while simultaneously providing possibilities for domestication to integrate into national media systems. Netflix' transnationalism is also closely tied to online media, which provides infrastructures for transnational audiences to relate to each other. Chapter 13, a new chapter added for the Second Edition, grapples with the ways Netflix establishes textual networks of meaning via what I call the 'transnational streaming franchise'. This chapter focusses on Netflix' use of the franchise model and fictional formats by looking at *Criminal* and the *Money Heist* texts. It also seeks comparison with Amazon's transnational strategy in *LOL: Last One Laughing*. Chapter 14 then conceptualises the transnational 'Netflix audience'. Due to the structure and mode of address of national television, many conceptualisations of television audiences are assumed to be national audiences. Chapter 14's discussion shows that no conceptualisation of Netflix can fully reject notions of national audiences or national media systems. Yet, a Netflix audience is simultaneously addressed as a transnational audience. This adds a different layer to regimes of control and power within the system of Netflix as transnational broadcaster.

This study is focussed on Netflix' self-produced Originals. This has several reasons: first of all, it allows the exploration of the transnational dimensions of Netflix. The misleading use of the term 'original' in the label 'Netflix Originals' disguises the fact that these texts will not be 'original' everywhere and the term only describes exclusivity in some national markets. Netflix' in-house productions, however, can be accessed wherever Netflix is available. Another, more practical, reason for looking at these texts exclusively is that I am hoping to avoid a study too much skewered by an algorithm adjusted to my personal taste. My specific focus here is serialised programmes as a format largely used to justify Netflix' 'status' as TV. Much like linear television channels, Netflix also offers a number of other genres, such as film, documentary or even reality TV and late-night shows. Yet, the serial format has been crucial to position itself within the television market. Though texts are referred to and analysed across this study, this book's primary focus is not individual texts, but more on how Netflix' in-house productions function as part of its reconception of television.

Aside from the many keynotes, conference panels and articles dedicated to the topic, a range of fascinating books have been produced on Netflix and the broader implications of Video-on-Demand. Perhaps most prominently, Lotz has offered a seminal in-depth study on the challenges the US television industry faces in *The Television will be Revolutionized* (2007 and 2014), now in its second edition, and almost annual in-depth industry explorations since the 2017 *Portals*. Lotz' emphasis on industry is helpful and explains her exploration of the US context. Yet, this US-centric view, even a broader anglo-centric view, can only tell a small part of the story. Derek Johnson's edited collection *From Networks to Netflix* (2018 and 2022) has a more international outlook, but its industry studies approach makes it necessary for each discussion to remain nationally bound. This leads to fascinating debates about the continuing importance of television channels, but the relevance of Netflix as transnational broadcaster remains under-explored. Since the publication of the First Edition of this book, Catherine Johnson's *Online TV* (2019) and Roman Lobato's *Netflix*

Nations (2019), both seminal studies on the way streaming restructures media landscapes. Johnson adopts an industry perspective with a focus on British TV while Lobato considers a more transnational industry perspective. An early exploration of binge-watching comes in the form of Perks' *Media Marathoning: Immersions in Morality* (2014), whose conceptualisations of flow feature prominently in this book. The edited collections *The Netflix Effect* (McDonald and Smith-Rowsey 2016) and *The Age of Netflix* (Barker and Wiatrowski 2017) include important interventions from the fields of online research, audience and reception studies, textual analysis, television studies, film studies, genre studies, industry studies and so on. Even before Netflix became an important cultural force, the seismic shifts taking place in television hardly went unnoticed as evidenced by edited collections such as *Television Studies After TV* (Turner and Tay 2009), *Relocating Television* (Gripsrud 2010), *Television as Digital Media* (Bennett and Strange 2011), *Ephemeral Media* (Grainge 2011) or *After the Break. Television Theory Today* (de Valck and Teurlings 2013). A number of other works touch upon the shifts and help theorise it, most notably the works of Kompare (2005), Newman (with Levine 2012, 2013 and 2017), Dawson (2008), Nick Couldry (2012) or Joseph Straubhaar (2007). *Netflix and the Re-invention of Television* seeks to add to these explorations, linking Netflix to a specific history of television and control, exploring its structure and positioning it as transnational. This does not run counter to the body of theory that came before, on VOD, TV IV or Netflix, but rather, adds to these explorations. This book explores the current reconception of television by analysing Netflix in relation to regimes of control and its relationship with commercial and cultural power. Overall, this book offers a specific perspective on what television in a TV IV era is. It focusses the discussion on Netflix and, thus, offers a perspective as viewed through a specific interface and company brand. In some respects, this makes its view limited. At the same time, it also makes this discussion specific to a particular part of the process of TV IV. The narrow focus allows for a more concrete debate than a discussion of general shifts in the current television landscape with a view on companies that often operate in more limited geographical spaces. As such, this book can only explore a small part of what television in the TV IV era is. Yet, so far, Netflix has been a significant force within the process of TV IV, making this discussion highly pertinent.

Bibliography

Allem, Joe Patrick. 2017. "Why the Creators of '13 Reasons Why' should Pay Attention to the Spike in Suicide-Related Google Searches." *The Conversation*. https://theconversation.com/why-the-creators-of-13-reasons-why-should-pay-attention-to-the-spike-in-suicide-related-google-searches-79162.

Barker, Cory, and Wiatrowski, Myc (eds.). 2017. *The Age of Netflix*. Jefferson: McFarland.

Bellamy, Roger V., and James R. Walker. 1996. *Television and the Remote Control: Grazing on a Vast Wasteland*. New York: Guilford Press.

Bennett, James, and Niki Strange (eds.). 2011. *Television as Digital Media*. Durham, NC: Duke University Press.

Benson-Allott, Caetlin. 2015. *Remote Control*. New York: Bloomsbury.

Bolter, J. David, and Richard A. Grusin. 1999. *Remediation: Understanding New Media*. Cambridge, Mass.: MIT Press.

Brunsdon, Charlotte. 1990. "Television: Aesthetics and Audiences." In Patricia Mellencamp (ed.), *Logics of Television: Essays in Cultural Criticism Bloomington*, 59–72. London: Indiana University Press; BFI.

Brunsdon, Charlotte. 2010. "Bingeing on Box-Sets: The National and the Digital in Television Crime Drama." In Jostein Gripsrud (ed.), *Relocating Television: Television in the Digital Context*, 61–75. London: Routledge.

Chun, Wendy Hui Kyong. 2016. *Updating to Remain the Same: Habitual New Media*. Cambridge, MA: The MIT Press.

Chun, Wendy Hui Kyong. 2006. *Control and Freedom: Power and Paranoia in the Age of Fiber Optics*. Cambridge, Mass.: MIT Press.

Cohn, Jonathan. 2019. *The Burden of Choice: Recommendations, Subversion, and Algorithmic Culture*. New Brunswick: Rutgers University Press.

Couldry, Nick. 2012. *Media, Society, World: Social Theory and Digital Media Practice*. Cambridge: Polity.

Couldry, Nick, and Hepp, Andreas. 2017. *The Mediated Construction of Reality*. Cambridge, UK: Malden, MA: Polity Press.

Creeber, Glen. 2013. *Small Screen Aesthetics: From TV to the Internet*. London: BFI.

Curtin, Michael. 2009. "Matrix Media." In Jinna Tay and Graeme Turner (eds.), *Television Studies After TV: Understanding Television in the Post- Broadcast Era*, 9–19. London: Routledge.

Dawson, Max. 2008. *TV Repair: New Media Solutions to Old Media Problems*, edited by Lynn B. Spigel, Jennifer Light and Jeffrey Sconce ProQuest Dissertations Publishing.

Dixon, Wheeler W. 2003. *Streaming: Movies, Media, and Instant Access*. Lexington, Kentucky: The University Press of Kentucky.

Deleuze, Gilles. 1992. "Postscript on the Societies of Control." *October* 59 (Winter): 3–7.

de Valck, Marijke, and Jan Teurlings (eds.). 2013. *After the Break: Television Theory Today*. Amsterdam: Amsterdam University Press.

Epstein, Michael M., Jimmie L. Reeves, and Mark C. Rogers. 2002. "The Sopranos as HBO Brand Equity: The Art of Commerce in the Age of Digital Reproduction." In David Lavery (ed.), *This Thing of Ours: Investigating the Sopranos*, 42–57. London: Wallflower Press.

Ellis, John. 2000. *Seeing Things: Television in the Age of Uncertainty*. London: I.B. Tauris.

Franklin, Seb. 2015. *Control: Digitality as Cultural Logic*. Cambridge, Mass.: MIT Press.

G.-Stolz, B. 2021, "National, Transnational, Transcultural Media: Netflix—The Culture-Binge." In M. Jenner (ed.), *Binge-Watching and Contemporary Television Studies*, 145–61. University Press, Edinburgh.

Gamula, Lea, and Lothar Mikos. 2014. *Nordic Noir: Skandinavische Fernsehserien und Ihr Internationaler Erfolg*. Konstanz: UVK Verlagsgesellschaft.

Gitelman, Lisa. 2006. *Always Already New: Media, History, and the Data of Culture*. Cambridge, MA, USA: MIT Press.

Grainge, Paul (ed.). 2011. *Ephemeral Media: Transitory Screen Culture from Television to YouTube*. Basingstoke: Palgrave Macmillan.

Gripsrud, Jostein (ed.). 2010. *Relocating Television: Television in the Digital Context*. London: Routledge.

Hartley, John. 1999. *Uses of Television*. London: Routledge.

Hass, Nancy. 2013. "Is Netflix the New HBO." *GQ*. Available online: http://www.gq.com/story/netflix-founder-reed-hastings-house-of-cards-arrested-development. Accessed: 06.08.2017.

Johnson, Catherine. 2012. *Branding Television*. London: Routledge.

Johnson, Derek (ed.). 2018. *From Networks to Netflix: A Guide to Changing Channels*. London: Routledge.

Johnson, Derek. 2022. *From Networks to Netflix: A Guide to Changing Channels*, Second Edition. London: Routledge.

Jurgensen, John. 2013. "Netflix Says Binge Viewing is no 'House of Cards'; Half the Users it Studied Watch an Entire Season in One Week." *Wall Street Journal (Online)*. Available online: https://www.wsj.com/articles/netflix-says-binge-viewing-is-no-8216house-of-cards8217-1386897939. Accessed: 30.12.2017.

Kompare, Derek. 2005. *Rerun Nation: How Repeats Invented American Television*. New York, N.Y: Routledge.

Landau, Neil. 2016. *TV Outside the Box: Trailblazing in the Digital Television Revolution*. New York: Focal Press.

Lotz, Amanda D. 2014. *The Television Will be Revolutionized*, 2nd edn. New York: New York University Press.

Lotz, Amanda D. 2017. *Portals*. Michigan: Maize Books.

McDonald, Kevin, and Smith-Rowsey, Daniel (eds.). 2016. *The Netflix Effect: Technology and Entertainment in the 21st Century*. New York: Bloomsbury.

McCarthy, Anna. 2001. *Ambient Television: Visual Culture and Public Space*. Durham: Duke University Press.

Murphy, Sheila. 2011. *How Television Invented New Media*. New Brunswick, NJ: Rutgers University Press.

Newman, Michael Z. 2017. *Atari Age: The Emergence of Video Games in America*. Cambridge, MA: MIT Press.

Newman, Michael Z. 2014. *Video Revolutions on the History of a Medium*. New York: Columbia University Press.

Newman, Michael Z, and Elana Levine. 2012. *Legitimating Television: Media Convergence and Cultural Status*. Abingdon: Routledge.

Pearson, Roberta. 2011. "Cult Television as Digital Television's Cutting Edge." In Bennett, James and Strange, Niki. (eds.), *Television as Digital Media*. Durham, NC: Duke University Press. Kindle, location 1248–1592.

Perks, Lisa Glebatis. 2015. *Media Marathoning: Immersions in Morality*. Lanham, Maryland: Lexington Books.

Petruska, K., and Woods, F. 2019. "Traveling Without a Passport: 'Original' Streaming Content in the Transatlantic Distribution Ecosystem." In H, M. Hilmes & R.E. Pearson (eds.), *Transatlantic Television Drama: Industries, Programs, & Fans*. Oxford University Press, Oxford, pp. 49–67.

Proctor, William. 2017. "Why Psychologists have Got it Wrong on 13 Reasons Why." *The Conversation*. Available online: https://theconversation.com/why-psychologists-have-got-it-wrong-on-13-reasons-why-79806. Accessed: 01.01.2018.

Salecl, Renata. 2010. *The Tyranny of Choice*. London: Profile Books.

Santo, Avi. 2008. "Para-Television and Discourses of Distinction: The Culture of Production at HBO." In Cara Louise Buckley, Marc Leverette, and Brian L. Ott (eds.), *It's Not TV: Watching HBO in the Post-Television Era*, 19–45. London: Routledge.

Straubhaar, Joseph D. 2007. *World Television : From Global to Local*. Thousand Oaks, Calif.: Sage Publications.

Tay, Jinna, and Graeme Turner (eds.). 2009. *Television Studies After TV: Understanding Television in the Post- Broadcast Era*. London: Routledge.

Ward, Sam. 2016. "Streaming Trans-Atlantic: Netflix, Imported Drama and the British Digital Television Ecology." In McDonald, Kevin and Smith-Rowsey, Daniel (ed.), *The Netflix Effect: Technology and Entertainment in the 21st Century*, 219–234. New York: Bloomsbury.

Williams, Raymond. 1974. *Television. Technology and Cultural Form*. Glasgow: Fontana

Wolff, Michael. 2015. *Television is the New Television*. New York: Portfolio/Penguin.

Television

Reasons Why (2017–20), USA: Netflix.
America's Got Talent (2006–), USA: NBC.
America's Next Topmodel (2003–), USA: The CW.
Alfred Hitchcock Presents… (1955–62), USA: CBS, NBC.
Arrested Development (Fox, Netflix), USA: 2003–6, 2013–19.
Buffy the Vampire Slayer (1997–2003), USA: WB, UPN.
Club de Cuervos (2015–19), MX: Netflix.
Columbo (1971–2003), USA: NBC.
Dancing with the Stars (2005–), USA: ABC.
Dr. Horrible's Sing-Along-Blog (2008), USA: iTunes.
Farmed and Dangerous (2013), USA: Hulu.
Fuller House (2016–20), USA: Netflix.
G.L.O.W (2017–19), USA: Netflix.
Grace and Frankie (2015–22), USA: Netflix.
Handmaid's Tale, The (2017–), USA: Hulu.
Hemlock Grove (2013–15), USA: Netflix.
Hill Street Blues (1981–7), USA: NBC.
House of Cards (2013–18), USA: Netflix.
Kaun Banega Crorepati? (2000–12), IND: KBC.
Lilyhammer (2012–14), NO: NRK.
Love (2016–18), USA: Netflix.
*M*A*S*H* (1972–83), USA: CBS.
Master of None (Netflix, 2015–21), USA: Netflix.
Orange is the New Black (2013–19), USA: Netflix.
Ranch, The (2016–20), USA: Netflix.
Sopranos, The (1999–2007), USA: HBO.
Squid Game (2021–), KR: Netflix.
Twin Peaks (1990–1), USA: ABC.
Twin Peaks: The Return (2017), USA: Showtime.
Who Wants to be a Millionaire? (1998–2014), UK: ITV.
X-Files, The (1993–2018), USA: Fox.
X Factor, The (2004–), UK: ITV.

Film

Spielberg, S. 1975. *Jaws*. USA: Universal Pictures.

PART I

Controlling Television: TV's Ancillary Technologies

CHAPTER 3

Controlling Television: TV's Ancillary Technologies

Part I of this book focusses on the concept of control to explore how television's ancillary technologies have increased individual control over entertainment technology. This involves the movement from broadcasting to narrowcasting or from mass medium to niche medium, targeted at smaller and smaller audience segments. As Milly Buonanno, who introduces the terminology of narrowcasting, puts it:

> the dynamic of expansion that drives the path to abundance turns out to be exactly reversed: that is to say, it becomes a dynamic of contraction made crystal clear in the terminology itself, which indicates the sequential passage of broad televisual diffusion (to the widest possible audience) to a narrow diffusion (to smaller sections of the public). (2008, 23)

In other words, texts are geared at smaller audience segments, but this increases the overall number of texts in immense proportions. This movement is enabled by different technologies that allow increasingly direct communication between viewers and industry and a modelling of television content that more closely resembles audience desires. Netflix' system supposedly offers a (momentary) high point of audience control in exchange for detailed information on how, when and where viewers consume television content. This is conceptualised here via a history of television and its ancillary technologies and the kind of communication it enables. The current reconception of television, in which Netflix plays

M. Jenner, *Netflix and the Re-invention of Television*,
https://doi.org/10.1007/978-3-031-39237-5_3

a dominant part, is a continuation of previous negotiations of the kind of control audiences have over television. This is part of a negotiation of power between industry and audiences. Yet, television and its ancillary technologies also often become the locus of broader social debates surrounding ideas of power and control. Part I functions as a pre-history to Netflix and its relationship with control and power, which will be discussed in Part II. Instead of a detailed history of technological developments, it offers a brief history of control and power in relation to television. More specifically, it focusses on control and choice, power and subversion in relation to ancillary technologies, not the television set itself. Neither control nor power are understood as stable and monolithic systems. Thus, the terms also change meaning in different contexts. This also grounds further debates in this book in television history to explain how Netflix' marketing deliberately plays on concepts of control used throughout television history to market its most successful ancillary technologies. This necessarily links in with questions of how they transform the medium. This negotiation of power and control necessarily includes varying meanings of power and control in different social, political and technological contexts.

Dawson argues in his PhD thesis *TV Repair* (2008) that ancillary technologies to television were often part of a broader discursive project to offer solutions to television's flaws. Thus, the control that devices such as RCDs, VCRs, DVD players, DVRs, etc. give to viewers all offer possibilities to 'repair' television. Mediated through marketing discourses that emphasise technological innovation, these technologies also emerge as sites of neoliberal discourses surrounding ideas of autonomy and control:

> This unflagging belief in technological progress, as well as the conception of remediation as rehabilitation or reform that it engenders, is frequently mobilized by technology manufacturers or retailers in order to justify the considerable expenses of replacing fully functioning media technologies and systems with new and unproven ones. But [...], it is just as often invoked by critics, policymakers, pundits, and viewers. This ideology of progress is about more than just moving units. It is also an expression of a desire for substantive change that is rooted in a dissatisfaction with the media technologies and systems of the present day. (Dawson 2008, 19–20)

An important discourse is the paradigm of control as linked to free market capitalism. Particularly the ancillary technologies pushed in the 1970s and 1980s were placed within a Cold War context in which individual freedom was largely defined as participating in free market capitalism (and opposition to Soviet state 'control' of its subjects). Newman positions the cultural discourse and marketing surrounding video games in the 1970s as part of Cold War anxieties surrounding mass culture:

> One of the key formal dimensions of broadcast media that allowed for this kind of rhetoric was radio and television's transmission from one to many. The audience can have its mind programmed by radio and TV only as long as the medium allows for no feedback from the viewer. Video games made it possible to see TV as a participatory rather than a one-way medium, and this contrast tapped into a line of thinking about mass society during the era of protest and counterculture of the 1960s. (2017, location 1399)

In other words, the various technologies that introduced levels of autonomy, control or participation to television tapped into several discourses: on the one hand, they counteracted fears about being indoctrinated through mass media. But on the other hand, they also solicit participation in consumer culture and the idea that the individual can exert more autonomy the more money they spend. This ties in with Chun's argument that, in relation to the internet, 'freedom' is often used interchangeably with free market capitalism (2006, location 143). To participate in free markets translates to individual freedom and, thus, control. Technological developments grow out of social discourses: a new technology can only be successful if an actual need for them exists, as Williams puts it (1974, 28), or a need can be constructed via marketing. A major anxiety surrounding television has always been its perceived ability to manipulate its viewers, be that on a technological level, through radio waves that can be used (and misused), ideological control via texts, or by generating anti-social behaviours in viewers, such as violence. Ancillary technologies often come with a promise to escape the negative effects of television, possibilities to avoid advertising and escape other 'bad' television that can elicit these negative responses. Successful ancillary technologies let viewers exert control themselves rather than being controlled. Oftentimes, these discourses of control switch to discourses of self-control or self-discipline as it becomes clear that the technology itself cannot eradicate 'bad' behaviour (see Dawson 2008). Thus, discourses of control and power change and shift constantly in reaction to new technological, but also ideological, social or political realities.

Possibly the most obvious technology of control is, as the name suggests, the remote control. Though remote controls for television sets were available since the late 1940s in the US, they took on an increased importance in the 1980s. Improved and more affordable infrared technology meant that they were quickly included with television sets as a matter of course (Benson-Allott 2015, 81). At the same time, they also took on a new function: previously marketed as technologies to help avoid advertising, the increasing adoption of cable and the proliferation of available channels meant that RCDs were now predominantly used to manage this increased choice. Renata Salecl (2010) links the idea of choice with neoliberal narratives of self-improvement: the 'right' choice about diet, parenting style, partner, but also cultural product will lead to the 'right' human being. Yet, an abundance of choice, as offered in neoliberal societies, commonly leads to paralysis and an inability to make choices at all, for fear of making the 'wrong' one. This kind of narrative can be easily translated to the cultural distinctions about the 'right' or 'good' TV and the 'wrong' or'bad' kind of TV: television advertising necessarily functions as 'bad' TV, along with more low-brow programming, such as soaps or reality TV. Television has relied on ideas of 'quality' from its early years, but the remote control promises ease of access to this 'good' television and the easy avoidance of 'bad' programming. In Salecl's argument, the ability to choose is synonymous with control over one's own environment. RCDs allow viewers to sample choices more easily, but they do not actually enable viewers to make 'good' choices. The figure of the couch potato, caught up in a constant loop of surfing channels without making a choice, is emblematic of the paralysis that critics like Salecl link to an abundance of choice. Benson-Allott discusses the activity suggested by the term 'channel-surfing' as an ultimately passive act (2015, xix). In the face of abundant choice, viewers do not necessarily choose 'good' TV or subvert the commercialism of US free-to-air television. The choices made by viewers, in the first instance, are choices that affect a viewer's immediate environment and are not intended to effect broader social change. Thus, RCDs enable viewers to manage choice, but the control exercised in making these choices remains without social reach. For example, as discussed in Chapter 1, anxieties surrounding 'couch potatoes' are not linked to the amount of power those who control their television from the couch yield, they are linked to fears about political apathy: exactly a lack of power or will to exercise it. Thus, the lack of power implicated in the control RCDs enable is widely recognised in these discourses. As has been argued by a number of critics in relation to more contemporary digital technologies, such as the DVR, YouTube or streaming platforms, most notably in fan studies, increased control over the scheduling of programming also often comes with increased responsibilities and various kinds of labour for the viewer (Andrejevic 2008; Jenkins et al. 2013). Tasks previously performed by industry are now the viewer's responsibility, such as organising how much of a specific television text viewers are shown each week, when they can see it, how long instalments should be, or in what order texts are placed in. Furthermore, with more recent technologies, viewers are tasked with the responsibility to protect their own data, for example, by installing and possibly paying for additional software. As Dawson points out, much of the task of 'repairing' television is also given to viewers by emphasising that it is their responsibility to put the technology to use to produce a 'better' television (2008, 200). In other words, the responsibility for 'bad' television (and its assumed effects) is no longer put on the producers, but the consumers of television. This neoliberal logic creates a meaning to the word 'control' that relegates it squarely to the private sphere and severely limits its social impact.

As Franklin argues in the introduction to *Control: Digitality as Cultural Logic*:

> The logic under which cultural worlds are reconceptualised as information processing systems is here defined as *control*. Control, as it is theorized in this book describes a set of technical principles having to do with self-regulation, distribution and statistical forecasting that is extended to the conceptualization of sociality through a series of subtle historical transformations. (2015, 1, italics in the original)

Franklin understands control "...as fundamentally digital but not necessarily confined to social practices that are directly mediated by electronic digital computers" (ibid.). Many technological advances in personal computing take place around the same time the technologies of TV II discussed here became popular. Yet, these technologies highlight that the practices of control are only marginally linked to digital technologies, though later developments would employ the digital to increase control. In fact, Franklin's definition shows how much metaphors of individual control in neoliberal societies are applied to the digital. This kind of control is embedded in broader socio-political structures, as discussed in much depth by theorists like Deleuze (1992), Castells (2009), Chun (2006) or Couldry (2012). In these contexts, control is often associated with the control of the state or the capitalist system. Yet, as much as this kind of ideological, state and economic control is acknowledged, this study focusses more on the control exercised by the subjects of control societies, to use Deleuze's terminology. Thus, the focus here is on the kind of control these technologies allow in relation to power associated with media industries. Another emphasis to illuminate this control is on how objects like television function as symbols in social discourses surrounding power. A critical idea here is that various kinds of control, even within a broader ideological framework of neoliberalism, take on different meanings. These meanings inform the way television is understood and reconceptualised. Thus, control, as concept, is not used in the broader senses of theories of 'control societies' or 'network societies', but the control individuals can exercise with the help of television's ancillary technologies. This is not to contradict theories of control societies, but rather, to understand control in differing contexts and in relation to different technologies. Even if control does not overturn power structures, it remains a crucial concept for an understanding of TV IV and Netflix.

Acknowledging the importance and relevance of control necessitates a revisiting of the relationship between power and control. This relationship is more complex than its packaging in neoliberal discourses suggests. As Foucault notes, power is a multi-sided relationship:

> ...when one speaks *of power*, people immediately think of a political structure, a government, a dominant social class, the master and the slave, and so on. I am not thinking of this at all when I speak of *relations of power*. I mean that in human relationships, whether they involve verbal communication [...], or amorous, institutional, or economic relationships, power is always present: I mean a relationship in which one person tries to control the conduct of the other. So I am speaking of relations that exist at different levels, in different forms; these power relations are mobile, they can be modified, they are not fixed once and for all. [...] These power relations are thus mobile, reversible, and unstable. (Foucault 1997, 291–292)

RCDs and other ancillary technologies do not allow a reversal of power relations, but they allow viewers to formulate a speech act within a discourse of power, potentially subverting or destabilising commercial power structures. As discussed in Chapter 5, the VCR spawned entirely new industries that destabilised commercial power structures of Hollywood and the television industry. It also served to reconceptualise the object of television as a 'hub' of media convergence. Yet, commercial power has hardly been reversed in the US since remote controls and VCRs were first introduced. Thus, the kind of control linked to RCDs or VCRs cannot be understood as synonymous with power. Nevertheless, they are tools that enable viewers to negotiate the conditions under which power is organised in relation to television. As such, they allow a multi-way system of communication rather than the one-way system of mass communication. The act of controlling television, thus, serves as communicative act. At the same time, what is at stake here is not only commercial power. In a binary system of 'the audience' vs 'the industry', a number of questions about power and control go unasked and unanswered: an audience's consumer power can be responded to by changing the structure of advertising, for example. This ultimately only changes delivery systems for advertising rather than a reorganisation of broader power structures, though it may already satisfy some viewers. The audience is a complex aggregate of social processes and hierarchies with different interests. Equally, the industry consists of creative personnel and personnel in charge of creating revenue as well as various connected industries with differing interests. As discussed in Chapter 12, conventions of adjacent industries, such as the translation industry, also shape texts. Furthermore, governments provide regulatory frameworks that guide many decisions. Thus, negotiations of power and control are not communicative processes that take place between two monolithic blocs, but complex processes that are guided by often contradictory social, political, economic or cultural discourses. Because of this, television and its ancillary technologies can emerge as important objects through which social issues not immediately linked to television can be debated. These can range from gender discourses to discussions of democracy and democratic values to public health issues.

Linked to these concepts of power, choice and control, the term subversion takes on a significant role. Chapters 4 and 5 discuss the various ways the television and advertising industries reacted to RCDs and VCRs by changing programming, ranging from commercials to home shopping to the aesthetics of prime-time television. Thus, RCDs, VCRs and later digital technologies allow viewers to erode the power structures of commercial television through grazing, zapping, zipping of advertising or time-shifting. Yet, this subversion doesn't mean a long-term overturning of power structures. The term 'disruption' is in many ways more appropriate as it suggests a more short-term nature of the way these technologies come to disturb existing structures of the media industries, which reorganise to re-establish their hegemony. Yet, the hegemonic system itself ultimately remains intact. This points to the way the control associated with these technologies is embedded in the structures of neoliberal capitalism, rather than significantly subverting them. In other words, the VCR may offer possibilities to subvert existing media systems, but its reliance on commercial television (for time-shifting) or the home video industries means that it cannot significantly overturn these systems. Nevertheless, the dynamics of this control in relation to television allow for an analysis of the specific assumptions about audiences and understandings of the medium that underpin this cultural logic.

The television set is viewed here as a point where various technologies intersect and reconceptualise the medium of television. As Kompare argues,

> Whether playing or recording, however, video devices are physically and culturally connected to television sets, forcing television – as both technology and cultural form, to borrow Raymond Williams' description – into a complex new relationship that foregrounds its function as an audiovisual display device, rather than its more established role as dominant modern cultural institution. This link destabilizes the direct presentation of scheduled television events, and enables people to use their personal media technology to create or access programming on their own terms, rather than stay locked to the fare and schedule dictated by the broadcasting industry. (2005, 198–9)

Thus, the ability of viewers to decide what the television set is for—to watch Hollywood films, pornography, home movies, advertising or prime-time dramas, play video games or stream content—makes it into an increasingly flexible medium. Of course, the central 'hub' of media convergence is the internet—as broad and blurry as this term may be in a world that can hardly be imagined without it—but it is worth remembering that before online access was widely available, the television set already enabled its owners to do a variety of things with it. Murphy positions television as 'middletext':

> In its very pervasiveness and abstraction of form, as well as its ability to contain and present other media, television is well positioned in the (historical, aesthetic, and technological) middle of our media system today. (2011, 8)

The 'middletext' is largely located on a textual level with different TV texts referring to various media forms, but the text is also extended beyond television to include various incarnations online through 'official' and 'unofficial' material. This negotiation is not conceptualised here via texts, but, rather, via the media convergence that takes place through television's ancillary technologies. Even with the shift online, the TV set remains central to our experience, enabled via cable boxes, game consoles and other technologies that allow the display of online media on the set. Thus, television, in its reconceptions, is understood as an important site where media convergence takes place. In fact, the history of television is a history of media convergence where both, technology and content, are fluid and constantly shifting.

Part I of this book displays an undeniable anglo-centrism. This is determined by a number of factors. First of all, there is a dominance of media studies in the UK and the US. This is particularly true when it comes to available data and interpretations of ancillary technologies from the 1980s and 1990s that inform how, for example, RCDs are integrated in gender discourses. There is an argument to be made for the need for historical research into the reception of RCDs, cable and VCRs in other cultural contexts, but this lies outside of the scope of this study. Beyond this, as the largest market in 'the west', as immigrant nation with diverse communities, a heavy emphasis on free market capitalism and relative economic stability throughout the twentieth century, a new technology's fate often gets decided in the US market. If a technology is successful in the US, it can often be sold elsewhere and promoted through exported programming.[1] Another element of the anglo-centrism of Part I is the almost hyper-commercial nature of US television. Much of the reasoning used to explain the success of some technologies and the failure of others, as well as the industry panics and changes determined by them, are assigned to the technologies' abilities to help viewers avoid advertising (remote controls, VCRs, DVD box sets, DVR). Yet, this function is much less

[1] An example of this is the prominence of the DVR TiVo in the *Sex and the City* episode 'Great Sexpectations' (06/02).

important in a number of national TV markets than it is in the US, where advertising occurs at comparatively extreme frequencies. This may serve to explain why it took some technologies, such as the remote control or the DVR, longer to catch on outside of the US. Nevertheless, the increasing availability of commercial channels outside of the US, though advertising still occurred at a lower frequency, allowed these technologies to catch on elsewhere. This was accompanied by similar cultural discourses of advertising as 'bad' television and ancillary technologies as a means to avoid it. Still, the American history of television and its ancillary technologies is not understood as universal experience, even though the US history of technology guides this discussion.

Part I of this book is largely organised chronologically, though Chapters 3 and 4 discuss the same era of TV II. The guiding question is how ancillary technologies enable communication about control and power between viewers, industry and function as symbols within broader cultural debates. The technological shifts of the TV II era and the ways the RCD and the VCR enabled negotiations of control and power are, thus, central to a pre-history of Netflix this part describes. Chapter 5 moves on to discuss the ways the TV III era and digital technologies offered different ways to negotiate power and control. Thus, this part offers a framework for the next part, which focusses on binge-watching as a way to market, structure and brand Netflix. These debates of control and power in relation to the medium of television also carry important ideas of how television is reconceptualised in the TV II and TV III era. If control is closely linked to neoliberal discourses of power relations, then this necessarily has consequences for the way the medium needs to be understood, both historically and in its more contemporary iterations. This also ties in with the kind of control exercised by nation-states and the way this is reconceptualised by transnational television, as discussed in Part III.

Bibliography

Andrejevic, Mark. 2008. Watching Television without Pity. *Television & New Media* 9 (1): 24–46.

Benson-Allott, Caetlin. 2015. *Remote Control.* New York: Bloomsbury.

Buonanno, Milly. 2008. *The Age of Television Experiences and Theories*, Bristol: Intellect.

Castells, Manuel. 2009. *The Power of Identity the Information Age: Economy, Society, and Culture Volume II*, 2nd ed. ed. Hoboken: Hoboken: Wiley.

Chun, Wendy Hui Kyong. 2006. *Control and Freedom: Power and Paranoia in the Age of Fiber Optics*. Cambridge, Mass.: MIT Press.

Chun, Wendy Hui Kyong. 2016. *Updating to Remain the Same: Habitual New Media*. Cambridge, MA: The MIT Press.

Couldry, Nick. 2012. *Media, Society, World : Social Theory and Digital Media Practice*. Cambridge: Polity.

Dawson, Max 2008. *TV Repair: New Media Solutions to Old Media Problems*, eds. Lynn B. Spigel, Jennifer Light and Jeffrey Sconce. ProQuest Dissertations Publishing.

Deleuze, Gilles. 1992. Postscript on the Societies of Control. *October* 59 (Winter): 3–7.

Foucault, M. (1997 [1984]). The Ethics of the Concern of the Self as a Practice of Freedom. In P. Rabinow (Ed.), *Ethics: Subjectivity and Truth* (pp. 281–301). London: Penguin.

Franklin, Seb. 2015. *Control: Digitality as Cultural Logic*. Cambridge, Mass.: MIT Press.

Jenkins, Henry, Sam Ford, and Joshua Green. 2013. *Spreadable Media : Creating Value and Meaning in a Networked Culture*. New York: New York University Press.

Kompare, Derek. 2005. *Rerun Nation: How Repeats Invented American Television*. New York, N.Y: Routledge.

Murphy, Sheila. 2011. *How Television Invented New Media*. New Brunswick, NJ: Rutgers University Press.

Newman, Michael Z. 2017. *Atari Age: The Emergence of Video Games in America*. Cambridge, MA: MIT Press.

Salecl, Renata. 2010. *The Tyranny of Choice*. London: Profile Books.

Williams, Raymond. 1974. *Television. Technology and Cultural Form*. Glasgow: Fontana

CHAPTER 4

Managing Choice, Negotiating Power: Remote Controls

The remote control can be viewed as a rather reactive technology, developing further in accordance with other technologies rather than forcing change and innovation itself. Bellamy and Walker describe it as an 'invisible' technology used to operate other technologies rather than playing or displaying its own content (1996, 10). Yet, the remote control enables viewers to manage technological change, from the commercialisation of television to the proliferation of channels in the TV II era to the vast expansion of ancillary technologies in relation to television from the VCR to the DVR. For Netflix, the integration of the app into the television set (via DVRs or other technologies) has been important insofar as it allows for management via a remote control. Thus, remote controls are considered here as a technology that, as reactive or invisible as it may be oftentimes, is central for the way television can be manged and understood.

The enormous shifts in technology, viewing behaviour, industry and programming that take place in relation to television in the 1980s and 1990s are almost 'common sense' within television studies. These changes often cite the introduction of cable in the US and the VCR as main drivers of these shifts (see, for example, Kompare 2005, Buonanno 2008 or Lotz 2014). What often gets lost in these accounts is the importance of the remote control. This can be explained by a number of factors: early remote controls were already introduced for radio in the late 1920s and

M. Jenner, *Netflix and the Re-invention of Television*,
https://doi.org/10.1007/978-3-031-39237-5_4

for television in the late 1940s. RCDs are also often used to control non-broadcast technologies, such as garage doors. There is also a qualitative difference in the kind of technology a remote control is in comparison to VCR and cable: both offer extended choices, either through the way programming can be watched (time-shifting), what kind of programming can be watched (pre-recorded tapes) or the amount of channels available. In other words, cable and the VCR are more radical disruptions that force more visible changes, while the remote control's function appears to be to operate both. Yet, the remote control, in its most optimistic interpretations, offers the possibility to interrupt 'flow' and build individualised schedules (see Bellamy 1993). RCDs, thus, significantly impact on the structure, perception and definition of television and associated ideas of control (or lack thereof). In their introduction to the 1993 collection *The Remote Control in the New Age of Television*, Bellamy and Walker argue:

> Although remote control devices were designed to make existing television operations more convenient, the technology has been used by the consumer to facilitate grazing and multiple program viewing and to change the relationship of viewer to the television medium. [...] Grazing [later known as channel surfing], 'zapping' (using RCDs to avoid commercials), and 'zipping' (avoiding commercials by rapidly scanning recorded programming) are means by which the audience exerts control over television programming and, by extension, the television industry. (1993, 4)

This claim highlights how much RCDs have been invested with ideas of control, choice, power or subversion of the existing commercial structures of television. As this chapter will argue, several anxieties around social control and power have also been formulated via the object of the remote control. This chapter explores issues surrounding control, power, choice and subversion and their relation to RCDs. It starts out by exploring the kind of control RCDs allow viewers. Julian Thomas argues:

> The remote is designed to embody a carefully crafted set of technological and commercial compromises, enabling the viewer certain degrees of control over content available but restricting certain critical options. The viewer can fast-forward through advertising [on time-shifting technologies like the VCR], but cannot jump past them. [...] A remote may control a specific task well, but it is designed to do so in a particular way that may benefit some users, but not others. (2011, location 797–802)

This indicates that the kind of control given to viewers is always situated in broader discourses of what television *is* and what it is *supposed to be*. Secondly, this chapter looks at changes to television content in response to RCDs. As much as Bellamy and Walker as well as other theorists are hopeful about the possibilities the increased choices for consumers bring, the commercial structures of television are not subverted. Television content changes, but commercial television remains. In fact, the thrust towards deregulation in 1980s America generally worked to enable the building of media conglomerates in the 1990s. This context highlights that the commercial power structures of television are not disrupted in any significant way through the RCD. In a last step, the social anxieties formulated via the RCD, particularly in the 1980s when remote controls became common household gadgets, are explored. Anxieties around the commercial power of television, gender or political and physical apathy are expressed, highlighting the symbolic power of the RCD as an extension of television, even if this does not translate to real power. Yet, what is implied in these discourses are the hopes and fears associated with new technologies. Thus, this chapter does not argue for RCDs as tools of subversion of existing power structures. However, it positions RCDs in relation to discourses that aim to position them as such.

Negotiating Power via Television Remote Controls

The remote control has a history that goes back to the 1920s when it was introduced as a means to control radio. As Benson-Allott describes in her detailed history of the remote control in the US context, it was marketed even then as a means to control commercial radio programming and allow listeners to avoid advertising. The first television remote, the Telezoom, was introduced in 1948 and allowed viewers to zoom into the centre of the screen. It remained relatively unsuccessful when compared to the Zenith Lazy Bones, introduced in 1950 and included functions like volume control and changing channels (Benson-Allott 2015, 32). Zenith's president was a vocal adversary of television advertising and the development of Zenith's Lazy Bones remote control is often viewed as a deliberate expression of this:

> Zenith's founder and president, Eugene F. McDonald Jr, was particularly averse to television commercials and used his company to fight them. He believed that if television manufacturers made it easier for audiences to

> tune away from or mute commercials, advertisers and broadcasters would have to improve their pitches or find a new business model altogether. (ibid. 34)

McDonald's and Zenith's role in the development of the remote control as technology to subvert commercial media carries important implications: on the one hand, the belief that the main function of the RCD was to avoid or silence advertising shaped Zenith's marketing campaigns, which proved successful enough to provide a general guideline on how to market television's ancillary technologies. On the other hand, the notion of a media system that is in need of subversion or 'repairing', as Dawson (2008) puts it, is used to sell another item. As such, the remote control has never meant a subversion of capitalism, or commercial media, itself, but more control as a means to individualise the schedule. Thus, what is on offer is a technology of control, not a technology of subversion. Though this is, of course, part of how neoliberal capitalism works, the idea of control in the absence of power has remained central to how television, it's ancillary technologies and its reconceptions function.

Infrared technology was introduced in the 1950s, but became much cheaper in the 1980s, which made it possible to integrate the technology into consumer electronics. Much more reliable than previous wireless remote control technologies, the first of the 'new generation' of infrared remote controls were introduced by Viewstar in 1980. By 1985, the technology had supplanted others for wireless remote controls. More importantly, with the costs for remote control manufacturing relatively low, manufacturers could include them with an increasing amount of technologies (TVs, VCRs, hi-fi systems, cable boxes) without having to increase the price (ibid. 81). Benson-Allott even goes as far as calling infrared technology as contributing to a 'democratization' of television culture, as it meant equal access to expensive, and previously 'elite' control over television. Remote controls quickly became integral to television culture. Bruce Klopfenstein notes that the growth of RCD use throughout the second half of the twentieth century is linked to three technologies: television sets, VCRs and cable television. The vast diffusion of remote controls visible throughout the 1980s is very much linked to the proliferation of channels made possible by cable television and the addition of an ancillary technology to the television, the VCR. Klopfenstein's detailed analysis of sales data refers to technologies sold with remote controls, rather than RCDs themselves (due to the lack of available data). In relation to cable, Klopfenstein points out:

> Cable operators had significant economic incentives to promote converter box remote controls in the home. First, converter boxes generally were necessary for subscribers to get additional basic cable channels progressively made available in the 1980s. Second, converter boxes were specifically necessary for subscribers to receive otherwise scrambled pay services including pay-per-view. Third, many cable operators charged a premium to subscribers with remotes. (1993, 29)

Though Klopfenstein cannot present exact numbers in his study, it is clear that viewers became increasingly accustomed to RCDs throughout the first half of the 1980s, many owning more than one by the late 1980s as all ancillary technologies became more affordable (see also Benjamin 1993). Klopfenstein links this more to cable than the VCR, presumably as the proliferation of channels makes RCDs more necessary to manage choice.

As Jennings and Rockwell note,

> ...when a viewer is armed with an RCD, the selection process becomes more complex than simply choosing one program from the universe of available options. Typically, the user is able to utilize the remote control to maximize gratification both between different programs (e.g., easily selecting among competing options) and within programs (e.g., adjusting the volume). Most critical for the preponderance of viewers, no longer do commercials have to cause interruptions to the viewer; another choice can be made simply and effortlessly. (Jennings and Rockwell 1993, 74–5)

Of course, programmes are still interrupted, even if viewers choose to change channels during ad breaks. Nevertheless, the quote points to the complex negotiations of power at stake in RCD use. As a technology that makes the television experience more interactive, RCDs necessarily democratise the process of television viewing, shifting more power onto the viewer, even though it remains asymmetrically distributed. Nevertheless, this process needs to be viewed as a negotiation of power rather than a subversion: RCDs do not fundamentally change the existing power structures but force the industry to respond to new conditions of television viewing. RCDs enable this negotiation through the ease with which attention is shifted from one channel to the next. This is not to suggest that industry had the ability to monitor viewing beyond Nielsen ratings.[1] However, these figures along with assumptions made about RCD use, most importantly that RCDs would be used to avoid advertising, heavily influenced programming.

Negotiating Power Through Programming

The negotiation of power enabled by RCDs is far from straightforward: first of all, the ability of audiences to respond to the programming offered to them is relatively limited. Nielsen and other rating agencies offer important insights, but broadcasters generally cannot measure where audiences switch to if they change channels or if there are some advertising spots that capture viewer attention better than others. A common assumption by researchers, industry and popular discourse alike in the 1980s and 1990s was that RCDs would be used to avoid advertising. Bellamy and Walker view the technologies of cable television, VCRs and RCDs as significantly shifting power relationships between viewers and medium (1993, 6). In fact, they argue that before these technologies were introduced, the television industry configured audiences as passive. Considering programmers' reliance of Least Objectionable Programming this seems, at the very least, simplistic: an audience capable of being offended by programming can hardly be thought of as passive. Considering daytime television's address towards housewives and the programming's reliance on aural cues to alert audiences to important scenes, these audiences are also not perceived as physically inactive, but possibly distracted (Ellis 1992). Male prime-time viewers might have been understood as more attentive, but physically inactive and unwilling to change channels as soon as one had been settled on for the night—or at least for the course of a programme. Programming strategies supposed an audience that would be unwilling to change channels once they had settled on one. This suggests that negotiations of power and control in a TV I era were not easily grasped through an active/passive binary. Hence, the assumptions made about audiences in a TV II era would be no less contradictory. Where, in a TV I era, the audience response was assumed to be more affective, the activity assumed for a TV II audience would be

[1] Of course, the viewing behaviour of audiences directly monitored by Nielsen could be analysed in more detail. Nevertheless, ratings for ads would not be introduced until the DVR (see Curtin 2009).

to stay in front of the TV but change the channel. With increased competition, migration to a different channel would be worse for a broadcaster than leaving the room or switching off the set: after all, the TV I audience is assumed to be 'unreachable' for advertising messages whereas the TV II audience's attention moves to the competition, which can make significant financial gain from another broadcaster's loss.

The main assumption in relation to RCD use was that it would be used to avoid advertising. This could significantly challenge the financing model for commercial television in the US and even overturn power structures. Yet, this supposed 'power' of the consumer needs to be put in perspective. As Bellamy and Walker point out: "The reality is that advertising avoidance is a problem of long standing for all commercial media" (1996, 51). This reasoning led television advertisers early on to develop strategies to stand out among other advertising, such as jingles, animation or other aesthetic and narrative ploys. In a study on VCR use, Carolyn Lin points out:

> ...viewers who more frequently recorded and played back programs did appear to absorb more information presented in TV advertisements or announcements for personal activities (e.g. sports, events, charity functions) and product purchases. [...] This might occur despite the association between post-viewing purchases and commercial pausing, as such censorship requires the viewer to pay close attention to the commercial messages being paused from recording. (1990, 89)

Lin's finding easily explains a rather relaxed attitude of advertisers towards the VCR, and, by extension, also the RCD. Someone who is grazing also needs to pay attention to what is on the screen. Numbers published by Nielsen on the time spent in front of the television throughout the 1980s also suggest that screen time was slowly extended throughout the decade.[2] Longer screen time further increases the possibility of viewers developing familiarity with advertising spots. Furthermore, the proliferation of channels meant that advertisers could direct their messages straight to a desired or likely consumer base, rather than spend high sums of money to address a mass audience that may not be interested or unable to afford the product. Despite this, reports of viewers watching

[2] Data taken from Nielsen: http://www.nielsen.com/content/dam/corporate/us/en/newswire/uploads/2009/11/historicalviewing.pdf.

pre-recorded tapes or even playing video games during ad breaks probably did not go reported without some anxieties for the television and advertising industry (see Newman 2017, location 1550). In fact, there is a marked shift in advertising in the era of the 1980s and 1990s. As Lotz points out, changes "in dominant advertising practices can substantially affect television programming and, consequently, the stories the medium provides" (2014, location 3924). Though Lotz focusses more on contemporary shifts, the changes made in the 1980s and 1990s, from product integration to infomercials, remain relevant to the themes and aesthetics. In the arena of the 30-second spot that dominated television from the 1950s onwards, there is a lot of innovation to convince viewers to watch specific spots, even though, as Lotz points out, the format itself did not fundamentally change (ibid.). Advertising blocs are hardly homogenous and producers of advertising try to convince viewers to watch their spot rather than the entire advertising bloc. This is even more true in an age of RCDs and grazing than previously. The era features a range of innovative spots, on the one hand aesthetically interesting, but even going as far as telling long-term stories, such as the romance between neighbours in the Taster's Choice coffee commercials (Jicha 1998). Other strategies are the accomplished aesthetics of Levi's 501 or Pepsi commercials that mimic short-form music video aesthetics (see Chandler 2015). Bellamy and Walker identify five strategies used by advertisers to respond to grazing: targeting, spot length, placement, programming control and creative changes (1996, 57–62).

Maybe most remarkably, the infomercial became a common format for programming on mainstream channels, usually in time slots where most viewers could be assumed to be asleep. Infomercials are essentially long-form programmes designed to sell one specific product, such as knives, fitness equipment or a line of cosmetics. They consist of a filmed programming element, which introduces the product and has presenters and guests show how it works and what its advantages are as well as a direct response segment that allows viewers to call in and buy the product. Both segments can be repeated indefinitely. As August Grant and Jennifer Meadows point out, long-format commercials had been prominent on US TV in the 1950s but were outlawed by the FCC in 1973 and allowed again in 1984 (2002, 257). Two years later, in 1986, the shopping channel QVC started broadcasting, which divided up 30-minute slots to companies selling different products:

> One might assume that a home shopping channel like QVC produces 'programming' like any other television channel, but it only really provides a type of long-term commercial. [...] So, while QVC may resemble traditional programming (it does, for example, share aesthetic similarities with daytime TV), this perhaps only allows it to skilfully conceal its harsh commercial imperative from viewers who may be put off by too obvious a hard sell. Although, for example, its presenters may appear relaxed, informal and even able to ad-lip freely on live TV, everything on screen is carefully choreographed and orchestrated to produce maximum profit, with each presenter being told (via an earpiece) what to do and say by a producer in the control room who knows precisely what the sales per minute (SPM) are. (Creeber 2015, 210)

QVC also works with elements reminiscent of the game show when it lowers sale prices live on air. Shopping channels and infomercials, often several hours long, may mark the most significant structural change to how television advertising changed in the 1980s. This can be linked to grazing: while few viewers might settle in for an evening of infomercial, grazers might get 'hooked' by a specific product or presenter. Even if viewers only stay for a few minutes, they may still be persuaded to buy something, as "this genre is typified by offering a virtually continuous stream of sales pitches" (Grant and Meadows 2001, 256). Furthermore, the effect of the advertising can instantly be measured in sales numbers and products taken out of the line-up, if necessary. This shift in strategy for advertisers is significant, even if it is relatively marginalised and rarely discussed TV genre.

The idea of 'quality' television was also re-introduced to attract viewers. As Thompson outlines, this development reaches back to the 1970s and television series throughout the 1980s would strive towards a unique style and distinctiveness. Series like *Hill Street Blues* or *Miami Vice* (NBC, 1984–9) are examples of series with a specific style and aesthetics. Particularly *Hill Street Blues* would also achieve considerable critical acclaim, which would further emphasise its significance (see Jenkins 1984; Thompson 1996, 59–74, Gitlin 1994). But beyond a broad idea of 'quality' TV, more 'middlebrow' series like *Magnum, P.I.* (NBC, 1981–8) or *Dynasty* (ABC, 1981–9) would develop visual styles that clearly set them apart from competing programmes.

Aside from qualitative changes to programming, scheduling became more important. This refers to the way advertising blocs are organised to keep viewer attention as well as how programmes are arranged within the schedule. Bellamy and Walker (1996) discuss the following strategies: strong lead-ins (a successful programme at the beginning of the time bloc), hammock (a less successful programme in-between two strongly rated ones), tent-pole (a less successful programme is placed before more successful ones), blocking and stacking (series of the same genre or with the same demographic appeal are programmed together). These strategies are not new to television, but they took on a new significance with the rise of the RCD. As Susan Tyler Eastman and Jeffrey Neal-Lunsford point out:

> Even without cable television, viewers now jump between pairs of programs, graze along dozens of channels, and generally show little station or network loyalty, paying scant attention to choosing a single source for a daypart's viewing (if, indeed, they ever consciously 'choose' a channel or network to view). (1993, 189)

The authors move on to argue that this led to top-loading, meaning the allocation of high production values to the beginning of a programme. *Hill Street Blues*, for example, would start episodes with its famous 'roll-call' scenes: these scenes were shot in documentary style with hand-held cameras (see Gitlin 1994, 293). In line with this, Eastman and Neal-Lunsford point to opening scenes that often postpone increasingly elaborate opening credits until after the first commercial break. A common strategy for television, starting in the 1970s, was also to put a teaser before the actual beginning of the episode, which gave a taste of upcoming plots, possible guest stars and action scenes, such as exciting car chases or moments of romance. The 'MTV style' of series like *Miami Vice*, following the quick edits and fast-paced narratives of music videos and other MTV programming, can also be attributed to assumptions about grazing. Eastman and Neal-Lunsford also observe:

> It is widely believed that between-program clutter such as credits, commercials, promos and public service announcements are an invitation to change channels. Interstitial, or non-program, matter facilitates grazing as viewers look for more interesting fare or avoid selling messages. To keep viewers from reaching for their RCDs, programmers and producers increasingly focus their efforts on rapid and arresting transitions between programs. (1993, 193)

There are different strategies to cut closing credits short or keep viewers interested as they are guided to the next programme. Some episodes of *Roseanne* (ABC, 1988–97), for example, end on bloopers as the credits roll over them. The still common (even on Netflix) squeezed credits move them to the side of the screen as previews or other programming takes up the majority of the screen. Kimberley Massey and Stanley Baran point to an episode of the relatively conventional legal drama *Matlock* (NBC, 1986–95) where viewers were asked to "phone in and vote on who was the murderer" (1990, 101–2). This interactive strategy has proven much more successful in live shows but is testament to the lengths broadcasters would go to solicit continued viewer attention.

Another way the television industry responded to RCDs was by developing stronger channel brands communicated through logos, idents, programming strategies, visual style and other features:

> In the USA from the mid-1950s to the mid-1980s the national networks had an oligopoly on broadcasting. The networks endeavoured to attract undifferentiated mass audiences and it was common practice for a network to imitate programming innovations of its rivals. Any brand identity that was too specific or too defined could potentially alienate viewers, and so branding functioned primarily as a shorthand device for indicating the general identity of a network. (Johnson 2012, 5)

The efforts to construct more consistent and refined brand identities in the 1980s worked to tie viewers to individual channels. Channel logos function as shorthand to communicate to viewers which channel (and associated brand identity) they are watching:

> Channel branding was valuable in an expanded programming environment to allow viewers to know what they could expect to be 'on' a particular channel. (Lotz 2017, location 525)

These strategies indicate the relevance of RCDs in negotiating the relationship between viewers and industry. These negotiations are predominantly concerned with the maintenance of the financing model of commercial television. In this, the system of commercial television is not subverted, and power structures are not overturned. Yet, the system adapts to new conditions in which viewers exert more control over their environment. This can be viewed as a result of negotiations of power relations via the RCD.

Remote Control Anxieties

Though originally introduced to limit the power of advertisers and enable viewers to exercise control over their television experience, RCDs quickly became objects around which broader cultural anxieties were formulated. Part of this is likely linked to their name and the associations with science fiction or horror, where 'remote control' of another person is often used as a story device. Yet, when they were first introduced for television, they were marketed as a solution to anxieties surrounding commercial television. With television becoming increasingly popular in Western post-World War II societies, anxieties about ideological influences and annoyance with television commercials only seemed to grow and the remote control was offered as a technology to offer relief. This idea became even more popularised in the late 1950s with the publication of Vance Packard's *The Hidden Persuaders* in 1957, which offers insights into the psychological strategies used by advertisers. Packard likens some television advertising to brainwashing and compares it to strategies used by communist regimes. In the US, there also was a prevailing myth that advertisements were presented at a louder volume than other programming. The FCC debunked this in a 1956 inquiry, but the fact that the myth existed at all shows that viewers must have perceived television advertising as extremely annoying and possibly harmful (see Dawson 2008, 56). Some viewers took the problem into their own hands and sold on kits to help other viewers mute the TV.[3] Yet, more commercial interests were also at play:

> In certain situations, viewers were joined in their struggles against advertisers by networks eager to mount a power play over their sponsors. However, for reasons that should be obvious, the networks could never commit themselves fully to the anti-advertising cause. Television receiver manufacturers, on the other hand, did not face this same dilemma. Zenith in particular reached out to viewers in their ongoing battles with advertisers, enlisting the audience in its own campaign against advertiser-supported television. (ibid. 59–60)

[3] The 'Blab-Off', for example, a kit for home-made devices to shut off the sound during ads is prominently mentioned on the website of the Early Television Foundation (see http://www.earlytelevision.org/blab_off.html).

With the introduction of cable, the function of the RCD changed from a device to avoid advertisement to a device to manage choice and switch between programmes. This increased choice, managed via RCDs, made avoiding advertising easier than ever. Yet, instead of resolving anxieties about commercial television, new anxieties developed and old ones re-emerged.

An important focus of academic and popular discussion surrounding RCDs in the 1980s and 1990s emphasises gender. This is linked to now somewhat clichéd debates along the lines of 'who has control in the household?', but is also embedded within feminist debates, specifically the backlash to feminism, from the second half of the 1980s onwards. Yet, these gendered discourses reach back further. As critics who analysed remote controls in the US have pointed out, the emphasis on control in the marketing of early remote controls had decidedly gendered aspects:

> At a moment when critics and pundits accused television of making men soft, and television programs of making men out to be impotent idiots, electronics manufacturers promoted remote control devices as a technological means of shoring up the control they had sacrificed when they had welcomed television into their homes. (ibid. 45)

Keir Keightley (2003) outlines how much the television, from its early years, was conceptualised as commercial, low culture and 'feminine' in opposition to hi-fi systems that relied on 'masculine' user choice and accumulation of vast record collections. In this binary created in popular discourse, Keightley observes the traditional active/passive and individualism/mass culture binary for male and female consumption of mass media. Whereas male 'technology' was largely marketed as a 'hobby' and for technological tinkering, technology marketed at women was largely viewed as furniture, the 'electronic hearth' to bring the family together (see Spigel 1992). Thus, the remote control, suggesting activity, was bound to emerge as a site of gendered conflict: it allowed 'control' and 'activity', a masculine mastering of the 'feminised' object of television.

In the 1980s and 1990s gender discourse changed: as Julie D'Acci notes, white middle-class women spent less time at home as they increasingly sought to enter the public sphere through work. As a result, daytime viewership plummeted and advertisers became increasingly eager to address a 'working women's market' (1994, 71). This resulted in a shift in prime-time programming in an effort to address (white, middle-class) women, which might have informed popular discourse about issues of who gets to control the television. Further, in the 1970s and 1980s, as patriarchal power structures were strongly challenged by second-wave feminism in the US, the available programmes proliferated, making RCDs important technologies to control television. This is particularly relevant for the second half of the 1980s, which is a period Susan Faludi (1992) describes as a period of backlash against feminism. In this context of coinciding developments, remote controls emerged as sites of dissent over who controls what is watched, rather than a site of dominance over a commercial medium. This discourse is qualitatively different from the questions of control in the era of TV I. Early remote controls would have essentially been used to control sound or the on/off button. They would have been understood as objects to control the 'flow' of the television schedule. The control wielded by remote control users would have been over advertisers, not the rest of the family (as patriarchal power was implicit). In other words, rather than being a technology to *literally* control the television set, the remote control's status shifted to an object to *symbolically* dominate the family in the TV II era. Thus, at least in hindsight, it may be less productive to ask if there are gendered differences in how remote controls are used than to ask about the kinds of discourses these questions are embedded in. If a broader popular discourse asks what kind of discord feminism brings to the family, the remote control functions as one site where male power and dominance becomes visible. Nevertheless, it is also a site where it becomes contested as other family members may voice dissent and frustration. Gary Copeland and Karla Schweitzer (1993) confirm David Morley's (1988) findings that, in family viewing situations, a male member of the family is more likely to control the remote:

> In this study, females controlled the remote during family viewing situations in only 15.2 percent of families. Domination of the remote control also strongly suggests domination of the program selection process. (Copeland and Schweitzer 1993, 165)

Furthermore, Elisabeth Perse and Douglas Ferguson argue that men feel empowered by the remote controls while women feel disenfranchised (1993). Following this, empirical research does not tend to find that remote controls are the cause of much dissent within the household, as women give up control willingly. This points to the symbolic role RCDs take on in public discourse rather than their actual role in family life. In other words, what is at stake is a broader discourse around gender and power. This fits neatly with Keightley's research comparing use of hi-fi systems and the television in 1950s America. The RCD allows for 'control', for 'tinkering' with television programming, volume and image. This status as 'technology' rather than 'home appliance' may also influence the gendered differences at play in this specific discourse. The remote control emerges as symbol for other forms of social control and power. As such, it enables communication about control and power that goes beyond discourses about commercial media. Nevertheless, male domination over the private sphere impacts on women in the public sphere. Thus, the symbolic function of RCDs as objects to 'take back control' is a powerful feature of the broader backlash against feminism. The control RCDs enable in gender discourses only makes sense as part of a broader discourse where they can be symbolically linked with patriarchal power.

A further anxiety is related to issues of audience activity and time spent watching television as remote controls become affordable for all in the 1980s. The equal access to television across social class and taste cultures, especially in a TV II world with its massive proliferation of channels, was soon widely interpreted as problematic. In the late 1980s and 1990s remote controls were no longer marketed as items to control mass media and make active choices about avoiding unwelcome programming. Instead, it became symbolic of passive subjugation to broadcasting flows and an inability to switch off. This shift is important: early remote controls could increase the price of a set by a significant amount, making the avoidance of advertising a privilege for elites. In relation to Zenith's Lazy Bones, Benson-Allott points out:

> It added $30 to the price of any Zenith television set at a time when sets ranged in price between $269 and $629. It could also be purchased separately and installed by a handy homeowner or television repairman. $30 in 1950 is equivalent to nearly $300 today, though, so the Lazy Bones remote still represented an extravagant expense for middle-class consumers. (2015, 33)

In the 1980s, the manufacturing of RCDs became so cheap remote controls were quickly included automatically with the purchase of a television set. With this shift comes also the reconceptualization of an object of empowerment and control to an object that allows for physical passivity. In the contradictory assumptions surrounding audiences in the TV II era, this physical passivity is also often understood to suggest cognitive passivity. Part of this is linked to the greater choice of programming and channels: even the most disciplined mind may find it challenging to deal with this much choice. Additionally, particularly newer cable channels would only be able to produce relatively cheap original programming. For example, as David Andrews outlines, softcore porn films could function as cheap late-night programming for cable television (2006, 79–89). Thus, the available choices were often of relatively low quality, even 'disreputable', so grazing through channels would expose viewers to more 'bad' television—and not just in the form of advertising. This, of course, went against promises and hopes that RCDs could 'repair' television. Ros Jennings notes in relation to the spread of satellite and cable in the UK:

> In discussions of television, there seems to be little notion of self-regulating and discerning viewers, but rather discourses of moral panic circulating around the figure of the 'couch potato'. Satellite and cable systems with their promise of multiple channels and fears about dubious quality control encapsulated all these fears about excess and lethargic slavery to television viewing. (2003, 112–3)

The shift of RCDs as objects only accessible to elites to a 'mass' object is heavily informed by contemporary class-based assumptions about television. The roots of the term 'couch potato' to describe habitual television viewers who would spend most of their free time on the couch in front of the TV are largely satirical. The term was trademarked in the US by cartoonist Robert Armstrong in 1976, who would go on to publish a successful cartoon of the same name with Jack Mingo in the form of *The Official Couch Potato Handbook* in 1983. A *New York Times* story from 1987 reports on the availability of couch potato board games and dolls (see Home & Garden Editorial, *New York Times*, 12.11.1987). This story describes a decidedly urban middle-class (or yuppie) version of the couch potato where hard-working young adults assemble in New York's fashionable clubs to watch contemporary 'quality' TV, such as *L.A. Law* (NBC, 1986–94). The story suggests ironic re-appropriation, but also activity: after all, these young adults go out to watch TV in a communal viewing experience, rather than in isolation at home. However humorous, as Laurence Scott's analysis in a piece for *The New Yorker* in 2016 outlines, "Though full of puns and ironic triumphalism, [Armstrong's] lighthearted book betrays the social anxieties that surrounded television", which were widely expressed in the television of the era. From Darlene's (Sara Gilbert) teenage depression on *Roseanne* to *Beavis and Butt-Head* (MTV, 1993–2011), from *Married... with Children* (Fox, 1987–97) to *The Simpsons* (Fox, 1989–), anxieties around young people and the working class would be expressed via the figure of the physically inactive viewer on decidedly unfashionable couches. Much like the term 'couch potato' itself, all these texts are satirical, but as much as they satirise how the middle-class views youths and the working class, they do not tend to question anxieties around television viewing. De-constructing 'moral panics' or 'popular anxieties', Graham Murdock points to the prominence of class-based assumptions in which the 'mass' in mass media is equated with 'working class' (2001, 153–8). Murdock traces the idea that the working class is usually an 'other', outlined by journalists as different from a 'respectable' middle class, that is vulnerable to the effects of mass media. As Julian Petley notes,

> Debates about media effects tend to focus on how children and young people are supposedly affected – usually for the worse. But lurking behind these fears about the 'corruption of innocent minds' one finds, time and again, implicit or explicit, a potent strand of class dislike and fear. (2001, 170)

Thus, the tradition of linking fears surrounding young people with classist assumptions is common and recurs often in relation to anxieties and moral panics around television. In the 1980s/1990s iteration of these anxieties the remote control and the resulting physical passivity of the viewer is central. In these debates, RCDs function as symbols for apathy, subjugation and powerlessness. Physical inactivity is equated with cognitive inactivity and willing acceptance of oppression through mass media, rather than using the RCD as a tool of subversion or negotiation of power. In the case of the remote control, there isn't a specific moment of 'moral panic', but in the symbol of the couch potato, broader anxieties surrounding the assumed effects of mass culture and assumed media effects on the 'othered' working class come to the surface. Scott assigns the decline in the usage of the term 'couch potato' in the early 2000s to the ubiquity of online media. Yet, this is also a cultural moment when television reached a moment of legitimation which made binge-watching on DVD box sets an acceptable practice for middle-class audiences (see Chapter 9). Thus, anxieties dissolve as practices are adopted by the 'gatekeepers' of culture.

The RCD's function within broader debates surrounding power and control, thus, varies. For (presumably) white, middle-class families, the remote control functions as symbol within gender struggles in the 1980s. Meanwhile, in relation to young people and the working class, it functions as a symbol of subjugation to the ideological messages of mass media. In this context, the remote control is not a technology of agency that helps viewers avoid 'bad' television in the form of advertising or qualitatively inferior programming. The remote control is less an object that enables negotiation of power, but a symbol of subjugation. Unlike in gender discourses, holding the RCD does not translate to holding power over the family unit, but lack of agency. These contradictory connotations of RCDs speak to its complicated role in negotiating power and control.

Conclusion

This chapter explored RCDs and issues of power and control associated with it. It discussed the technology's new function in the TV II era, its role in a negotiation of power and control between audiences and industry and its symbolic power in broader social discourses of the era. These various roles of the remote control indicate how much of its power was assumed rather than real: though scheduling techniques and programmes changed in the era, much of this was based on assumptions about audience's attitudes to advertising. Additionally, the symbolic role the remote control assumes in popular discourses surrounding the family, gender and broader anxieties about class, age and television has implications for this analysis. These discourses also highlight how limited control is: in gender- and class-based anxieties in which the remote control is important, control is limited. Gender discourses surrounding remote control use in the home may work as a powerful metaphor for a broader power struggle, but its role in the actual power struggle against patriarchy is more or less non-existent. Its role in the expression of class and age-based anxieties makes this even clearer: the assumption is that remote controls invest no one with social power. Yet, these discourses also fail to recognise that various branches of the television industry did perceive the remote control as disruption that merited changes to television scheduling and advertising. This is not to over-emphasise the power of the consumer, but to recognise where the effects of control of the television viewer lie. They cannot be understood as equating real social power, but RCDs enable a negotiation of how power is organised in the context of television.

Bibliography

Andrews, David. 2006. *Soft in the Middle: The Contemporary Softcore Feature in its Contexts*. Columbus: Ohio State University Press.

Armstrong, Robert, and Jack Mingo. 1983. *The Official Couch Potato Handbook: A Guide to Prolonged Television Viewing*. Santa Barbara: Capra Press.

Baran, Stanley J. and Massey, Kimberly K. 1990. "VCRs and People's Control of their Leisure Time." In Dobrow, Julia R. (ed.). *Social and Cultural Aspects of VCR Use*. Hillsdale, N.J.: L. Erlbaum Associates, 93–106.

Benson-Allott, Caetlin. 2015. *Remote Control*. New York: Bloomsbury.

Bellamy, Robert V. 1993. "Remote Control Devices and the Political Economy of a Changing Television Industry." In Robert V. Bellamy and James R. Walker (ed.), *The Remote Control in the New Age of Television*, 211–220. London: Praeger.

Bellamy, Robert V., and James R. Walker. 1993. "The Remote Control Device: An Overlooked Technology." In Robert V. Bellamy and James R. Walker (ed.), *The Remote Control in the New Age of Television*, 3–14. London: Praeger.

Bellamy, Robert V., James R. Walker, and James R. Walker. 1996. *Television and the Remote Control: Grazing on a Vast Wasteland*. New York: Guilford Press.

Benjamin, Louise. 1993. "At the Touch of a Button: A Brief History of Remote Control Devices." In Robert V. Bellamy and James R. Walker (ed.), *The Remote Control in the New Age of Television*, 15–22. London: Praeger.

Buonanno, Milly. 2008. *The Age of Television Experiences and Theories*. Bristol: Intellect.

Castells, Manuel. 2009. *The Power of Identity the Information Age: Economy, Society, and Culture Volume II*. 2nd ed. ed. Hoboken. Hoboken: Wiley.

Chandler, Daniel. 2015. "The Levi's 501 'Launderette' Commercial." In Creeber, Glen (ed.), *The Television Genre Book*, 3rd ed., 209.

Copeland, Gary A., and Karla Schweitzer. 1993. Domination of the Remote Control during Family Viewing. In Robert V. Bellamy and James R. Walker (ed.), *The Remote Control in the New Age of Television*, 155–168. London: Praeger.

Creeber, Glen. 2015. "QVC." In Glen Creeber (ed.), *The Television Genre Book*, 209–211. London: BFI.

Curtin, Michael. 2009. "Matrix Media." In Jinna Tay and Graeme Turner (ed.), *Television Studies After TV: Understanding Television in the Post- Broadcast Era*, 9–19. London: Routledge.

D'Acci, Julie. 1994. *Defining Women: Television and the Case of Cagney & Lacey*. Chapel Hill; London: University of North Carolina Press.

Dawson, Max. 2008. *TV Repair: New Media Solutions to Old Media Problems*, eds. Lynn B. Spigel, Jennifer Light and Jeffrey Sconce. ProQuest Dissertations Publishing.

Eastman, Susan Tyler, and Jeffrey Neal-Lunsford. 1993. "The RCD's Impact on Television Programming and Promotion." In Robert V. Bellamy and James R. Walker (ed.), *The Remote Control in the New Age of Television*, 189–210. London: Praeger.

Ellis, John. 1992. *Visible Fictions Cinema: Television: Video*. Hoboken: Taylor and Francis.

Faludi, Susan. 1992. *Backlash: The Undeclared War Against Women*. London: Vintage.

Gitlin, Todd. 1994. *Inside Prime Time*. Berkeley: University of California Press.

Grant, August E., and Jennifer H. Meadows. 2002. "Electronic Commerce: Going Shopping with QVC and AOL." In Carolyn A. Lin and David J. Atkin (ed.), *Communication Technology and Society : Audience Adoption and Uses*, 255–278. Creskill, N.J.: Hampton Press.

Home & Garden Editorial. 1987. "Catering to a Couch Potato's Every Need." *The New York Times*, Available online: http://www.nytimes.com/1987/11/12/garden/catering-to-a-couch-potato-s-every-need.html. Accessed: 23.12.2017.

Jenkins, Steve. 1984. "Hill Street Blues." In Jane Feuer, Paul Kerr, and Tise Vahimagi (eds.), *MTM: 'Quality Television*, 183–199. London: BFI.

Jennings, Bryant, and Steven C. Rockwell. 1993. "Remote Control Devices in Television Program Selection: Experimental Evidence." In Robert V. Bellamy and James R. Walker (eds.), *The Remote Control in the New Age of Television*, 73–87. London: Praeger.

Jennings, Ros. 2003. "Satellite and Cable Programmes in the UK." In Michelle Hilmes and Jason Jacobs (eds.), *The Television History Book*, 112–115. London: BFI.

Jicha, Paul. 1998. "Coffee Commercial Romance Grinds to A Halt." *Chicago Tribune*. Available online: http://articles.chicagotribune.com/1998-04-25/news/9804250021_1_scene-taster-s-choice-spot. Accessed: 23.12.1017.

Johnson, Catherine. 2012. *Branding Television*. London: Routledge.

Keightley, Keir. 2003. "Low Television, High Fidelity: Taste and the Gendering of Home Entertainment Technologies." *Journal of Broadcasting & Electronic Media* 47 (2): 236–259.

Klopfenstein, Bruce C. 1993. "From Gadget to Necessity: The Diffusion of Remote Control Technology." In Robert V. Bellamy and James R. Walker, (ed.), *The Remote Control in the New Age of Television*, 23–39. London: Praeger.

Kompare, Derek. 2005. *Rerun Nation: How Repeats Invented American Television*. New York, N.Y: Routledge.

Lin, Carolyn. 1990. "Audience Activity and VCR Use." In Julia R. (ed.), *Social and Cultural Aspects of VCR Use*. Hillsdale, N.J.: L. Erlbaum Associates, 75–92.

Lotz, Amanda D. 2014. *The Television Will be Revolutionized*, 2nd ed. New York: New York University Press.

Lotz, Amanda D. 2017. *Portals*. Michigan: Maize Books.

Morley, David. 1988. *Family Television: Cultural Power and Domestic Leisure*. London: Routledge.

Murdock, Graham. 2001. "Reservoirs of Dogma: An Archaeology of Popular Anxieties." In Barker, Martin and Petley, Julian (eds.), *Ill Effects: The Media/Violence Debate*, 2nd ed. London: Routledge. 150–169.

Newman, Michael Z. 2017. *Atari Age: The Emergence of Video Games in America*. Cambridge, MA: MIT Press.

Packard, Vance. 1957. *The Hidden Persuaders*. Longman.

Perse, Elisabeth M., and Douglas A. Ferguson. 1993. Gender Differences in Remote Control Use. In Robert V. Bellamy and James R. Walker (ed.), *The Remote Control in the New Age of Television*, 169–186. London: Praeger.

Petley, Julian. 2001. "Us and Them." In Martin Barker and Julian Petley (eds.), *Ill Effects : The Media/Violence Debate*, 2nd ed., 170–185. London: Routledge.

Scott, Laurence. 2016. "What Ever Happened to the Couch Potato?" *The New Yorker*. Available online: https://www.newyorker.com/tech/elements/what-ever-happened-to-the-couch-potato. Accessed: 23.12.2017.

Spigel, Lynn. 1992. *Make Room for TV. Television and the Family Ideal in Postwar America*. Chicago: University of Chicago Press.

Thomas, Julian. 2011. "When Digital was New." In Bennett, James and Strange, Niki (eds.), *Television as Digital Media*. Durham, NC: Duke University Press. Kindle, location 640–938.

Thompson, Robert J. 1996. *Television's Second Golden Age*. Syracuse, N.Y.: Syracuse University Press.

Traudt, Paul J. 1993. "Surveillance and Cluster Viewing: Foraging through the RCD Experience." In Robert V. Bellamy and James R. Walker (eds.), *The Remote Control in the New Age of Television*, 57–72. London: Praeger.

Television

Beavis and Butt-Head (1993–2011), USA: MTV.
Dynasty (1981–9), USA: ABC.
Hill Street Blues (1981–7), USA: NBC.
L.A. Law (1986–94), USA: NBC.
Magnum, P.I. (1980–8), USA: CBS.
Married… with Children (1987–97), USA: Fox.
Matlock (1986–95), USA: NBC.
Miami Vice (1984–90), USA: NBC.
Roseanne (1988–97), USA: ABC.
Sex and the City (1998–2004), USA: HBO.
Simpsons, The (1989–), USA: Fox.

CHAPTER 5

New Regimes of Control: Television as Convergence Medium

If RCDs enable control over the television experience, time-shifting technologies offer more substantial options to avoid dealing with the television schedule or commercial television. Whereas RCDs enable interactivity and negotiation of power and control, time-shifting technologies enable viewers to fast-forward and skip advertising altogether. VCRs and later DVD players even allow viewers to forego commercial television content in favour of pre-recorded content. Where the RCD allows control over choice, time-shifting allows control over time and content. As Lotz argues:

> The VCR is one of the first technologies to trouble our understandings of 'television'. The distribution of the VCR as an affordable technology, which achieved mass diffusion at the same time as the remote control, significantly expanded viewer's relationship with and control over television's entertainment. [...] The recording devices allowed viewers to negate programmers' strategies through time shifting and introduced new competitors such as the home video and purchase market. (2014a, b, 1378)

The two dominant functions of the VCR are the recording and time-shifting of television broadcasts and the viewing of pre-recorded tapes. As Newman argues:

M. Jenner, *Netflix and the Re-invention of Television*,
https://doi.org/10.1007/978-3-031-39237-5_5

> Video was often positioned similarly to cable in this period [the 1970s and 80s] as a liberating, culturally uplifting, and democratizing medium. It promised to be a kind of Robin Hood of media, redistributing power in communication from corporations and institutions to individuals. (Newman 2014, 25)

Where cable extends choice and RCDs work as tools to manage that choice, VCRs have the potential for more significant subversion (or at least disruption) of commercial television. Time-shifting means that broadcasters have little knowledge about if a programme is watched at all and what is fast-forwarded and what may be re-watched. The viewing of pre-recorded tapes, whether rented or bought, lies even further outside of the sphere of knowledge of the television industry. The reaction is less a reorganisation of schedules, as with RCDs, but a more profound restructuring of media industries via conglomeration and a focus on pre-recorded programming.

As Newman points out, in the 1950s and 1960s, video was largely imagined to be synonymous with television rather than ancillary technology (2014). Yet, when Sony started advertising the Betamax in 1975, its emphasis was on time-shifting:

> Like their ancestors, the first Betamax cassettes could only record an hour of video, an embodiment of Sony's assumption that the machine would primarily be used for time-shifting broadcast television shows (which generally lasted an hour at most). Tape length was a crucial factor in the early skirmishes between Sony's Beta format and its rival, Matshushita's VHS – the story goes that RCA, the major producer of VHS recorders in the United States, refused to start manufacturing the machines until a tape could record not just an hour-long serial drama, but a full football game (Greenberg 2008, 44)

Frederick Wasser cites *New York Times* critic Jack Gould as writing in 1967 that:

> By far the most interesting aspect of the innovation is its promise to introduce into the television medium the element of individual selectivity that up to now has been lacking. (cited in 2001, location 1386)

The VCR was understood and marketed as a technology that would provide previously unknown control, choice and power to subvert existing media systems. Cable extended competition within the framework of the free market, though broadcast channels had more (financial) resources to compete than most newer cable channels. RCDs proved more challenging, but changes to programming and content and structure of advertising could also deal with grazing consumers. The VCR offered viewers possibilities to spend their time in front of the TV watching pre-recorded tapes. It allowed viewers to zip through advertising. As with RCDs, the assumption that viewers would do this was likely more influential than actual data.

The kind of control offered by the VCR was not only unprecedented, it could even put audiences out of the reach of commercial television. As Joshua Greenberg (2008) argues, the VCR experience in the US was largely modelled after the cinema experience. Considering the high sale prices, it may not be surprising that most VCR owners preferred to rent tapes. Rental stores also developed the convention of selling popcorn and other food associated with the cinema experience. This positioned videotapes as somewhere between the cinema and TV experience: it involved going out, selecting a film (with a wider choice than even at the biggest multiplex) and buying movie snacks, but viewing at home, being able to take a break to go to the bathroom or get something from elsewhere, making loud comments and viewing on the small screen. The positioning of the VCR as a different version of the cinema possibly made it a more substantial threat to the cinema than to television. Nevertheless, it also substantially changed how the television set would be used.

Greenberg (2008) argues the VCR is a medium in its own right, at least partially based on the associated video-rental and straight-to-video film industry. As much as the VCR disrupts Hollywood hegemony through the video-rental industry, this point is more complicated to make for television. The VCR is a relatively useless technology if it is not plugged into a television set, so the object of the television set is central and continues to be used. In relation to television, time-shifting also cannot unequivocally be assumed to replace, or even modify, the experience of broadcast television: VCRs time-shift television, but viewers cannot be assumed to forego television viewing altogether. Though zipping through advertising is made possible, it is not known how much of a practice it actually was. This means that the threat was more direct for cinema, as viewers would rent tapes instead of buying movie tickets. Viewing pre-recorded tapes might take time away from television viewing, but commercial or academic research does not appear to have been concerned with the question if that would cost the television industry more viewers than cinema did. The interventions from the television and advertising industry discussed in the last chapter have been designed to address the triple threat of the RCD, VCR and cable. Nevertheless, the uncertainty of how viewers were using their VCRs made for less precise interventions. Thus, this chapter is less concerned with how the television industry addressed issues arising from the VCR via programming, but more with how viewers used the possibilities offered by the VCR to manipulate the television schedule.

This chapter continues the exploration of power and control through ancillary technologies by looking at the various ways the VCR changes understandings of what television is. In this, it conceptualises the VCR as time-shifting technology. Various studies and conceptualisations of VCR viewing are given here to emphasise the complex possibilities time-shifting allows for, particularly in a pre-digital era. What is implicit in the way viewers put the VCR to use, even if it is often only small audience segments, is viewer desire for control. More specifically, it is about the *kind* of control viewers seek. This is often literal as well as symbolic systems of ownership over a product: the recording, repetitive viewing and archiving of texts. Thus, viewers may have little control over the means of production, but a form of ownership over the finished product. The chapter then moves on to discuss the way the VCR enabled the development of industries and programming that was, at least initially, independent of Hollywood and television, though later incorporated into these systems. In a last step, this chapter positions television as convergence medium, furthered by the VCR, but with various media forms displayed on the television screen that enable more interactivity. This reconception of television as convergence medium also had consequences for the gendered metaphors and conceptualisations of television described in the last chapter. Thus, this chapter understands the television set as 'hub' of media convergence in an era when more and more ancillary technologies rely on the set to display their content.

Time-Shifting Television

The so-called 'Betamax Case' is instructive in how time-shifting was understood and perceived by viewers and industry in the 1970s and 80s:

> MCA/Universal Studios and Walt Disney Productions filed a lawsuit in a California Federal District Court in 1976, charging the Japanese company with copyright infringement. They alleged that Sony (through its Betamax VCR advertising) was encouraging Americans to use Betamax machines illegally to videotape television shows produced and owned by the two studios. (Secunda 1990, 18)

As Secunda notes, typical Betamax advertisements would, indeed, emphasise that viewers could 'build their own schedule' by recording and replaying content (ibid.). Nevertheless, at the heart of the case was the question of whether recording content directly from broadcast television was, indeed, copyright infringement. After the case had moved back and forth between different courts with contradictory findings, the US Supreme Court finally decided in 1984 that taping for home use was not copyright infringement. By this time, the home video market had been established, posing different regulatory hurdles, and the VHS format had already proven more popular than Betamax. Nevertheless, early Betamax advertising and the 'Betamax case' are significant in what they tell us about the perceived use of the new technology.

Because relatively little data is available on how viewers would use the VCR as time-shifting technology to manipulate different aspects of television throughout the 1980s and 1990s, the studies that offer this kind of information are of particular relevance. Ann Gray's study of British female VCR users is indicative of time-shifting behaviours: she identifies different strategies for time-shifted viewing. For example, several of her subjects report recording programmes for short-term use. They may record an episode of a favourite series in order to 'keep up' with it. One woman even reports recording as she watches, both, when viewing on her own and when watching with her partner, in case her viewing is interrupted or the programme turns out to be worth archiving (1992, 119). This behaviour is later also reported by Bjarkman in her 2004 article on video collectors. In her study, the simultaneous viewing and taping serves the purpose of preserving and archiving the television programme (more than the television flow) (2004, 225). Several of Gray's study subjects reported recording television flow, so not just the programme they wish to record, but also preceding and following programmes. Gray also finds time-shifting to avoid conflict, allowing one party in the household to watch one programme while another is recorded.[1]

Content recorded from television, however, largely seems to be archived when films are recorded, at least in Gray's study. When flow remains intact, this is more commonly linked with poor organisation and archiving skills. Nevertheless, Bjarkman notes in her study on VHS collectors about 12 years later:

> With steady advances in video technology over the past two decades, more and more viewers refuse to accept that celebrated television moments are doomed to disappear forever. Programs we miss (in either sense) need not slip out of our grasp now that VCRs are a domestic staple. Video recorders seize texts out of the ether and give them material form so that they may be preserved, circulated, recollected, and relived. Beyond entertainment value, these recordings serve as exterior memory, cultural relic, and resource in the home. (2004, 218)

Thus, in the course of the 1990s, the practice of recording and archiving television seems to have become more common, even if this is only true for relatively small and marginalised fan communities. From Gray's gendered perspective, the archives are more commonly the territory of the women's male partners than their own:

> The organization and maintenance of an archive would seem to be a predominantly male and middle-class activity. The limit which economic circumstances place on the number of tapes is significant here, but the gendered nature of this practice requires some examination. Obviously the question of available time as well as inclination is important, but some of the women reported their partner's concern to review tapes, especially movies. The women themselves did not share this preference. The whole concept of an archive is based on the assumption that there will be more than one viewing of the product, something that would appear to be a predominantly male activity. Even those women who did have archived films of their own [...] reported that they were much more prepared to 'wipe' than their partners. (1992, 132)

[1] The taping of a programme while watching another one to avoid conflict confirms the view voiced in the last chapter that dissent within household over who controls the remote may have been more an imagined problem within cultural discourse in the context of anti-feminist backlash than a real issue.

Partly, this seemed to be due to a preference for repetitive viewing by male partners. Bjarkman's study on repetitive viewing and archiving is of particular interest here, as her study points to the archiving and exchange of recorded television among collector-fans. This suggests an already established predecessor to the DVD box set that started to emerge as dominant force around the time of her study. Though the VHS collectors she deals with may be a relatively small audience segment, it suggests that recording and collecting of television was already a practice before studios learned to fully capitalise on it with DVD box sets.

Repetitive viewing is a dominant topic in discussions of time-shifting.[2] In Dobrow's study, which included almost 200 interviews in the context of a larger survey, but included questions on VCR use, she found:

> ...virtually each person interviewed reported that he or she used the VCR to view things more than once; what was surprising was the variety of programming viewed multiple times, and the similar reasons given for multiple viewings across demographic and ethnic groups. Movies (rented, purchased or prerecorded videocassettes, or taped off of network or cable television) led the list of programs watched more than once. Of television programs other than movies time-shifted and played back later, surprisingly many respondents reported viewing sports games [...], news programs [...] situation comedies [...], and soap operas. (1990, 186, emphasis removed)

Her respondents also report rewatching DIY, cooking or exercise tapes, home movies, music videos, and even advertising spots. The breadth of material recorded and re-viewed indicates that viewers not only enjoy deciding when to watch what, but also how many times it should be watched. Much of the material that is being watched several times is closely linked to the 'low culture' status of television. As Dobrow finds, beyond educational uses (learning English, particularly in immigrant families) or the performance of rituals for children, VCR users seem to enjoy repeat viewing of 'trivial' television content. Barbara Klinger (2010) traces the importance of re-viewing films using *The Big Lebowski* (Coen and Coen 1998) as an example of films that 'become cult' thanks to re-viewing practices.[3] The VHS era certainly produced a number of films that did

[2] The 'ritual' of rewatching clearly predated the vast diffusion of VCRs in the US in the 1980s (see Klinger 2006, 135–7).

[3] As suggested above in relation to archiving, Klinger also links the practice to male viewers. Though often studied less, the practice of repeat viewing is also common among

badly at the box office, but generated a fan following, for example due to their, as Klinger calls it, 'ritual importance' to fans. A 1986 story in the *New York Times* by Leslie Bennetts also reports on the practice of copying tapes, illegal practice in the US at the time, but seemingly widely accepted. This also suggests repetitive viewing, even though it features mainly as a way of saving on rental fees in Bennetts' story. Replay culture, along with increasing possibilities for fans to congregate and communicate online, significantly changes the process of 'cultification' for film. As Kompare (2005) argues, the repetitive structures of television in terms of genre formulas, spin-offs or reruns already suggest how repeat viewings can easily fit into the broader repetitive structures of television. Kompare notes that, though feature films dominated the VHS market, television also played a role in this market:

> In lieu of 'officially released' television on home video, unauthorized television collecting (via VHS) has flourished, albeit on the margins of television culture, with very little impact on the business of television. Even early on in the home video era, however, the fact that [VHS collectors] wished to preserve their favorite television shows on video suggested that a potential market existed for commercially released (i.e., officially published) home video copies of television series. (2005, 203)

In terms of sell-through videos, this obviously posed problems: only a few episodes of a series can be included on a VHS tape and the object of a tape takes up significant space. Only few series popular with fans and in reruns, such as *The X-Files*, *Buffy, the Vampire Slayer* or *Friends*, would be worth publishing. Yet, television is, of course, also easily recorded via the VCR, either for time-shifting or to archive. Importantly, Stevens (2021), studying fanzines and the ways fans of *Starsky and Hutch* (ABC, 1975–9) report viewing, notes that both behaviours take place: viewing several episodes in a row and repetitive viewing, as audiences would have already watched episodes on first broadcast or in repetition. These tapes would have also been archived. Of course, fans, like Bjarkman's fan collectors, are a marginal group of audiences, especially in the TV I and TV II eras. However, it is important to observe that these practices of binge-watching have historically existed and been made possible by recording

women, as cult films more associated with female viewers, from *Dirty Dancing* (Ardolino 1987) to *Clueless* to *Titanic* show.

technologies that give audiences more control over their own schedules. Thus, what developed in relation to the VCR were distinct viewing protocols related to time-shifting and new ways to engage with television through repetitive viewing. These different ways of engagement heavily inform later practices: from what Kompare calls 'accumulative repetition', meaning the purchase of DVD box sets for repeat viewings and building of large collections to the dominance of binge-watching as a means to watch television without abiding a schedule (see Part II). The practical use of the VCR for time-shifting purposes also significantly changes understandings of what the television set is for and the permeability of the television schedule through time-shifting. This suggests the movement of the television towards convergence medium.

Television and the VCR: Industries, Genres and Control

The industry that built around the VCR was the video-rental and sell-through market of pre-recorded tapes. This industry is closely linked to Hollywood, which introduced an entire aftermarket to cater to the VCR. Wasser points out that the so-called 'format war' between Betamax and VHS was ultimately decided:

> ...when the purchase and rental of prerecorded tapes became as important if not more important than recording programs off the television [...] the competition between Betamax and VHS was decided on the basis of video as an extension of the movie theatre.[4] (2001, location 1684–98)

Wasser and Greenberg both offer detailed analyses of how the VHS industries developed. The focus here is on the more televisual aspects of these industries: first, these industries inform an understanding of television as convergence medium. Second, they highlight the development of VHS-only genres which heavily draw on television as the screen that shows it. These genres also highlight some of the more gendered aspects of VHS culture, but also the way assumptions about television viewership, control and power become more contradictory and complex through the VCR.

[4] The so-called 'format war' was the competition between Betamax and VHS tapes as delivery format for pre-recorded tapes.

Megumi Komiya and Barry Litman argue:

> Since its inception, the prerecorded video program market has passed through two major stages and is now embarked on a third one. The first stage was the *development* of the industry, heavily reliant adult programming. The second stage was the *expansion* and legitimization of the industry, based on Hollywood feature film programming. The third stage, currently underway [in 1990], represents the further expansion, *maturation* and *diversification* of the industry based on nontheatrical movies and nonadult programming, such as children's material, instructional, and music videos. (1990, 27, italics in the original)

The authors move on to point out that Hollywood did publish a vast number of films as pre-recorded tapes in the US over the second half of the 1980s, indicating the speed at which the VHS industry grew in the era. Wasser (2001) is more specific in outlining these phases: 'The Early Years', 'Years of Independence', 'Video Becomes Big Business' and 'Consolidation'. These are chapter titles, rather than clearly defined 'phases' and only the 'years of independence' have a specific time frame attached (1981–6). Yet, these outlines offer a clearer idea of how Komiya and Litman's analysis can be understood. In both cases, more 'disreputable' genres play an important role in the development of the VCR industry. After the 1970s had seen adult films become veritable box office hits in the US with *Deep Throat* (Gerard 1972) or *The Devil in Miss Jonas* (Damiano 1974), producers recognised potential in productions published via VHS early on:

> The VCR easily captured the pre-existing porno audience and added a larger public composed of viewers who would never think of stepping into an adult movie theater. The concurrence of the Betamax and the new, more plot driven erotica led to adult titles becoming the first big genre for prerecorded cassettes. Customers were willing to buy sex videos for $100 or more in order to view them at home. [...] Merrill Lynch reported that through the end of the 1970s 'X-rated' cassettes accounted for half of prerecorded sales. As late as 1980, German and British video distributors reported that pornography accounted for 60 to 80 percent of their sales. These same figures are reflected in various anecdotal reports about the U.S. market. (Wasser 2001, location 2095–2104).

Thus, pornography made up a significant part of the pre-recorded video market, emphasising the importance of the home context. More than just a 'home cinema' in the sense that it allows a cinematic experience at home, the privacy of the home can play an important role for viewers. Productions quickly shifted away from the theatrical release model to straight-to-video productions as the genre diversified to cater to a variety of audience tastes (see ibid. and Greenberg 2008, 95). Throughout the 1970s, a number of extremely violent horror films, ranging from *The Last House on the Left* (Craven 1972) to *I Spit On Your Grave* (Zarchi 1978) were released. These films also did well in the home video market and spurred on a lively straight-to-video industry for horror films. This stage of what Komiya and Litman describe as the development of the industry through largely adult content also means that an infrastructure is developed for the sale of pre-recorded tapes, allowing major movie studios to join into the industry. Critical evaluation tends to focus on more 'disreputable' genres, Johnny Walker (2022) points out in relation to the UK, that the video industry was associated with London's seedy East End, which supported video's image.

At the same time, VHS was always more complex. For example, there are also other ways in which pre-recorded straight-to-video content can trouble television. Regulatory systems could be introduced to deal with horror or pornography, but the film and television system was also threatened in other ways, less troubling to social norms. The most remarkable aspect of the VHS industry at this point was the development of programming previously unavailable either on film or television. Workout videos, how-to-videos to explain DIY repairs in the home or cooking videos, and children's videos became popular formats. Most literature also mentions music, though Wasser notes that, beyond *Michael Jackson: Thriller* (Landis 1983), this programming was not profitable (2001, location 2794). As Lin notes,

> It appears that TV viewing no longer stands only for watching TV programs provided by TV programmers; instead, it may suggest watching a special-interest video, such as gardening guide through the use of a VCR and TV monitor. (1990, 88)

The change in programming to special-interest videos also indicates how neatly this fits with the shift towards infomercials mentioned in the previous chapter: the aesthetics and voiceover narrative are similar, despite the change in genre. In this regard, infomercials can be viewed as a response to the VCR as well as RCDs. These genres specific to VHS developed largely following the success of *Jane Fonda's Workout* (Galanty, 1982):

> This how-to-tape was produced and distributed by the entrepreneur Stuart Karl and released in the spring of 1982. Three years later, it had earned $34.2 million for the supplier on sales of 950,000 units. The tape had several unique aspects. It was sold at the relatively high price of $59.95, and yet most of its sales were to individual customers rather than rental stores. It had a relatively strong shelf life, developing strong steady sales for a sustained period. Many other companies engaged in the sincerest form of flattery by putting out their own 'how-to' cassettes featuring celebrities. (Wasser 2001, location 2778)

Jane Fonda's Workout also has a number of gendered implications for the relationship of television and its ancillary technology and broader cultural debates of 'high' and 'low' culture. The video quite clearly addresses a female audience despite the fact that two male participants can be seen in the video. The exercises are aerobics but are also clearly reminiscent of ballet dancing. For women, the home is a workplace where housework and chores need to be performed (whether they also work outside of the home or not). The aerobics video can be counted as among these chores. The activity suggested by aerobics videos suggests women's labour of conforming to beauty standards, rather than a 'hobby', which is a terminology commonly used in associated with male labour in the home. The fact that it is performed and marketed by Jane Fonda, Hollywood star and, thus, embodiment of its beauty standards, highlights the notion that the performance is essential for conforming to these standards. This labour is brought to the foreground more than in broadcast television: it is literally the subject matter of the video. This tension between the emphasis on labour and activity, displayed on the 'feminised' television set, highlights some of the contradictions inherent in any gendered understanding of television constructed through binary oppositions. Yet, it also brings to the foreground the main aspect of how the VCR questions any gendered notions of television. After all, the VCR is often understood as 'masculine': theorists like Greenberg (2008) or Newman (2014) point to the importance of 'hacking' or 'tinkering' with the VCR, positioning it as 'technology' rather than home appliance. As mentioned above, the building of archives is also important. As Keightley (2003) points out, this positioning has gendered implications: the building of collections of 'high culture' music or pre-recorded film suggests an interest more along the lines of a 'hobby'. This is performed in leisure time away from the workplace. Gray notes in her study on women's use of the VCR that "VCRs were marketed from the outset as hi-tech equipment which had to be mastered, thereby apparently addressing the male consumer" (1992, 18). Exercise tapes trouble this distinction significantly.

This troubling of the more gendered binaries of television shows that such a distinction is being de-constructed in the TV II era as more ancillary technologies are introduced. The 'how-to' genre works to deconstruct the various connotations of television by highlighting labour and activity. This disruption of cultural binaries very clearly positions the television set as a place of media convergence: there may be different kinds of tape from the more masculinised ideas of high culture to more feminised low culture. Yet, this only highlights that the television set is now a place where different forms of culture converge. Of course, this has always been true of broadcast television content, but the VCR emphasises this point even more. The content of the how-to video is troubling to television as they often require regimes of repetitive, self-scheduled viewing that were impossible on broadcast television. Programmers addressed this issue by scheduling their own aerobics content, but the convenience of the VCR allowed for audiences to self-schedule when to do their exercise or do other tasks linked to the 'how-to' video genre. More than collections of films and the display of cinema on television screens, the VHS-only genres indicate a level of activity uncommon for television or anything viewed on the television screen.

Television as Convergence Medium

Hollywood and the television industry could accommodate various branches of the industry that developed around the VCR, particularly as conglomeration became more common. Yet, what became more difficult to manage are the various ways the meaning of television changed: through straight-to-video genres, time-shifting and other ancillary media, concepts of what television *is* and how (and by whom) it could be controlled radically shifted.

Aside from the VCR, video games introduced another way to question and control television. Game consoles have always been perceived as 'not

TV', but a medium unto itself, even more so than the VCR. At the same time, they seem to have been at the forefront of changing ideas of what a television set can do and what viewers can use television for. As Tristan Donovan notes in his more journalistic account of the history of video gaming, the development of game consoles is linked to developer Ralph Baer's desire to do something with a television set other than receiving broadcasts (2010, 18). As Newman points out:

> As a device to plug into a television set, video games intervened in television history by giving broadcast audiences an alternative to watching TV shows. (2017, location 242)

If television is viewed here as a 'hub' for convergence, then video games functioned as one way in which the television could be experienced as something other than the broadcasting schedule. Much like with the VCR and RCDs, first iterations of the game console became available in the 1970s, at the start of the reconception that took full effect throughout the 1980s as ancillary technologies became more affordable. Gaming is, in many respects, positioned as more radical disruption of commercial television than the VCR. Gaming not only allows for the viewing of non-broadcast material, but it allows for an alternative way of interacting with the medium. To start with, those who play video games are called 'users', 'players' or, to use a more recent terminology, 'gamers', suggesting a more active position than 'viewers' or 'spectators'. Even the 'how-to' genre for the VCR does not reconfigure its viewers as athletes, chefs, homemakers or builders, even though these activities—however amateurish performed—are clearly expected of viewers. By reconceptualising the viewer as active participant with accompanying descriptors, gaming, thus, goes further in questioning the meaning of television than the VCR. The cognitive activity of grazing may be similar to that of playing tennis on an Atari 2600, but the interactivity of gaming is conceptualised as going beyond RCD use. As Newman (2017) shows, discussion of video games in the 1970s put the supposed passivity of watching television in opposition to video games. These were not only positioned as interactive, but 1970s marketing even framed gaming in relation to athletics by introducing games like 'tennis' or 'basketball' for the Atari. Advertising campaigns in the US included NFL players or baseball stars. Though there are gender discrepancies in how this activity is framed as different from that associated with workout tapes, it ties into the same discourse: ancillary technologies as a way to create a more 'active' way to use the television set. As discussed in the last chapter, a major anxiety linked to RCDs was the physical inactivity it promoted. This links in with fears relating to television and its effects on the working class. If, as Dawson (2008) suggests, ancillary technologies function as a way to 'repair' television and its social ills, the physical activity promoted by workout tapes or the cognitive activity of video gaming clearly offers solutions.

Despite technological differences between the various media forms, the practice of gaming took place at a number of sites. The first home console, the Magnavox Odyssey became available in 1972. In the same year, Atari also brought out its first 'hit' coin-operated game to be played in more 'public' spaces, *Pong*. This association of games as part of the public sphere in bars or arcades, but also the private, may be why its primary association is as its own medium rather than as part of TV II:

> Unlike many new media, video games emerged as multiple objects in different kinds of spaces. They were both computer and television technology. They were both a public and a private amusement, played in taverns and living rooms. In some ways, they were like pinballs or pool, and in others they were like watching television or playing checkers. (Newman 2017, location 268)

That these different iterations of gaming were all constructed as part of the same medium, computer games, rather than as part of the distinct media they occur in (computers, television, gaming machines), is not just a matter of technology, industry, timing or marketing, but, as Newman outlines, a specific discourse that ties them together. Because video games are located in a variety of spaces and take different forms, developing into a distinct medium, they play an important part for reconception of television that severs the link between the concept of television and the television set. Yet, particularly the various iterations of Microsoft's Xbox have positioned the game console more and more as a 'hub' for home media systems, still largely mediated through the television screen. In fact, Wolff (2015) terms contemporary television 'consolivision', pointing to the potentially vast amount of different consoles connected to the television set. Though it may be possible to screen DVDs or Blu-Rays, watch Netflix and even make skype calls via the Xbox, ultimately, none of this is possible without a television set. Thus, the ties between television and gaming are still extremely close. Video games further an understanding of television as convergence medium.

This goes hand in hand with straight-to-video genres, which also trouble the understanding of television. The VCR and video games, thus, serve as a reconception of television as convergence medium. This reconception is largely led by concepts of interactivity that draw into question any ideas of television as singular, feminised medium. Television as convergence medium is not easily understood via an active/passive binary and gendered connotations. This is not only due to changing understandings of gender or audiences, but the idea of television as convergence medium that allows for a variety of rituals and practices, many of which are interactive. Thus, television as convergence medium also means an understanding of television as pluralistic medium.

Conclusion

To tie the discussion of this chapter back to the guiding concepts of Part I, the reconception of television as a hub of media convergence extends choice. Control can then be exercised over this choice, so the immediate environment of viewers can be affected. What this suggests is a radical shift in the kind of control viewers can assume over the television. The control viewers can enact is vastly extended via the VCR and game consoles. The choice is not limited to the channels available on network, cable or satellite television, but also to which ancillary technology to use and which kind of interaction with the set to enact. Thus, the possible regimes of control are extended vastly. Much more than the RCD, this kind of control can even be conceptualised as subversion as it puts interactive viewers out of the reach of commercial television. In fact, in a *New York Times Story* from 1986 on "One Day in the Video Rental Whirl", one interviewee notes:

> I don't watch television because television is boring. And why should I go to the movies if I can rent? I can watch these movies in my own house, and call my friends and say: 'Come on over. We'll watch video all night, play 'Trivial Pursuit,' cook and eat and play music'. (Bennetts 1986)

This indicates how much the VCR can change the perception of the medium. The VCR allows for more significant options than RCDs to evade the broadcasting schedule and disrupt the television industry.

Time-shifting even allows viewers to zip through advertising, potentially threatening the financing model of commercial television. Though this never manifested in the TV II era, TV III started to fulfil this potential with digital technologies, forcing advertisers to re-think strategies on advertising.

The VCR was less a technology to negotiate power between industry and audiences but gave viewers the option to ignore at least some parts of the industry, such as advertising or other undesirable parts of the television flow. VHS-only genres are a potent example of how much viewers could take advantage of avoiding television. Because the VCR allowed viewers to use their television set for something other than watching linear television, it developed as a significant technology to further television's role as 'hub' of media convergence. Along with video games, it developed as a technology to further different versions of audience activity and interactivity. This illuminates how much the TV II era reconceptualised television from mass medium to convergence medium. Control, and the various kinds of control enabled by various ancillary technologies, is a key concept to understand this reconception. In some instances, this showed subversive potential, though media companies soon adapted, largely by building large media conglomerates in the 1990s.[5] On a broader social level, television as convergence medium troubles a range of gendered assumptions about television, which may be the reason why the VCR does not feature as prominently in many social debates about television as the RCD. Though interactivity remains a largely 'male' domain, as outlined by Newman, straight-to-video content, specifically how-to videos, confuses such distinctions even more. At the same time, it is important to acknowledge that the VCRs and game consoles also came at significantly higher financial cost than RCDs in the TV II era. As such, they were more strongly associated with social 'elites', rather than the working class.

[5] In the US, the Telecommunications Act of 1996 lifted many restrictions for large corporations to own a range of media companies across sectors. This led to a vast expansion of media companies, both within the US and internationally, referred to as conglomeration.

Bibliography

Bennetts, Leslie. 1986. "One Day in the Video Rental Whirl." *New York Times*. Available online: http://www.nytimes.com/1986/08/13/arts/one-day-in-the-video-rental-whirl.html. Accessed: 07.02.2018.

Bjarkman, Kim. 2004. "To have and to Hold: The Video Collector's Relationship with an Ethereal Medium." *Television and New Media* 5 (3): 217–246.

Dawson, Max. 2008. *TV Repair: New Media Solutions to Old Media Problems*, Lynn B. Spigel, Jennifer Light and Jeffrey Sconce (eds.). ProQuest Dissertations Publishing.

Dobrow, Julia. 1990. "The Rerun Ritual: Using VCRs to Re-View." In Dobrow, Julia R. (ed.) *Social and Cultural Aspects of VCR Use*. Hillsdale, N.J.: L. Erlbaum Associates. 181–94

Donovan, Tristan. 2010. *Replay: The History of Video Games*. Lewes: Yellow Ant.

Gray, Ann. 1992. *Video Playtime: The Gendering of a Leisure Technology*. London: Routledge.

Greenberg, Joshua M. 2008. *From Betamax to Blockbuster: Video Stores and the Invention of Movies on Video*. Cambridge, Mass.: MIT Press.

Keightley, Keir. 2003. "Low Television, High Fidelity: Taste and the Gendering of Home Entertainment Technologies." *Journal of Broadcasting & Electronic Media* 47 (2): 236–259.

Klinger, Barbara. 2010. "Becoming Cult: "The Big Lebowski," Replay Culture and Male Fans." *Screen* 51 (1): 1–20.

Klinger, Barbara. 2006. *Beyond the Multiplex Cinema, New Technologies, and the Home*. Berkeley: University of California Press.

Kompare, Derek. 2005. *Rerun Nation: How Repeats Invented American Television*. New York, N.Y: Routledge.

Kumiya, Megumi and Litman, Barry. 1990. "The Economics of the Prerecorded Videocassette Industry." In Dobrow, Julia R. (ed.) *Social and Cultural Aspects of VCR Use*. Hillsdale, N.J.: L. Erlbaum Associates. 25–44.

Lin, Carolyn. 1990. "Audience Activity and VCR Use." In Julia R. (ed.) *Social and Cultural Aspects of VCR Use*. Hillsdale, N.J.: L. Erlbaum Associates, 75–92.

Lotz, Amanda D. 2014a. *Cable Guys: Television and Masculinities in the 21st Century*. New York: New York University Press.

Lotz, Amanda D. 2014b. *The Television Will be Revolutionized*, 2nd ed. New York: New York University Press.

Lotz, Amanda D. 2017. *Portals*. Michigan: Maize Books.

Newman, Michael Z. 2017. *Atari Age: The Emergence of Video Games in America*. Cambridge, MA: MIT Press.

Newman, Michael Z. 2014. *Video Revolutions on the History of a Medium*. New York: Columbia University Press.

Secunda, Eugene. 1990. "VCRs and Viewer Control Over Programming: An Historical Perspective." In Dobrow, Julia R. (ed.), *Social and Cultural Aspects of VCR Use*. Hillsdale, N.J.: L. Erlbaum Associates. 9–24.

Stevens, E.C. 2021. "Historical Binge-Watching: Marathon Viewing on Videotape." In M. Jenner (ed.), *Binge-Watching and Contemporary Television Studies*, 23–39. Edinburgh: Edinburgh University Press.

Walker, J. 2022. *Rewind, Replay: Britain and the Video Boom, 1978–92*. Edinburgh: Edinburgh University Press.

Wasser, Frederick. 2001. *Veni, Vidi, Video: The Hollywood Empire and the VCR*. Austin, Tex.; Chesham: University of Texas Press; Combined Academic.

Wolff, Michael. 2015. *Television is the New Television*. New York: Portfolio / Penguin.

Television

Buffy the Vampire Slayer (1997–2003), USA: WB, UPN.

Friends (1994–2004), USA: NBC.

Starsky and Hutch (1975–9), USA: ABC.

X-Files, The (1993–2018), USA: Fox.

Film

Ardolino, Emile. 1987. *Dirty Dancing*. USA: Vestron Pictures.

Cameron, J. 1997. *Titanic*. USA: Twentieth Century Fox.

Coen, J. and Coen, E. 1998. *The Big Lebowski*. USA: Polygram Entertainment, Working Title Films.

Craven, W. 1972. *The Last House on the Left*. USA: MGM.

Damiano, G. 1974. *The Devil in Miss Jones*. USA: Pierre Productions.

Galanty, S. 1982. *Jane Fonda's Workout*. USA: Karl Video Corporation.

Gerard, J. 1972. *Deep Throat*. USA: Bryanston Pictures.

Heckerling, A. 1995. *Clueless*. USA: Paramount Pictures.

Landis, J. 1983. *Michael Jackson: Thriller*. USA: Vestron Video.

Zarchi, M. 1978. *I Spit on Your Grave*. USA: Cinemagic.

CHAPTER 6

Digital Television and Control

The TV III era may be easiest understood through the legitimation of television and the rise of a new kind of 'quality' TV that went along with an increased audience fragmentation. Yet, it is also characterised by increased storage size of DVDs and DVRs as opposed to VHS tapes as well as the portability of content and devices. Viewing on laptops became possible through DVDs and online catch-up services that allowed viewers to schedule their own viewing. As this suggests, the TV III period also meant a shift towards the digital and associated technologies (PC, laptop) as central convergence medium. This went along with the re-branding of the internet in the early 2000s, after the dot-com bubble had burst and left investors wary. Though the internet had been participatory early on, it was now re-branded on these terms as Web 2.0. As marketer Tim O'Reilly put it:

> Web 2.0 is the network as platform, spanning all connected devices; Web 2.0 applications are those that make the most of the intrinsic advantages of that platform: delivering software as a continually-updated service that gets better the more people use it, consuming and remixing data from multiple sources, including individual users, while providing their own data and services in a form that allows remixing by others, creating network effects through an 'architecture of participation', and going beyond the page metaphor of Web 1.0 to deliver rich user experiences. (O'Reilly cited in Fuchs 2013, 32)

M. Jenner, *Netflix and the Re-invention of Television*,
https://doi.org/10.1007/978-3-031-39237-5_6

YouTube is a particularly vibrant example of this participatory culture: to survive, YouTube needs its users to upload their own self-made videos or comment on other users' videos. Social media also rely on participation. Axel Bruns describes these users who both, use and produce their own content, as produsers (2002). Whereas the television was a central 'hub' for media convergence in the TV II era, the period following the internet's re-branding as Web 2.0 in the mid-2000s also meant a reconceptualization of the way television was consumed. This could mean the consumption of DVDs on a laptop rather than a television set, serial formats on YouTube or even streaming of TV episodes. As Lotz points out[1]:

> The various post-network technologies produced complicated consequences for the societies that adopted them. Viewers gained greater control over their entertainment experience, yet became attached to an increasing range of devices that demanded their attention and financial support. Many viewers willingly embraced devices that allowed them greater authority in determining when, where, and what they would view [...]. In many cases, the 'conventional wisdom' forecasting that the new technologies would have negative consequences for established industry players proved faulty; technologically empowered viewers used devices to watch *more* television and provided the industry unexpected new revenue streams at the same time they eroded old ones. (2014, location 1350–7, italics in the original)

Yet, even though the threat to television as business was not substantial, this shift had significant consequences for television as medium: the link between television as medium and the television set was severed as television content increasingly moved towards other media forms. The television set remains central, particularly as gaming consoles work to extend its function within the home by making it a central locus of home media systems, as the various iterations of Microsoft's Xbox show. Yet, this suggests a reconception of television as part of broader PC systems, converging dominant media forms. The central 'hub' of this convergence is an unspecified location called 'the digital', accessible through various devices, not (only) the television set. The kind of control given to users/viewers is remarkable. Yet, this is often received in exchange for increasingly minute data. The direct communication not possible via

[1] Lotz uses the terminology of post-network television, which is specific to the arrangement of the US television industry and is used here synonymously with TV III.

the RCD is possible as narrowcasters can collect increasingly minute data on viewing behaviour via DVRs or online catch-up services. This data is used to produce content based on specific audience segments' tastes and to advertise directly to them. Yet, giving this data to industry is not likely to produce substantial shifts in power structures. Nevertheless, it is a communication process based on detailed information on customers' wishes. This chapter explores how control is reconceptualised and re-organised via ancillary technologies in the TV III era.

Re-establishing Industry Control: DVD and DVR

The functions of the VCR to play pre-recorded tapes and to record content from linear television were more or less divided up between two different technologies: the DVD player and the DVR. DVDs were introduced in 1997 and quickly dominated the market (see Kompare 2005, 197; Lotz 2014, location 3276). If the VCR managed to disrupt power structures in the sense that it allowed viewers to time-shift television or rent pre-recorded tapes, then DVD largely worked to re-establish industry power. Maybe most importantly, DVD players do not allow for recordings, all discs need to be bought or rented—alternatives are illegal in most Western countries.[2] As Greenberg outlines,

> ...the DVD represents an attempt by Hollywood studios to reclaim the control of their products that they lost to mediators and consumers in the 1980s. Unlike videocassettes, movies on DVD are encoded with a proprietary algorithm called Copyright Scrambling System (CSS), which is created, owned and regulated by the DVD Copy Control Association (DVD CCA), a consortium of movie studios and hardware manufacturers. [...] Motion picture studios have found other ways to even more explicitly control the distribution and sale of movies on DVD; for example, the DVD standard divides the world into seven regions. (2008, 157)

Furthermore, since the rise of DVDs (and in fear of viewers who may copy their content), motion picture companies have lobbied for stricter copyright laws worldwide (see Strangelove 2015, 48–73). Because piracy, at the time, was more commonly framed as a problem for the film

[2] Though not discussed here, Michael Strangelove's *Post-TV. Piracy, Cord-Cutting and the Future of Television* (2015) offers valuable insights into piracy as alternative way to access television content and industry efforts to gain control over these alternatives.

industry, it is largely neglected here. Meanwhile, the DVR digitally stores information on programming and viewers can record it. Unlike the VCR, it allows for skipping rather than zipping of advertising. Nevertheless, the digital generally allows industry to monitor viewer activity more closely than previous technologies. Though this enables industry to respond more directly to viewer behaviour, it also means viewers relinquish a significant amount of data in exchange.

Klinger views DVD as a 'relative' of the VHS tape, at least in respect to its function in home viewing culture as a medium for repetitive viewing (2006, 59). The enhancements DVD makes to time-shifting are also significant: improved image quality, the possibility to change language settings and subtitles or jump to individual scenes, and the option for producers and distributors to add bonus material like making-offs, behind-the-scenes or blooper reels. For Kompare, focussing on the aspect of data storage and reproduction in technological developments,

> DVD is not only a 'spin-off' or upgrade from VHS, but rather the first significant media format of the twenty-first century, and a major development in the history of media repetition. (2005, 206)

Though the business of DVD was built on industry structures initially designed for VHS tapes, such as the rental business, a number of other changes also occurred. Publication windows were changed, largely due to fear of piracy made possible by online infrastructures and the ease with which DVDs could be ripped. DVDs also opened up another market for television as DVD box sets became increasingly popular. As Kompare notes,

> Home video's primary medium, VHS tape, was portable, permanent, and easily accessible to most consumers, and while particularly well suited for film distribution and exhibition, it was incompatible for the mass distribution of entire television series. However, the rapid adoption of Digital Versatile Disc (DVD) technology at the end of the 1990s prompted a reconception of television on home video. The enhanced technical standards and new industrial practices developed for the new format allowed for the delivery of hours of television to consumers in small, tangible packages that also happened to look rather nice on a bookshelf. (ibid., 197)

The space saved by DVDs relative to VHS tapes would allow for larger collections. Over the following decade, packaging of DVD box sets would become smaller and smaller: many season box sets now take up the same space on the shelf as a single film. The affordable pricing of DVDs also supported this point (ibid., 208). DVD box sets also allow for the playing of DVDs on portable devices and, thus, changed where television could be viewed. What Kompare calls acquisitive repetition, the replaying of bought content at a time convenient for viewers, established new regimes of ownership that made television less ephemeral. The display of DVD box sets on shelves meant that TV series could be used as cultural capital to show to visitors. Through these strategies, DVD encourages acquisition to enable the flexible viewing of television content. Thus, the DVD signals a return to the hegemony the VCR had disrupted. Yet, it also signals a significant shift in what television is: viewing becomes increasingly self-determined, increasing choices and control over what is watched, when it is watched and where it is watched. At the same time, the medium allows viewers increased control without threatening the television industry: what is not watched in TV ads is paid for in the more direct exchange of buying a DVD box set. Thus, the business model of television shifts to a mixture of direct-pay and ad-financed for commercial television (see also Chapter 5).

The DVR as a time-shifting technology that allows skipping (rather than zipping) of ads posed a more significant threat to the television industry. In its first few years of existence, DVR technologies were particularly dominant in the US, perhaps in response to the commercial nature of the system. More than the VCR, for the US television industry, it highlighted some of the major problems with an advertising model created for linear viewing. Though the emergence of the DVR and industry complaints that the technology made it easier to skip advertising coincided with experiments with and implementation of new advertising models, the matter is a bit more complex:

> Blaming the DVR for the experimentation in advertising techniques and program financing norms that emerged in the early 2000s makes for an elegant argument, but it is a grand overstatement of the impact of the device. Certainly the reassessment of advertising models was overdue long before DVRs enabled advertisement skipping. The future uncertainty fuelled by the DVR only helped the industry toward the 'tipping point'

> at which the risk of trying something new appeared less dangerous than blindly maintaining the status quo. (Lotz 2014, location 3871–8)

Other factors Lotz cites as part of these changes that led to a 'tipping point' are the 2008 recession and the rapid development of technologies like streaming. The wide array of problems the print publishing industry has faced since the late 1990s may also play into the development of new advertising models. Nevertheless, as discussed in Chapters 4 and 5, many of these problems were already visible in the 1980s and only became heightened with the increased control given to viewers, as well as more accurate tools to measure viewer behaviour. As Dawson points out:

> An additional feature of DVRs is that they may be connected via telephone lines to central computer databases, facilitating exchanges of information between television viewers, broadcasters, and sponsors. Connecting DVRs to these databases makes it possible for viewers to search television listings for their favorite programs, performers, or genres, much in the same way they do the Internet, and to receive programming suggestions based on the recommendations of collaborative filtering algorithms that cross-reference their viewing histories against those of millions of other DVR owners. (2008, 193–4)

Of course, this also implies the increasingly detailed viewer data that is being stored. This can be read as a closer communication between industry and audience about what kind of programming is being viewed and produced. At the same time, this power relationship is asymmetrical in the sense that industry can collect more data on viewers than vice versa. This is a reversal of the relationship established via RCDs or the VCR: these technologies allowed viewers to gather data on available offerings and choose which parts are desirable programming. As argued in Chapters 4 and 5, this does not subvert existing power structures, but disrupts them by giving more control to viewers within an asymmetrical system. The DVR gives even more control to viewers. Yet, in exchange viewers have to relinquish more information than previously, when information was largely collected via Nielsen (or other survey companies') boxes: of course, these companies would collect information on individual viewers. Yet, this involves an explicit agreement for the limited data to be collected, rather than the kind of data collection in the digital era when data is collected in bulk via IP addresses and services cannot be accessed without granting permission. This already poses some of the problems of 'big data' linked to online transmission systems. At the same time, the industry tends to put this more accurate data to use by devising programming that is more closely tailored to the taste structures of small audience segments.

Power was unequally distributed before the DVD and the DVR. However, the exchange of control for power is more obvious for those technologies. Yet, again, this is a negotiation: the industry has to respond to its data if it wants to attract audiences in an increasingly diversified field. The data collected is not necessarily weaponised but collected to create an increasingly individualised version of television. Much of what is foreshadowed here is the algorithmic construction of television discussed in Chapter 8 in relation to Netflix. DVD and DVR managed to restore hegemony by introducing stricter controls on how content could be used, what established theft (for example, the ripping and uploading of DVD content) and on what devices it could be used, or rather, which region of the world that device needed to come from. The use of two different devices to provide what the VCR previously offered also contributed to this control. Nevertheless, viewers also got to exercise unprecedented control over the conditions of their own viewing. This tension is visible throughout the TV III and into the TV IV era.

YouTube, Social Media and Narrative

As important as DVD and DVR are for the way television changed in the early 2000s, the internet also threatened previous conceptions of the medium. Technologically speaking, YouTube may be Netflix' closest relative in contemporary media. When Reed Hastings positioned Netflix in relation to HBO in 2013, he not only aligned it with a heritage of 'quality' TV, he also rejected the allegiance with YouTube, its reliance on videos created by 'amateurs', legal complications surrounding copyright law and its associations with a participatory version of online culture. It also denies the way YouTube paved the way for online streaming, both technologically and culturally. YouTube is essentially a hybrid: a streaming platform that increasingly followed the logics of television, but also a participatory medium that would solicit attention by highlighting the amateur video and allow comments on it.

YouTube is usually understood, in popular as well as academic discourse, within the context of a variety of participatory projects of Web 2.0 in the early 2000s. Launched in 2005, it sat comfortably within the context of other media platforms that explicitly solicited user engagement, such as Wikipedia (launched in 2001), Facebook (launched in 2004) or Twitter (launched in 2006). They are part of Web 2.0, which encourages viewers to interact, leave comments and share. The term produsers, which describes consumers who also produce their own content, is, of course, applicable to all these sites (Bruns 2007). Yet, the videos produced for YouTube are qualitatively different from individual tweets or Facebook statuses, even if these include photographs. In his helpful distinction between 'explicit' and 'implicit' participation, Mirko Tobias Schäfer points to the ease with which we upload a social media status (implicit participation) as opposed to the effort and deliberation involved in filming, editing and uploading a YouTube video, research and write a Wikipedia article or contribute to software development (explicit participation) (2011, 41–54). These distinctions help conceptualise the various kinds of participation linked to Web 2.0. Even those users who only 'watch' YouTube videos are logged as 'views', which helps position a video according to popularity and establish more implicit participation. Jean Burgess and Joshua Green argue:

> While it would eventually seek premium content distribution deals and, once utilized, a tiered access program that provided paying users with the ability to upload longer videos, YouTube has always oriented its services toward content *sharing*, including the sharing of mundane and amateur content, rather than the provision of high-quality video. [...] Consumer co-creation [...] is fundamental to YouTube's value proposition as well as its disruptive influence on established media business models. (2009, 4, italics in the original)

The discursive framing of YouTube as site for participation has impacted on the way users interact with it and integrate it into their everyday media practices, even as they consume content made for television, but uploaded to the site. Thus, to state that YouTube is discursively tied to Web 2.0 while Netflix is discursively tied to television is more than just an academic debate. These discursive framings influence how they are culturally positioned, how people interact with it, what expectations they have and what aesthetic forms can emerge from them. It also heavily influences how money and data are exchanged between viewers and industry.

Wolff (2015), controversially, argues that it was YouTube which positioned 'the internet' as a place for narrative video. He even goes so far to argue that, more than amateur videos, it was pirated videos that made YouTube successful. As legal suits against individual users mounted—in addition to a long-term litigation with Viacom—YouTube's model shifted more towards amateur videos (see Burgess and Green 2009, 1–15). Much of these productions are, at least in some ways, similar to the VHS-only genres of DIY or aerobics videos. In fact, how-to genres like make-up tutorials are highly successful on YouTube. It also was the amateur-produced content that developed unique, 'authentic' aesthetics and narrative structures for online video. Creeber aligns the aesthetics and narrative forms that emerge on YouTube with the forms of television (2013, 130–7). A number of YouTube series mix the aesthetics of the YouTube video and its direct address with fictional serial narratives that unfold over several episodes. A production like *The Lizzie Bennett Diaries* (Agreeable Entertainment, Pemberley Digital, 2012–14) is a prime example for this format, with each episode 3–5 minutes long and filmed like a confessional video, but essentially emulating the narrative of *Pride and Prejudice* (Austen 1836). Particularly the adaptation and popularity of serial narrative forms for YouTube imply that the consumption of YouTube is linked, not only to the aesthetic forms, but the habits of television viewing. However, the short length of episodes of YouTube series plays an important role in the way they can be structured into everyday life in a way decidedly different from television. José Van Dijk offers the terminology of 'snippets' to describe the short length of YouTube clips (2013, 118). The concept draws attention to the importance of time in relation to online content. The short length of individual snippets allows for the possibility to 'squeeze them in' while doing other things on the computer. This aspect points to one of the ways in which YouTube destabilises the power structures of television: there is no centralised schedule and no real way to establish prominence in the same way a high-budget prime-time series might. Communal viewing is not possible in a traditional sense, though videos are often shared on social media, establishing a system of 'recommendations' by friends or family. Though slightly longer with episodes of around 15 minutes, the format of snippets would re-emerge on BBC iPlayer with *Staged* (BBC, 2020–1) during the Covid-19 lockdown in the UK. The programme featured actors Michael Sheen and David Tennant and their wives emulating a private conversation on Zoom. This was mostly due to the limited production possibilities during lockdowns, but is also a powerful example of the way YouTube has influenced the structures of television. Established industry may produce some content, but much is produced by produsers.

Van Dijk argues that Google's takeover of YouTube was followed by an extensive redesign that highlighted its similarities to television through the introduction of channels, a visual de-emphasis of comments and the use of narratives of YouTube stars who managed to acquire fame within the parameters of traditional music or television industries (2013, 112–5). As Wolff notes, the site also increasingly relied on the advertising models familiar from television (2015, location 1654). Yet, YouTube is also set apart from television through its associations with Web 2.0, produsing and social interactions. Its failed attempts to move into more professional television productions show how viewer expectations also set it apart from television—even if many users do not participate in produsing, or even commenting. Nevertheless, though decidedly distinct from television, YouTube taught viewers to watch TV-like formats online. Much of its serialised formats may be amateur productions, but its narrative forms are still akin to television. They were later widely copied in episodes that emphasised communication via video call platform Zoom during national lockdowns to manage the Covid-19 pandemic. Individual episodes in series like *Mythic Quest* (Apple, 2020–) as well as the example of *Staged* make this influence obvious. Thus, YouTube adopted a model close to television as broadcasters made use of platforms like iTunes or Hulu to offer alternative sites for viewing. As a result, the link between television and the set became even more fragile than in the TV II era and, in some respects, disappeared.

YouTube is still set apart from television in a number of ways, largely linked to its discursive positioning closer to social media. Yet, it informs how online viewing can be organised and new videos can be recommended. The deliberation it suggests to viewers in choosing videos to watch, particularly snippets that are only 'squeezed in', allows for a qualitatively different experience of control than time-shifting. Unlike the RCD, the main focus is not on 'sampling' choices but watching a whole short video. Unlike pre-recorded content on VHS or DVD, it is not associated with going to a store or waiting for shipment (in rental systems or when buying them). Unlike recorded viewing, it lies outside the television schedule. YouTube may not be television, but it foreshadows streaming platforms in all these ways.

Catching up on Television: BBC iPlayer and Hulu

Curtin (2009) argues that the introduction of the BBC iPlayer in 2007, two years after YouTube, marked an important moment in the development of what he terms 'matrix media', a system of a number of different media streams and a substantial shift in media convergence. The DVD box set was already an important delivery system for TV series, so the option for viewers to catch up on missed episodes online served as an acknowledgement of audience desires and needs. The iPlayer can also be viewed as a reaction to counter piracy and keep viewers interested in PSB in the UK. In the same year, in the US, NBC-Universal and News Corporation launched a joined venture internet portal, with ABC-Disney joining later, Hulu. Lotz pinpoints 2009, the year Hulu doubles its content library and adds Disney as partner, as the year when it becomes relevant on a broader cultural level (2014, location 1727). The iPlayer and Hulu are both highly relevant developments, not only because they provide first online catch-up services to television. Both are also content aggregators, the iPlayer uniting programming from the various channels under the BBC brand and Hulu uniting programming from various US network channels. Both are also distinct in the way they represent templates for how PSB and commercial broadcasting worldwide can reorganise themselves to remain relevant in a TV III and TV IV era. Importantly,

> The nonlinear convenience of these services made clear how television distributed by internet protocol could rival and surpass the experience of broadcast- or cable- distributed television, and countered the experience of internet-distributed video to that point as slow loading and pixelated. (Lotz 2017, location 303)

Thus, these services also presented online television as a viable option and made it possible for viewers to accept streaming as technology to deliver television. Thus, Hulu in the US and iPlayer in the UK would serve for viewers as examples of 'good' (meaning technologically relatively high-standard) online television.

Johnson describes Hulu as a service brand, meaning it originally provided a specific service (catch-up TV), fed from other sources, rather than producing its own original content. In this, it is similar to earlier iterations of Netflix. Hulu would start producing original content in 2013—even though its programming would not reach the same critical acclaim as that of Netflix until 2017's *The Handmaid's Tale*. In its original version, Hulu would offer access to recently aired episodes of TV programmes as well as selections from involved channels' back catalogues. This system would later inform the organisation of other platforms into libraries of content: curated rather than programmed or scheduled (Lotz 2017, location 258). The co-existence of recent and historical television content is important as other platforms would copy this structure. Evan Elkins notes,

> ... at its founding in 2007 [...], Hulu aimed to draw viewers away from pirate activities like torrenting as well as the practice of watching unauthorized clips on YouTube by building an over-the-top (OTT) service that offered a more clearly official and authorized online television experience. (2018, 336)

As Johnson observes, channel branding is absent on the site and users cannot search the catalogue via channel brands (2012, 54). Instead of branding itself via 'quality' TV, as HBO did at the time and Netflix would soon do (see Chapter 10), the range of available programmes would be central to the platform's identity. Hulu, emulating commercial television, always did include advertising and established it as part of 'watching Hulu'. However, it also introduced different tiers later on, thus allowing viewers to pay more for less advertising, a practice common for a variety of catch-up platforms worldwide. Considering the fears of the television industry linked to advertising, this is surprising: going back to RCDs and VCRs, the common assumption was that television's ancillary technologies would be used by audiences to avoid advertising. Hulu gives control over what is watched when, but the viewing of ads was long non-optional, even if ads are overall more targeted (based on viewing history or location). Much of contemporary US network programming has been at the forefront of developing alternatives to the 30-second spot as advertising (see Lotz 2014, location 4162–4262). The use of product integration in storylines of series like *Modern Family* (ABC, 2009–20) and other sitcoms is particularly striking (see Gillan 2015, 32–5). Thus, the use of the non-optional 30-second spot on Hulu is a deliberate choice to position the platform in relation to network television, assuming its dominance over online platforms as originator of content. Yet, it also contradicts assumptions about audiences and advertising commonly made in relation to ancillary technologies: Hulu assumes that control over scheduling is more important to audiences than advertising avoidance.

As outlined by Johnson, internet portals function as possibilities for 'relationship building' in the context of branding for television channels (2012, 49). This ensures brand loyalty, and possibly more awareness of the branding of specific channels as viewers have to navigate directly to the channel's website (such as cbs.com, nbc.com or 4od.co.uk). Though this is important for commercial channels, it is equally relevant for PSB channels which are also increasingly asked to provide justification for the license fee in an age of narrowcasting. Thus, catch-up streaming platforms offer a possibility for broadcasters to control their own brand. For Johnson, brands function as interfaces to mediate viewer interaction with specific channels. Chun points to the various ways software is constantly being re-programmed in response to audience responses, made possible by the direct communication online portals allow for (2006, location 229–51). Johnson and Chun discuss different elements of contemporary branding, Johnson discussing television branding in relation to its importance to linear broadcasting and Chun debating online protocols. Nevertheless, their work is equally important to understanding streaming platforms: Johnson's focus on branding makes it possible to consider the importance of channel brands to online streaming and Chun's work positions interactions between these brands and software as direct interaction and, thus, a site for power struggle. Yet, in relation to catch-up services, the relationship between power and control remains complex. Viewers are given increased control, but this control does not overturn existing power structures. In fact, the data viewers relinquish in exchange for control can serve to solidify existing power structures rather than subvert them. As Chun's work shows, assigning ultimate power to software misunderstands how it works and gathers data, just as much as it misunderstands audiences and the complexity of their lived experience. The increased data can be used by the TV industry to adapt programming, though this does not imply an overhaul of financing systems.

Though these platforms offer unprecedented control over when content can be viewed, their strict use of geoblocking also limits this control in important ways. Geoblocking suggests how nationally bound the iPlayer and Hulu, as well as other catch-up services, are. This is also highlighted by links to specific channels or channel brands. Hulu may not highlight these brands, but still shows the limitations of the catch-up system by insisting on national boundaries of television programming:

> Geoblocking exemplifies a fundamental truth about television—that in spite of the McLuhanesque discourses of unfettered globalization we've seen emerge again and again throughout its history, the medium usually has a limited spatial reach. As a structural component of contemporary transnational viewing, geoblocking evokes and manages long-standing anxieties about media's transgression across political and geographical borders. (Elkins 2018, 338)

Geoblocking can be understood as an essential and visible site of power struggle: on the one hand, channel branding allows for foreign viewers to navigate to relevant websites, possibly with a view somewhat tinted by the exoticism of different national media systems. For example, the BBC is a well-known institution outside of the UK and cultural exports from the US have built a general familiarity with Hulu. However, geoblocking software has made it increasingly difficult for foreign users to evade existing geoblocking systems to stream content from these sites. Apart from reinforcing national media systems, the constant push-and-pull of the effectiveness of geoblocking software, often in competition with various providers of VPN software (that links users to proxy servers to access information blocked in the 'home' territory), makes it an important site to understand power struggles between users and various software providers, as well as national and international legal institutions and policies. Yet, it also shows the porous nature of the hegemony governing national media systems. As outlined in Part III, Netflix would later work to re-negotiate transnational and national media for its own purposes. In parts, this is in response to its own, very similar issues with national broadcasting licenses, audience desires and VPN software.

The level of control that can be exercised by internet-based programmers has increased vastly. Thus, the negotiation of control takes on a different form: communication between industry and audience becomes much more immediate and direct. The industry can collect more data points, even though it would take a few more years until this 'big data' would be interrogated more closely. Yet, audiences are given more control over the experience of television content.

Conclusion

This chapter has focussed on the various ways in which digital television has increased viewer control and shifted the structures of commercial media. At the same time, it also emphasised the way industry has taken back some of the control lost to the VCR. The two main functions of the VCR, time-shifting and the viewing of pre-recorded material were divided between the DVD and the DVR. YouTube offered a different kind of control. This kind of control emerged largely as part of a wave of social media companies and not explicitly as a challenge to the hegemony of television as cultural object or associated industries. Yet, it allowed for audio-visual content on computers, significantly contributing to a public perception of the internet as 'hub' of media convergence. Catch-up services iPlayer and Hulu combined streaming and long-form narratives of television. This extends options for viewers to choose when to watch what. Yet, these increased options of control, much like the ancillary technologies before it, do not usually come in exchange for power. In fact, as argued throughout Part I, these technologies tend to tie in with neoliberal discourses that put increased choice and control over these choices in a direct relationship with responsibilities of self-care (see Salecl 2010). In Dawson's analysis, this also implies the responsibility to 'repair' television and the various social ills it is discursively connected with (2008). This is most commonly achieved by handing scheduling power to viewers. Thus, neither control over scheduling nor the increased choices available to viewers can equate to subversion of dominant media or a consumers' real social power. Even though the delivery system for television changes how advertising is brought into the homes (or laptops) of viewers, this substantial reconception of commercial media systems does not actually change financing models or the fact that advertising is an integral part of this power structure. If anything, it makes advertising more portable as texts that employ product placement or product integration are exported. Furthermore, the television industry's use of data usually means more targeted advertising and programming for small groups in exchange for viewers' control over what is watched. Thus, at least in some ways, regimes of control and power have shifted. First of all, money is not the only currency being exchanged: particularly YouTube, owned by Google, collects data rather than funds, and does not provide clarity on what this data is used for. Catch-up services like Hulu and iPlayer operate under established financing models (advertising and licence fee), but still collect data to target their programming better. The main form of control that is given to viewers is over schedules, and, as the case of Hulu shows, not necessarily over how much advertising interrupts those schedules. Yet, this control also means that viewers are less exposed to programming they do not like. This control over programming does not equal social power. In fact, it often means that politically or socially subversive programming is only consumed by audience segments that already agree with the views purported in the text, often limiting social impact. As discussed in Chapters 9 and 10, DVD and streaming are often discussed in relation to 'quality' TV and the liberal values linked to it, but less so in relation to the kind of social impact 'quality' TV can have. The narrowcasting of the TV III, and even more so, the TV IV era suggest that this impact is limited to those whose algorithm suggests specific taste structures. Additionally, the TV III era suggests a return to a hegemony in control over media that was disrupted by many ancillary technologies of TV II and often runs counter to the globalising narratives of the internet. Though different formats for VHS tapes had been used previously in different regions of the world, DVDs imposed further restrictions on the ways they could be shared across borders. Geoblocking is an even more obvious way to restrict where content can be watched and shared. Thus, media companies enacted relatively strict regimes that show the limits of control for viewers within a TV III environment. This aspect of national and transnational television will be interrogated further in Part III to position Netflix within these discourses.

None of the media forms discussed in this chapter have disappeared and all remain significant in the TV IV era. YouTube remains an important site for fan interaction, now usually without interference from rights holders (see Jenkins et al. 2013). It is also an important marketing platform for television, particularly for American late-night programming, which tends to make clips available internationally, and YouTube has become an increasingly important site for television to recruit new talent (such as Rachel Bloom). Catch-up television has only become more significant over the last few years as national broadcasters have developed increasingly sophisticated models (see, for example, Johnson 2017). Though this chapter was part of a broader theorisation of a pre-history of Netflix, these discourses are not finished or negated by Netflix. In fact, particularly YouTube and Hulu remain significant parts of the process of TV IV.

Bibliography

Austen, Jane. 1836. *Pride and Prejudice: A Novel.* London: Richard Bentley.

Bruns, Axel. 2007. "Produsage: Towards a Broader Framework for User-Led Content Creation." ACM. http://eprints.qut.edu.au/6623/.

Burgess, Jean, and Green, Joshua. 2009. *YouTube: Online Video and Participatory Culture*, Joshua Green (ed.). Cambridge: Polity.

Chun, Wendy Hui Kyong. 2006. *Control and Freedom: Power and Paranoia in the Age of Fiber Optics.* Cambridge, MA: MIT Press.

Creeber, Glen. 2013. *Small Screen Aesthetics: From TV to the Internet.* London: BFI.

Curtin, Michael. 2009. "Matrix Media." In Jinna Tay and Graeme Turner (eds.), *Television Studies After TV: Understanding Television in the Post-Broadcast Era*, 9–19. London: Routledge.

Dawson, Max. 2008. *TV Repair: New Media Solutions to Old Media Problems*, Lynn B. Spigel, Jennifer Light, and Jeffrey Sconce, eds. ProQuest Dissertations Publishing.

Elkins, Evans. 2018. "Geoblocking National TV in an on-Demand Era." In Derek Johnson (ed.), *From Networks to Netflix: A Guide to Changing Channels*, 333–42. London: Routledge.

Fuchs, Christian. 2013. *Social Media: A Critical Introduction* Los Angeles: Sage Publication.

Gillan, Jennifer. 2015. *Television Brandcasting: The Return of the Content-Promotion Hybrid.* New York; London: Routledge.

Greenberg, Joshua M. 2008. *From Betamax to Blockbuster: Video Stores and the Invention of Movies on Video.* Cambridge, MA: MIT Press.

Jenkins, Henry, Sam Ford, and Joshua Green. 2013. *Spreadable Media : Creating Value and Meaning in a Networked Culture.* New York: New York University Press.

Johnson, Catherine. 2017. "Beyond Catch-Up." *Critical Studies in Television: The International Journal of Television Studies* 12 (2): 121–38.

———. 2012. *Branding Television.* London: Routledge.

Klinger, Barbara. 2006. *Beyond the Multiplex Cinema, New Technologies, and the Home.* Berkeley: University of California Press.

Kompare, Derek. 2005. *Rerun Nation: How Repeats Invented American Television.* New York, NY: Routledge.

Lotz, Amanda D. 2014. *The Television Will be Revolutionized.* 2nd ed. New York: New York University Press.

———. 2017. *Portals.* Michigan: Maize Books.

Salecl, Renata. 2010. *The Tyranny of Choice.* London: Profile Books.

Schäfer, Mirko Tobias. 2011. *Bastard Culture!: How User Participation Transforms Cultural Production.* Amsterdam: Amsterdam University Press.

Strangelove, Michael. 2015. *Post-TV: Piracy, Cord-Cutting, and the Future of Television*. Toronto: University of Toronto Press.

Van Dijk, José. 2013. "YouTube Beyond Technology and Cultural Form." In Marijke de Valck and Jan Teurlings (eds.), *After the Break: Television Theory Today*, 147–60. Amsterdam: Amsterdam University Press.

Wolff, Michael. 2015. *Television Is the New Television*. New York: Portfolio/ Penguin.

Television

Handmaid's Tale, The (2017–), USA: Hulu
Modern Family (2009–20), USA: ABC
Mythic Quest (2020–), USA: AppleTV
Staged (2020–1), UK: BBC

YouTube

The Lizzie Bennett Diaries (2012–14), USA: Agreeable Entertainment, Pemberley Digital

PART II

Binge-Watching and the Re-invention of Control

CHAPTER 7

Binge-Watching and the Re-invention of Control

Following on from Part I, Part II considers the various ways Netflix reconceptualises control through the concept of binge-watching. Where Part I focusses on the pre-history of Netflix and the way ancillary technologies reconceptualised television via the concept of control, Part II explores Netflix in more detail in relation to binge-watching. Part II of this book discusses the centrality of binge-watching to the way Netflix structures, markets, explains and brands itself. Binge-watching, a practice where several episodes of a serialised programme are watched on a medium other than linear television, has become more than a mode of viewing to Netflix. It has become a publishing model that dictates how content is supposed to be watched on Netflix, explained by important figures in the entertainment industry, predominantly *House of Cards* actor Kevin Spacey, fired in 2107 due to sexual assault allegations, and *Arrested Development* creator Mitch Hurwitz in 2013. Binge-watching may be the term most closely associated with Netflix, which also developed the term 'binge model', meaning putting all episodes of a season online at once. But Netflix also strategically deployed the term and moved it from a relatively marginalised practice media fans and other enthusiasts of TV series engaged in into the 'mainstream' (see Jenner 2017). In fact, the year 2013 saw a number of headlines in US media outlets like *The Atlantic*, *Wired* or *Forbes* that suggest a 'normalisation' of the term (Lee 2013; McCracken 2013; Pomerantz 2013). Of course, this strong

M. Jenner, *Netflix and the Re-invention of Television*, https://doi.org/10.1007/978-3-031-39237-5_7

association between Netflix and binge-watching has made other streamers reluctant to use the term in a similar manner. Binge-watching can also be viewed as a term that encapsulates how control is offered to viewers in a TV IV era. As this suggests, binge-watching is not exclusive to Netflix, though I argue here that Netflix has employed it more centrally than other streaming services. In fact, it has so thoroughly created the impression that Netflix is synonymous with binge-watching that other streamers avoid using the term or publication model. As much as binge-watching, as company language suggests, offers unprecedented control to viewers, Netflix also clearly guides, or nudges, choices. Its algorithm even serves to limit choice by highlighting programmes it determines relevant to the viewer. In some ways, this tailored experience suggests less control and choice than offered through the RCD and the VCR.

Binge-watching is the concept that most strongly points back to Netflix' past as mail-order DVD-rental store. Founded in 1997, it made use of the size of DVD discs, delivering them by mail. As Ed Finn describes:

> Instead of paying extensive late fees to their local retail store, Netflix allowed customers to hang onto their copy of *Titanic* [Cameron, 1997] as long as they pleased for a fixed monthly subscription price. Rather than choose from a few thousand titles at their corner store they could select from tens of thousands in Netflix' vast library. And because the transactions were conducted by mail, customers no longer had to run a special errand, confront long lines or opinionated staff, or deal with the poor selection at their video store. (2017, location 1875)

The formula was adopted by a number of other companies around the world, such as Amazon affiliate Lovefilm or even UK supermarket chain Tesco. Streaming was initially an add-on to Netflix in the US to allow instant access to content. This continued the principle that a monthly subscription fee would buy as much content as viewers could watch. It has become company lore that one of the data points collected from the DVD business was how long customers needed to watch a disc of a DVD box set of a TV series and how quickly they wanted the next disc (see Jurgensen 2013). As Lotz notes,

> Beginning in 2004, feature articles in the popular press recounted the trend of audience members waiting until a full season of a series was available on

DVD and then watching the full season at a self-determined pace. (2014, location 1760–7)

In real numbers, by "2005, DVD sales of television shows reached $2.6 billion and accounted for nearly 20 percent of the overall DVD sales market [in the US]" (ibid., location 3276). As Lotz points out, this was a surprise to the industry. This is particularly true for the practice of binge-watching, a factor also evidenced by the fact that some DVD box sets of 'cult' or 'quality' TV, such as that of *Firefly* (Fox, 2002–3) or *Six Feet Under* (HBO, 2001–5), do not have a 'play all' function that automatically starts new episodes after one is finished. Thus, industry either did not expect viewers to desire this function or use DVDs for the purpose of binge-watching, or did not want to capitalise on it. At any rate, it did not make it easier for viewers to binge-watch without having to navigate back to the main menu. The amount of money and effort put into elaborately designed main menus, that often played like 30-second clips, as in the case of early DVD box sets of *CSI* (CBS, 2000–15), also indicates that industry did not consider the uninterrupted viewing of the text to be the main attraction of DVDs. This also stands in opposition to more recent DVDs, which tend to offer a minimum of menu design (often just a marketing logo) and extras. Netflix, however, came to the conclusion that audiences preferred watching a full disc in one sitting, rather than viewing DVDs as ancillary product for fans. Viewers seemingly sought viewing at their own pace more than ownership. Still, Netflix was hardly the only company with access to such data. Netflix' own deduction that binge-watching could interest more than just a few audience segments could have gone nowhere if it had not actively pushed the terminology and used the concept to structure and explain itself.

Defining binge-watching can be difficult. This is often due to the importance assigned to the number of episodes that need to be watched in order to establish a 'binge'. There are different ways to approach this issue. Binge-watching can be measured in relation to subjective viewing behaviour, as a number set by Netflix or other media institutions or in comparison to what linear television allows for in one sitting (see Jenner 2017). None of these are necessarily practical means to define binge-watching. Establishing binge-watching as 'excessive' compared to everyday viewing behaviour is almost impossible: 'everyday' media behaviour likely changes significantly over a lifetime. Ksenia Frolova (2017), for example, notes the limited time available to parents of young children to watch television series produced for adults. Based on this, the number of episodes needed to constitute a binge is subjective and heavily dependent on individual circumstances. A further complication of how to define binge-watching is noted by Andrew Wallenstein in *Variety*:

> Time and again, I hear of people polishing off a tonnage of TV time in a matter of days that takes me much longer to complete. It makes me wonder whether there's two separate breeds of bingers: We're both deviating from the typical week-by-week episodic allotment of live TV, but one type is engaging in marathon viewing sessions while the other spreads a smaller dosage across a greater number of days. (2013a)

Thus, viewers may engage in different forms of binge-watching, but still use the same terms to describe them. As a different way to define a binge, Netflix set the number of episodes at two watched in one sitting in a study conducted by Harris Interactive in 2013. This was based on qualitative research, but at a time when many viewers had already engaged in binge-watching on DVD box sets, often watching at least one disc in one sitting, this number seems low (see Feeney 2014). The third way to approach the issue is by comparing episodes watched to what is offered to viewers by linear television, so (usually) one episode of a series per week. As different transnational streamers have entered the market, discussion frequently focusses on publication models as dictating how content is watched. What all these definitions have in common, though, is an implicit assumption that serialised programmes are the object of binge-watching. The term does not describe watching several films in a row or episodes of different serialised programmes, but takes place as insulated flow, as Perks puts it, in the viewing of one series. Another implicit assumption is that the medium this is watched on is not linear television: even viewing a marathon or omnibus on TV is not classified as binge-watching. Instead, there is an emphasis on viewing on DVD or streaming. Brunsdon summarises that:

> The metaphors [of addiction implied in the term binge] demonstrate the shift from something that is rationed temporally (broadcast television), and which you must therefore get a fix from regularly, to something more like a box of chocolates which you purchase and consume in your own time. (2010, location 1626)

Though invoking addiction metaphors, the use of the term was originally relatively tongue-in-cheek. Wallenstein notes in the above-cited piece that many of his friends 'brag' about completing series in a minimum amount of time, rather than be ashamed of it, as is the case with, for example, binge-eating.

As argued in Chapter 5, some version of binge-watching has been a relatively common practice since time-shifting technologies have become available. As Matt Hills and Joanne Garde-Hansen (2017) explore, this can even include sound recordings. Stevens (2021), in her exploration of *Starsky and Hutch* (ABC, 1975–9) fandom, finds the use of the term 'binge' in 1985 by fans who watch several episodes in a row on VHS. Particularly the possibility of recording content from television meant that the collection and viewing of several episodes in a row was often relegated to the self-scheduled 'private' as opposed to the 'public' broadcasting schedule. Yet, officially distributed 'box sets' were rarely available before DVD (see Kompare 2005, 197–220). The DVD box set is discussed here as a 'binge medium' before streaming to illuminate how binge-watching can be conceptualised. Chapter 6 describes how DVDs offered industry a pathway to more control over time-shifted television content than previously possible. As a medium that plays content rather than record off broadcast television, the DVD allows producers to reframe content on their own terms. Jason Jacobs (2011) discusses the idea of a 'polluted' text, the idea that there is such a thing as a 'pure' text until it is interrupted or framed by advertising or other supposedly undesired programming. In other words, schedules, or even ad breaks on streaming platforms, serve as a means to dilute the 'pure' text. VHS recordings from television often cannot avoid recording at least some of that pollution. DVDs filter out the 'noise' of other television and offer this 'pure' text:

> ...digital television is promoted and to an increasing extent consumed, at least in part, in terms of its ability to purify the connective tissue of the schedule, to remove the adverts, promotional material, and other pollution that gets in the way of the 'pure' text. (2011, location 3095)

However, DVDs do not fully cancel out the 'noise'. Instead of advertising or idents, they offer (or, in some cases, used to offer) different material: DVD menus, making-offs, blooper reels, teaser trailers, and so on. Furthermore, the full-length closing credits and logos from producers are included, which usually are not shown any more on broadcast television (Eastman and Neal-Lunsford 1993). Much of this content may be desired while other features can be skipped or remain unwatched, but this poses some questions about what a 'pure' text is: it seems no less commercial or officially sanctioned by the television industry than texts positioned within a broadcast television schedule. Additionally, as Jacobs argues:

> Of course, digital television does not remove everyday life – indeed, it seems attuned to a particularly privatized and individualized everyday – but its online, onscreen variations allow users to mitigate or entirely remove the unwanted or surplus marks of the traditional schedule. (2011, location 3110)

Thus, the 'noise' of the everyday continues to exist, but it can be controlled how much it encroaches on the individual media experience. Newman and Levine discuss the perceived 'non-commercial' nature of DVD box sets, an impression created by the absence of ad breaks (2012, 136). However, considering that DVD box sets became a significant revenue stream for broadcasters like HBO, this supposed non-commercialism is (literally) bought and paid for. At the same time, the attraction of buying DVD box sets lies in the supposed textual purity just as much (if not more) as control over scheduling. The possibility to watch DVDs on laptops allows further independence. In fact, the autonomy to decide when to watch what, in a chosen language without ad breaks, at a chosen pace and at a convenient time to ensure attention, may be the most crucial aspect of binge-watching. This suggests that binge-watching implies control more than a dictated number of episodes to watch. At the same time, Johnson (2019) points out that: "across categories of TV, online and content natives a range of business models are in operation often utilising a combination of different sources of funding" (2019, 56). Thus, while binge-watching is defined via the 'pure text' without advertising on Netflix or DVD, this is not true for all streamers, as also pointed out in relation to Hulu in Chapter 6. In fact, in some markets Netflix operates a subscription tier with advertising, though this has not proven successful so far (see Peterson 2022). Different models exist, some of which serve to de-emphasise different aspects of binge-watching as concept.

Streaming heightens a number of aspects of binge-watching: for Netflix, binge-watching and insulated flow are a crucial structuring force (see Chapter 8). On Netflix, there are little extratextual materials: the exception are making-offs with interviews for some of its in-house productions. Blooper reels and other material is usually released through other means of distribution, such as DVD box sets or YouTube, meaning that viewers actively need to seek them out. Other streamers have taken this on board as well while DVD box sets offer less of this material. This means that Netflix offers a different kind of textual purity than DVDs previously did, aiming to remove even more 'noise'. However, text continues to be placed in a specific, industry-sanctioned context, such as the interface. At the same time—and paradoxically considering the addiction metaphors implied in the term—binge-watching also suggests increased control for the viewer. Embedded in a neoliberal capitalist system, the self-scheduled nature of binge-watching suggests unprecedented levels of control. The control industry maintains, again, indicates the problematic relationship between power and control. If the addiction metaphor can indicate anything in this context, it is an exploitative relationship between those in charge of 'supply' (industry) and 'addicts' (viewers). It implies that viewers may not be fully aware of what they give up in exchange for control over TV. Yet, this is, perhaps, to over-interpret these metaphors and to underestimate the levels of control audiences do exercise. As Chun (2006) argues, the power online companies have does not need to be interpreted in paranoid ways, though this does not mean ignoring the amount of data that is exchanged or the fact that power relations do not shift with audience's increased control. Systems through which data is exchanged are more detailed, allowing both, audiences and industry to formulate more elaborate responses through their viewing and marketing behaviour.

For Netflix, binge-watching has become a structuring concept. Perks describes this via her model of flow, which describes the two concepts of entrance flow and insulated flow. In her study, the concept links to different binge media, but it is remarkable how much Netflix is configured in accordance with this system. The structure of Netflix and its recommendation algorithm constantly introduces viewers to programmes that fit the individual users' taste structure (entrance flow). Once entrance flow to a serialised programme is established, the post-play (or auto-play) function, along with other features, such as 'skip intro', creates an almost seamless flow from one episode to the next (insulated flow). Serialised formats (self-produced and false Originals) are published as seasons, encouraging viewing as insulated flow.[1] Netflix' marketing campaigns for its first high-profile productions heavily emphasise and explain what binge-watching is (see Chapter 10). Most debates surrounding ancillary technologies and television discussed in Part I centred around control over the television schedule and advertising as what was assumed to be television's most disliked part. Binge-watching, as concept that signifies self-scheduling, illuminates that this dislike goes beyond advertising to include the weekly release of episodes of serialised programmes. Yet, unlike what some of the cultural logics surrounding Netflix may suggest, binge-watching is neither a 'pure' nor a 'natural' way of watching television content. Rather, it was deliberately marketed as such.

Thus, as Part II explores, the kind of control offered by Netflix and other streaming services, which follow the parameters set out by previous ancillary technologies without interrogating them. Overall, Part II analyses the structure of Netflix, its use of the concept of binge-watching and its overall branding. As young as Netflix, as content producer, is, it is involved in a constant reconfiguration of itself and its branding. This is likely linked to the increasing amount of algorithmic data collected in the context of its global expansion. The current focus on diversity and its quantification can also be related back to this, as discussed in Chapters 10 and 13. Yet, what does remain central is the concept of binge-watching. Part II develops an understanding of the way Netflix employs the term binge-watching to position itself in relation to linear television. A guiding question is how the concept of binge-watching guides the structure, marketing and cultural politics of Netflix. Chapter 8 explores the larger implications of Netflix' structure by comparing binge-watching to the schedule in linear television. In this regard, the broadcasting schedule is viewed as an organisational structure that also guides viewers and implicitly explains how the medium needs to be watched. Thus, content that may need more focus and attention is shown during prime time,

[1] There are exceptions to this, such as the final season of *Breaking Bad*, *Scream* or *Crazy Ex-Girlfriend* (CBS 2015–) which are licensed under a deal that permits the publication of new episodes in international markets shortly after they air in the US. Thus, the season is published in weekly instalments, allowing viewers to 'save up' episodes or watch them weekly. However, in these cases, viewers are ultimately left to self-schedule rather than being given a specific time slot each week.

whereas most daytime television may solicit attention in different ways. The chapter then moves on to explore what an equivalent to a schedule would be on Netflix. It analyses particularly the concept of entrance flow and how it can be established in relation to Netflix' algorithm and its use of genre to structure the experience. I focus here on binge-watching as structuring force for Netflix, its interface, production modules, marketing and viewer control. Many of these features are now expected for streaming platforms, which has seen Netflix shift marketing and programming emphases. Because of this, the platforms' focus on middlebrow TV and the use of quantification and social concepts like diversity have grown increasingly important. Chapter 9 discusses the way Netflix' content negotiates cultural value. It explores implicit linkages between binge-watching and 'quality' TV and Netflix' deliberate exploitation of these links. However, Netflix has more recently sought broader audience appeal transnationally by embracing more popular genres and programming (see also Jenner 2021). This negotiation between 'quality' and 'the popular' becomes particularly visible in Netflix' comedy strand, as is also made obvious in the opening credits of early Netflix sitcoms. Thus, this chapter explores these tensions in detail, with a particular emphasis on the role of binge-watching. Building on this, Chapter 10 discusses the role of binge-watching in marketing of its early in-house productions in 2013 and how Netflix more recently recalibrated its brand towards a specific version of diversity. The chapter also discusses how this emphasis on diversity is re-directed in specific ways in the streaming wars, now that control of the schedule has become a central feature of all streaming services. This is in line with the way Netflix positions itself transnationally. If, as Jennifer Gillan (2015) argues, the schedule is a central aspect of the branding of television channels, then the series Netflix publishes function as representatives of its brand. The terms under which diversity is understood, structured, produced and published are, thus, highly significant in understanding Netflix. Part II functions, on the one hand, as documenting how Netflix established itself via the concept of binge-watching in the past. However, it also emphasises more recent moves by highlighting how these relate to the company's recent past.

Bibliography

Brunsdon, Charlotte. 2010. "Bingeing on Box-Sets: the National and the Digital in Television Crime Drama". In Jostein Gripsrud (ed.), *Relocating Television: Television in the Digital Context*, 61–75. London: Routledge.

Chun, Wendy Hui Kyong. 2006. *Control and Freedom: Power and Paranoia in the Age of Fiber Optics*. Cambridge, MA: MIT Press.

Eastman, Susan Tyler and Jeffrey Neal-Lunsford. 1993. "The RCD's Impact on Television Programming and Promotion." In Robert V. Bellamy and James R. Walker (eds.), *The Remote Control in the New Age of Television*, 189–210. London: Praeger.

Feeney, Nolan. 2014. "When, Exactly, does Watching a Lot of Netflix Become a 'Binge'?" *The Atlantic*. Available online February. https://www.theatlantic.com/entertainment/archive/2014/02/when-exactly-does-watching-a-lot-of-netflix-become-a-binge/283844/. Accessed: 30.09.2017.

Finn, Ed. 2017. *What Algorithms Want: Imagination in the Age of Computing*. Cambridge, MA: MIT Press.

Gillan, Jennifer. 2015. *Television Brandcasting: The Return of the Content-Promotion Hybrid*. New York; London: Routledge.

Hills, Matt, and Joanne Garde-Hansen. 2017. "Fandom's Paratextual Memory: Remembering, Reconstructing, and Repatriating "Lost" Doctor Who." *Critical Studies in Media Communication* 34 (2): 158–167.

Jacobs, Jason. 2011. "Television, Interrupted: Pollution or Aesthetic?" In James Bennett and Niki Strange (eds.), *Television as Digital Media*. Durham, NC: Duke University Press. Kindle, location 3065–3399.

Jenner, Mareike. 2017. "Binge-Watching: Video-on-Demand, Quality TV and Mainstreaming Fandom." *International Journal of Cultural Studies* 20 (3): 304–320.

Jenner, Mareike. 2021. "Transnationalising Genre: Netflix, Teen Drama and Textual Dimensions in Netflix Transnationalism." In M. Jenner (ed.), *Binge-Watching and Contemporary Television Studies*. Edinburgh: EUP.

Jurgensen, John. 2013. "Netflix Says Binge Viewing Is No 'House of Cards'; Half the Users it Studied Watch an Entire Season in One Week." *Wall Street Journal (Online)*. Available online https://www.wsj.com/articles/netflix-says-binge-viewing-is-no-8216house-of-cards8217-1386897939. Accessed: 30.12.2017.

Kompare, Derek. 2005. *Rerun Nation: How Repeats Invented American Television*. New York, NY: Routledge.

Lee, Adrian. 2013. "How Netflix Stopped Worrying and Learned to Love the Binge." Available online https://www.theatlantic.com/technology/archive/2013/12/how-netflix-stopped-worrying-and-learned-love-binge/356159/. Accessed: 01.01.2018.

Lotz, Amanda D. 2014. *The Television Will be Revolutionized*. Second ed. New York: New York University Press.

McCracken, Grant. 2013. "From Arrested Development to Dr. Who, Binge-Watching Is Changing our Culture." *Wired*. Available online https://www.wired.com/2013/05/beyond-arrested-development-how-binge-watching-is-changing-our-narrative-culture/. Accessed: 14.01.2018.

Newman, Michael Z., and Levine, Elana 2012. *Legitimating Television: Media Convergence and Cultural Status*. Abingdon: Routledge.

Perks, Lisa Glebatis. 2015. *Media Marathoning: Immersions in Morality*. Lanham, MD: Lexington Books.

Peterson, T. 2022. *Netflix Lets Advertisers Take Their Money Back After Missing Viewership Targets*. In DigiDay. Available at https://digiday.com/future-of-tv/netflix-lets-advertisers-take-their-money-back-after-missing-viewership-targets/?utm_medium=email&utm_campaign=digidaydis&utm_source=daily&utm_content=221215&fbclid=IwAR3bR0-ApG2O0z5U2kkjZtqNa2LLi6izNsYEB2_WoMhy5Syg_HOay7Nma1U. Accessed: 01.03.2023.

Pomerantz, Dorothy. 2013. "Binge-Watching Is our Future." *Forbes*. Available online https://www.forbes.com/sites/dorothypomerantz/2013/05/29/binge-watching-is-our-future/#3f0229fc15ff. Accessed: 30.12.2017.

Stevens, E.C. 2021. "Historical Binge-Watching: Marathon Viewing on Videotape." In M. Jenner (ed.), *Binge-Watching and Contemporary Television Studies*, 23–39. Edinburgh: Edinburgh University Press.

Wallenstein, Andrew. 2013a. "Analysis: Why Netflix must Rethink Binge Viewing." *Variety*. Available online http://variety.com/2013/digital/news/analysis-why-netflix-must-rethink-binge-viewing-1118065356/. Accessed: 23.12.2017.

———. 2013b. "Why Everything You Know about Binge-Viewing Is Wrong." *Variety*, 13.08. http://variety.com/2013/biz/news/netflix-breaking-bad-everything-know-binge-viewing-wrong-1200586747/.

Television

Arrested Development (2003–6, 2013), USA: Fox, Netflix
Crazy Ex-Girlfriend (2015–19), USA: CBS
CSI (2000–15), USA: NBC
Firefly (2002–3), USA: Fox
House of Cards (2013–18), USA: Netflix
Johnson, C. 2019, *Online TV*. London: Routledge.
Scream (2015–16), USA: MTV
Six Feet Under (2001–5), USA: HBO
Starsky and Hutch (1975–9), USA: ABC

CHAPTER 8

Scheduling the Binge

The control viewers can exercise via ancillary technologies tends to be over the television schedule. RCDs, VCRs, DVDs, or online catch-up services all offer viewers the possibilities to change channels or time-shift television and avoid advertising and other unwanted material. Netflix abandons the linear schedule as framework to order content. Yet, this does not mean that it does not offer a structure that, at least in some ways, has much in common with the broadcasting schedule. Netflix does not offer up its texts in instalments of one episode per week (except in exceptional licensing deals), but rather in units of one season per year. It also does not prescribe when to watch what and only rarely publishes audience numbers to measure the immediate success of a film or series among viewers. Nevertheless, it structures the experience. It uses the auto-play function to ensure viewers 'stay tuned' for the next episode; it shows viewers where they left off watching to re-enter a text at any time, with the most recently viewed texts prominently positioned on the interface; and once viewers finish viewing one thing, it immediately nudges them towards similar texts. This structure has proven so successful that other streaming platforms widely adopted it. Netflix may not schedule in the sense of linear broadcasting, but it strongly urges, or in the terminology of data science, nudges viewers to make certain choices. And much like 'blocs' on linear television, its algorithm assumes that if viewers like one text of a specific genre, they are likely to want to watch others (see also

M. Jenner, *Netflix and the Re-invention of Television*,
https://doi.org/10.1007/978-3-031-39237-5_8

Gaw 2022). Binge-watching remains a strong factor as a way to ensure viewer attention. Perks divides this concept into a two-part flow model. Drawing on Williams' flow model, she theorises that digital television's system can be divided into 'entrance flow', which aims to get viewers to start watching a serialised programme in the first place, and 'insulated flow', which guides viewers through binge-watching that text. Lotz describes the organisation of content in what she calls 'portals' as an act of curation:

> ...portals have features that lead to differentiation in use, and the use experience of a single portal varies among viewers. The experience of logging in to Netflix differs from what a viewer encounters entering HBO Now so that not just programming, but also viewers' experience distinguishes portals to make portal features part of product differentiation. Some other features distinguishing portals as products include the strategy used to organize content, whether the last viewed content automatically played, and the particular sophistication of the search and recommendation functions. (2017, location 258)

In other words, the interface and Netflix' recommendation system are forms in which content is 'curated' or organised for the viewers, which are distinct from other streaming services (see also Johnson 2018). In the case of Netflix, the terminology of curation somewhat underestimates just how much concepts of insulated and entrance flow nudge viewers towards certain decisions. As Cohn points out: "Companies like Google, Amazon, or Netflix present their recommendation technologies as neutral, objective, benevolent, and natural" (2019, 10). This is in line with the way Netflix presents, for example, binge-watching as a 'natural' evolution of television viewing, when it is possibly best described as the most convenient way to consume content on certain technologies.

This chapter explores how Netflix employs binge-watching as a way to structure its interface and, through this, the experience of Netflix. To do this, this chapter will explore how the schedule of linear television has been theorised to analyse how Netflix is structured and what this organisational system means for the platform. Perks' insulated flow and entrance flow will serve as guiding concepts, but by applying the concept to Netflix and analysing how Netflix organises them, this analysis offers a much more specific view. This chapter will look at the television schedule to work out similarities and differences for Netflix and then move on to consider insulated flow (binge-watching) and entrance flow (the Netflix algorithm and its use of genre), in more detail. This analysis will highlight the organisational structure of Netflix to understand what role binge-watching plays in this.

Linear Television Schedules

Before going into more detail on how Netflix structures content, it is worth reflecting on the function of the schedule on linear television and the way it shapes and organises content. Roger Silverstone positions television as everyday in his 1994 book *Television and Everyday Life*. He draws on Anthony Giddens' work to argue that the ritualistic nature of the television schedule is structured into the everyday lives of viewers. What underlies his argument is an assumption that both, television and media habits, are stable. Chun defines habits as follows:

> Habits are strange, contradictory things: they are human-made nature, or, more broadly, culture becomes (second) nature. They are practices acquired through time that are seemingly forgotten as they move from the voluntary to the involuntary, the conscious to the automatic. (2016, location 249)

Television schedules are structured around the habits of viewers (afternoon television when children come home from school, prime-time television for families), but viewers also structure their habits around the schedule (switching on the television set at specific times, spending a night at home to watch a new episode of a favourite TV series). The broadcasting schedule is a major part of how television structures and is structured into everyday life. Broadcasting schedules are also complex in the sense that they do not just organise the content available to one channel, but always have to consider how the schedule of one channel competes with another. As Ellis notes,

> The sum total of schedules, locked in their competitive struggle, defines the character of a national television economy, or, to be more accurate, the character of a particular broadcasting market. From this perspective, the character of the national scheduling battle constitutes a formidable site of resistance and resilience in face of any globalizing tendencies that might bear down upon it. For television is always specific, however much it may be amenable to generalizations. (2000a, 145)

As such, television schedules are always nationally specific. This has often been a hurdle that transnational broadcasters have found difficult to tackle. The schedule is structured into nationally specific ways of structuring time, taking into account time zones, national holidays, common work or school hours, climate, etc., often making it difficult for transnational broadcasters to gain a far reach across borders. Thus, the schedule plays an important part in shaping communities, but is also integrated into the rhythms of everyday life of this community.

Gillan (2015) notes that scheduling practices across US television have remained surprisingly stable. She compares the practices used in the 1950s and 1960s by ABC with more contemporary scheduling practices on Showtime. She finds that the general practices of lead-ins, lead-outs, tent-poles, etc., have remained important practices to tie together thematically and tonally similar series. In fact, she argues that ABC's tween-focussed scheduling is surprisingly similar to the niche marketing employed by Showtime and its heavy reliance on dark comedy with female leads in the 2010s. Thus, scheduling can help build and maintain channel brands and establish links between programmes that, otherwise, might go unnoticed. Ellis (2000b) points to the relevance of audience demographics in guiding scheduling. In other words, guiding questions for scheduling are: 'who watches when?' and 'who is this programme aimed at?'. Thus, programmes aimed at children or whole family units are scheduled at times when children may watch alone, or the family is likely to watch together. But there are also aspects more driven by habits. For example, the German channel RTL showed the TV series *Deutschland '83* (RTL, 2015). In the US, the series was shown on the Sundance Channel, linking it to the prestigious film festival. In the UK, it merited weekly recaps in *The Guardian*, a purveyor of middle-class values and taste. In Germany, scheduled on a Thursday night on commercial channel RTL, the series rated poorly. As journalists Markus Ehrenberg and Joachim Huber (2015) suggest, this may very well be because the usual RTL scheduling for Thursday nights includes relatively light-hearted action dramas like the long-running *Alarm für Cobra 11* (RTL, 1996–) or American imports. *Deutschland '83* fits neither with the channel brand nor the expectations for its Thursday night slot and the audience the channel is likely to attract during this slot. Though the reasons for why programmes may be successful in some national contexts, but not in others are much more complex, the habits and expectations that build around schedules certainly form one aspect of such a discourse. This suggests that channels model viewers' expectations for specific slots, implying that schedules include a specific mode of address. The habits and rituals that build around broadcasting schedules are formed within the structures of a complex relationship. Ellis describes scheduling as "nothing other than editing on an Olympian scale" (2000a, 131). In other words, meaning is created through the ways programmes are 'ordered' to construct the television flow. In this, genres "are the basic building blocks of television, and the schedule is the architecture that combines them" (ibid.). Ellis summarises that the process of scheduling involves dividing a day into a grid of half-hour slots, to be filled with programming and 'surrounding materials', such as adverts. Commercial television is financed through the money advertisers pay for the audience a programme is assumed to attract, meaning that, in constructing a schedule, advertising is material that is 'filled in' after decisions on programming have been made. Scheduling can affect the success or failure of a specific programme beyond viewer expectations of a slot, as well. As Fiske outlines:

> The scheduling of *Cagney and Lacey* [CBS, 1981-8] provides a good example not only of its ability to build an audience, but also to affect meaning and popularity by influencing a show's generic affiliations. When CBS scheduled *Cagney and Lacey* after *Magnum* [CBS, 1980-8] on a Thursday evening, it rated poorly. But when scheduled on a Monday to follow *Scarecrow and Mrs King* [CBS, 1983-7], *Kate & Allie* [CBS, 1984-9] and *Newhart* [CBS, 1982-90] it topped ratings. Monday became known as 'women's night' and *Cagney and Lacey* was shifted away from masculine generic relations with *Magnum* and towards more feminine ones. Because *Cagney and Lacey* shows a particularly even mix of generic characteristics, its prime genre was in some doubt, and so scheduling was able to tip the balance away from masculine cop show towards soap opera or women's show.[1] (1987, 113)

This example illustrates well how scheduling is not only about genre or generic recognition, but also about more subtle features.

[1] Fiske's problematic understanding of gender and mode of address is visible throughout *Television Cultures*: *Magnum, P.I.*'s objectification of its male star points to something much more complicated and complex than terms like 'masculine' or 'cop drama' can describe (see Flitterman 1985). Similarly, *Cagney and Lacey*, visually and thematically much more cop drama than *Magnum, P.I.* with its Hawaiian setting and P.I. main character, cannot be classified as part of an elusive 'women's genre' based on the fact that it has female main characters.

There is limited time available to offer broadcasting, so the schedule functions as a way to ensure that broadcasters can use this time effectively by always attracting the maximum number of available viewers at any given time. In the system of commercial television, this is necessary to justify prices for advertising slots. Yet, the schedule also implicitly communicates to viewers how broadcast television needs to be watched: viewers might change channels, but they can never escape the way television flow is organised through time slots. As outlined in Part I, various technologies to re-organise and time-shift flow have been introduced, but there is no alternative to viewing linear television than to follow the schedule. This also speaks to the significance of the schedule for the way television is theorised and understood (see also Lotz 2017). Because of the relevance of scheduling for an understanding of what television is, it becomes important to understand and conceptualise how Netflix orders and organises its content.

The television schedule is crucial, not just to understanding how television is organised, but, as some theorists have argued, understanding television itself. Silverstone's argument about television's 'everydayness' in large parts hinges on the schedule. Fiske's example of the scheduling of *Cagney and Lacey* or the example of *Deutschland '83* point to the schedule's role in a programme's failure or success. Williams discusses 'flow' as central concept in how television functions in *Television. Technology and Cultural Form* (1974). Williams conceptualises television as a hybrid medium that draws on a variety of media. Flow is the means to organise these texts in a specific way. Williams argues that within this flow, different programmes are not organised into distinct units, but an ongoing structure where one programme almost seamlessly leads into the next. Ellis critiques Williams' notion of flow in much detail. He argues that:

> According to Williams' model of flow, then, everything becomes rather like everything else, units are not organised into coherent single texts like cinema films, but form a kind of montage without overall meaning [...]. Flow assembles disparate items, placing them within the same experience, but does not organise them to produce an overall meaning. This is a valuable insight; however, the problem lies in Williams' definition of 'items'. 'Items' are still separate texts, independent works like a cinema film. Finally, for Williams, flow is a feature of TV that severely compromises and alters the separate texts that TV has manufactured. (1992, 117–18)

Ellis argues for the concept of 'segmentation' where television is organised into 'segments' or 'items', meaning recognisably distinct parts. Ellis certainly invests viewers with more agency than Williams, arguing that they are fully capable of recognising differences between segments. Channel-surfing or grazing through different channels demands that viewers are able to quickly recognise the kind of 'segment' currently shown, specifically the genres of programming. Ellis' concept fits well for TV II where grazing viewers are constantly asked to identify the different genres of segments.

Binge-Watching Insulated Flow

Where Ellis' concept of segmentation may be more appropriate to grasp the experience of broadcast television in the TV II era (and later viewing of linear television), Williams' flow can easily be applied to the experience of 'textual purity' linked to binge-watching in the TV III and TV IV era. Williams describes being carried from one 'unit' of programming to the next without much distinction being made between programmes (Williams 1974, 91). Though this may somewhat simplify how the linear schedule functions, it is accurate in describing viewing on Netflix. The experience of being carried from one programme to the next, or, in the case of binge-watching, from one episode to the next without necessarily differentiating between episodes (it is, after all, the same text, following a broad narrative arc), is similar. Perks describes this experience as insulated flow: rather than from one programme to the next, viewers are guided from one episode to the next within the same programme:

> In the post-broadcast and post-television era characterized by convergence and exponential growth in competition from content providers, programmers' efforts to secure viewer attention at the beginning of flow can be seen as an increasing challenge. However, marathoning has resulted in an alternative model of flow, one that is assembling user-directed, self-perpetuating (because of technology and reader motives), and often self-contained (with little competition from other media flows). (2015, location 370–76)

In other words, distinct from Williams' flow, insulated flow describes a flow of a pure text.

The insulated flow may be understood as the defining feature of binge-watching. Insulated flow is a deliberate feature of the technology of streaming, particularly on Netflix. The most recent equivalent may be the 'play all' function on DVD box sets. Netflix' auto-play function, where the next episode automatically plays after a few seconds, makes this even easier than DVD box sets. As Perks puts it:

> This insulated flow announces itself, making viewers take ownership of their experience, but its automaticity makes it difficult for viewers to escape the insulated flow. They may already envision themselves as moving through that fictive world. Instead of having to opt-in to a marathon, viewers are made to opt-out. (2015, location 456)

Though similar insulated flow is possible on many DVD box sets and other streaming platforms, Netflix has used this model early on to structure the experience. Other than DVDs and several other streaming platforms, it shows thumbnail images of the next episode, without resolving cliffhangers. The organisation of Netflix is important here, specifically the auto-play or post-play function, which automatically starts the next episode after one is ended, and the skip intro function. The same way television explains itself by offering the schedule as the only means to watch it, Netflix presents insulated flow as suggested means to watch it and nudges viewers towards it. As shown in Chapter 10, Kevin Spacey often highlighted binge-watching when marketing the first season of *House of Cards* in 2013, indicating how important it is in explaining how to watch Netflix to new customers. Binge-watching, thus, functions as a way for Netflix to explain itself. Rather than searching for a new text to watch after each episode, viewers are meant to just stay within the insulated flow of a series. This is important as the absence of a broadcast schedule implies much more deliberate choices need to be made by viewers. Yet, having to make a new choice every 22–60 minutes (depending on what kind of programme is watched) could alienate viewers. Rather than making new choices over and over again, the post-play function ensures that viewers can just let a text run through. In other words, the various features that enable binge-watching on Netflix serve to mitigate the paralysis viewers might feel in the face of too much choice (see Salecl 2010). Instead, Netflix offers to make the choice *for* viewers. This does not necessarily mean giving less agency to viewers (as these are able to make these choices if they wish), but it means giving a control to viewers about how much agency they want to exert. The skip intro function removes one marker of distinction between episodes, making the flow from one episode to the next even more seamless. Thus, insulated flow, which nudges viewers towards binge-watching, is an important organisational feature for Netflix that helps explain how to watch it.

Netflix Algorithms, Genre and Entrance Flow

While insulated flow serves to keep viewers focussed on one series, entrance flow offers a model to understand what happens when a viewer is finished watching one text:

> Rather than being intertwined symbolic sequences, these forms of flow [insulated flow and entrance flow] are consecutive. Digital content delivery technologies make finding the sequence, a process I call *entrance flow*, seemingly more personalized and convenient. It is akin to using one 'preview channel' that is purportedly tailored to you, the reader, by cataloguing your history, making suggestions, and allowing you to maintain a queue. (Perks 2015, location 376–82, italics in the original)

Entrance flow is crucial for Netflix, as it guarantees viewers 'stay tuned' after finishing a series rather than just signing up for one month to watch the new season of *Orange Is the New Black* and cancelling their subscription immediately afterwards. It is also much more difficult to establish: insulated flow keeps audiences interested through textual features, but entrance flow works with comparatively elusive descriptors (thumbnail pictures, titles, brief plot descriptions). Netflix uses two techniques for establishing entrance flow: at the end of a text, it shows recommendations of generically and tonally similar texts and the texts featured on the front page of the interface as a viewer logs into their account. The entrance flow involves much more deliberate choices by viewers, who may search the catalogue for more options instead of relying on the recommendations given based on the last consumed text.

In the overwhelming amount of texts available on Netflix, the recommendation system 'orders' the catalogue for viewers and allows viewers to find texts suitable for entrance flow. The viewer recommendations, its familiar tone, the overwhelming sense that Netflix 'knows' us and acknowledges and addresses us as individuals, not as mass audience, is a key element of its strategies to create brand loyalty. Sarah Arnold summarises:

> This personalization is enabled by Netflix's analysis of vast quantities of user data, generated through the monitoring and interpretation of users' interactions with Netflix while viewing content. Netflix posits the use of data mining systems as beneficial for the consumer and suggests that such systems allow the company to better understand and respond to audience tastes through its recommendation system. (2016, 49)

Arnold describes these recommendations as "a schedule of sorts" (ibid., 51), suggesting that insulated flow and entrance flow go hand in hand to structure Netflix for viewers. Though the algorithm is hardly as prescriptive as a broadcast schedule, it nudges viewer choice by privileging one text (the recommendation) over others that may never appear anywhere on a viewers' page. Aside from branding or marketing, Netflix' recommendation algorithm is the most important building block in establishing entrance flow. As Finn notes,

> From the company's point of view, the entire apparatus is simply another exercise in abstraction, a way of thinking about the millions of different versions of Netflix as an algorithmic problem with a solution space: how can the offerings be personal enough while fitting business needs, licensing opportunities and creative content inventory on hand? (2017, location 2275)

This central task of balancing individualisation to establish entrance flow with the existing limits of the catalogue is taken on by Netflix' recommendation algorithm. Finn notes in relation to *House of Cards* that the series was recommended rather than advertised. The framing of series as 'recommended' based on previous searches rather than advertised to a broad audience is central: it sets Netflix apart from impersonal and abstract mass media to describe something individualised, as if it is recommended by someone close. The interface of Netflix frequently makes clear that its recommendations are individualised with headings like 'Because you watched…', 'Recommendations for [insert first name/screen name of viewer]', 'Because you added [a specific text] to your list'. Chun argues that networks, such as social media, "…capture subjects through users 'like YOU' – that is, users who like YOU ('friends') and those determined to be like YOU ('neighbors')" (2016, location 491). This is consistent with the way social media uses the 'you' or Amazon's 'customers who bought this also bought…' logic. Chun points to a double address towards the singular and the plural you. Yet, Netflix tends to address the singular 'you' by highlighting first names ('recommended for…') and pointing to past behaviour ('because you watched…', 'because you added … to your list', 'watch it again'). As Cohn (2019) makes clear, recommendation systems are never neutral, but usually based on skewed data sets that, for example, are more likely to be based on Caucasian, American tastes. Yet, Netflix makes much of its ability to 'know' the individual viewer. In an interview with *Atlantic* journalist Alexis Madrigal, Netflix' VP of product innovation Todd Yellin argues that knowing audience tastes is central to the company's ability to attract and keep viewers (2014). Of course, this is because it establishes entrance flow. As Alexander outlines:

> In a narcissistic manner, they [Netflix viewers] confuse the 'You' in 'Recommended for You' with a unique, complex individual, rather than with a group of strangers who all happened to have made similar choices. (2016, 86)

This points to the fact that audiences, even though organised in a different manner (see Chapter 15), are still massive. Considering that the 'you' is common in social media, it cannot be assumed that Netflix viewers automatically adopt the viewpoint suggested by Alexander, particularly as other versions of communal viewing remain common, such as discussion on social media or online articles (see Graves 2015; Grandinetti 2017). In fact, viewers may easily assume that recommendations to their friends look similar to their own. Nevertheless, Netflix emphasises individuation through company language when discussing the algorithm. The word 'recommend' may reach further than the 'you' as it suggests personal knowledge. Additionally, the Netflix algorithm is relatively accurate in its predictions, so recommendations, even if they are inaccurate may be likely to be close to desired texts (see also Gaw 2022). In other words, viewers who just watched *Clueless* (Heckerling, 1995) may not want to watch *Mean Girls* (Waters, 2004) or *Girlboss* (Netflix, 2017) afterwards (or ever), but still understand why it was recommended to them. Because such a mistake is easily made by humans, even those who know us intimately, it is relatively easy to forgive the algorithm and the mistake is not necessarily perceived as inaccuracy. Thus, the human associations of the term 'recommend' have consequences for viewer interactions with the algorithm. At the same time, Alexander is right in pointing out that individuation on Netflix only goes so far. Within our peer groups and shared taste cultures, we are likely to receive similar recommendations.

Nevertheless, these recommendations are not exactly the same for most viewers—partly due to the different content on Netflix in different countries, but also because of differing (if, in some cases, only slightly) viewing histories. Thus, the recommendations for viewers within the same taste communities are likely to look very similar, but in some respects also very different.

As this suggests, Netflix has unprecedented access to data about its audiences:

> Now Netflix can trace precisely how their customers watch, how long they hesitate between options, and perhaps even how much pausing, fast-forwarding, or rewinding goes on. The instant gratification of streaming creates a different kind of rating relationship – not the evaluation of a film I watched last week or ten years ago, but right *now*. (Finn 2017, location 1941, italics in the original)

The 'learning' algorithm records large amounts of viewing behaviour that go far beyond any commercial audience research, but operate as part of a broader 'big data' complex:

> Big data allows for more granular abstractions, constructs of consumer markets where we are targeted as individuals or as part of ad hoc groups that are so specific as to eclipse other important aspects of identity [...]. In marketing terms, this is the evolution of [audience] segmentation: the idea that by clustering consumers into particular categories, messages can be uniquely crafted to address their hopes and fears. (Ibid., location 2306)

The sinister implications of this can lead to somewhat alarmist headlines, as when journalist Andrew Leonard titles a 2013 story for *Salon* 'How Netflix is turning viewers into puppets'. In a less sensationalising tone, Uricchio suggests:

> In these predictive systems, the past is prologue, as the data generated through our earlier interactions shape the textual world selected for us. No 'surprises' or 'unwanted' encounters, just uncannily familiar themes and variations. (2017, 130–31)

Thus, many viewers may never be presented with Adam Sandler films or the various sitcoms produced by Netflix. Alexander (2016) voices similar concerns as Uricchio, particularly how older films that might challenge audience's tastes can escape attention. Uricchio takes his argument further in considering the role algorithms already play in artistic production, a factor not irrelevant considering Netflix' production of self-produced originals and its reliance on algorithmic data (see also Gaw 2022). Finn, outlining the role of algorithmic data in constructing *House of Cards*, points to the reinforcement of structures like authorship and stardom implicit in relying on data extracted from viewer responses to already existing texts (2017, location 2109). As such, Netflix' argument that it gives viewers what they want, or rather, what they are supposed to want based on past choices, can be highly problematic and point to a limitation of the algorithm: personal taste can be highly unstable and complex and dependent on circumstances beyond the knowledge of the algorithm. When company staff frequently outline that they are more interested in what you actually watch than what you say you watch (see Madrigal 2014 or Setoodeh 2017), they do not actually consider that these tastes are unlikely to stay stable for most of their customers. However, as Finn outlines, the data collected via algorithms heavily influences what texts are created. As such, cultural production based on algorithmic data does not challenge the boundaries of the medium in the way Netflix suggests. Texts that are produced based on past audience behaviours are bound to reproduce generic structures, existing systems of authorship and stardom, and so on. Yet, this past behaviour is used to establish new entrance flows. Though more data points are known to Netflix, this ties back to the practices of linear television: assumptions are made that viewers who like one programme are likely to 'settle in' for programmes of the same genre or with a similar tone. The principle that applies to programming strategies like lead-ins or lead-outs also informs algorithmic recommendations: if a viewer likes one programme, they are likely to choose a similar one to watch next. Since more national and transnational streaming platforms have become available, Netflix has access to fewer data points, as these are now 'spread out' among platforms. Thus, Netflix becomes even more specialised in specific genres and viewers become even more 'trapped' in specific genre structures as the recommendation algorithm is less aware when tastes shift. The national and international Top 10 Netflix introduced is one way to mitigate this problem.

A strongly related way Netflix' entrance flow is established is the use of genre. This aspect may link the algorithm most strongly back to the linear television schedule. Genre is central to the scheduling practices of linear television. Typically, programmes of the same genre will be scheduled together in the same 'bloc'. Lead-ins or lead-outs for weaker (in terms of audience numbers) programmes only work if all programmes concerned show some similarities in theme and tone, which are features genre structures. Genre necessarily needs some sort of communal consensus: a category like 'sitcom' or 'crime drama' means little if nobody recognises it. TV I and II, with their reach of a mass audience, can construct this consensus through scheduling and the creation of thematic or genre blocs. Scheduling can highlight some thematic commonalities or structural features (a specific kind of humour, stock characters, settings, etc.) over others, thereby constructing consensus. By this logic, in giving up control over the schedule, Netflix gives up its power to construct this consensus. Yet, Netflix heavily relies on genre to structure its interface. Its generic categories are based on an already existing consensus about genre, which Netflix does not challenge. Netflix' algorithm is structured around genre preferences more than other aspects—particularly for newer viewer accounts where more detailed knowledge of viewing behaviour has not been established, yet. Madrigal's often-cited 2014 article is instructive for this. This piece highlights Netflix' use of genre for the algorithms at work to determine not only viewers' professed genre tastes, but also subtle characteristics like 'romance factor':

> Using large teams of people specially trained to watch movies, Netflix deconstructed Hollywood. They paid people to watch films and tag them with all kinds of metadata. This process is so sophisticated and precise that taggers receive a 36-page training document that teaches them how to rate movies on their sexually suggestive content, goriness, romance levels, and even narrative elements like plot conclusiveness. They capture dozens of different movie attributes. They even rate the moral status of characters. When these tags are combined with millions of users viewing habits, they become Netflix's competitive advantage. (2014)

Netflix' system of genre moves beyond the familiarity of 'established' genres: this system tags content, not just in terms of genre, but according to a range of features that are often genre conventions (a certain kind of humour, a tone, a certain narrative structure). Yellin describes these tags as 'micro-tags' in his discussion with Madrigal, documenting miniscule or subtle details of the text. What emerges are micro-genres, categories the algorithm can use to individualise recommendations. At the time of Madrigal's writing, the specific genre categories created by the tagging system were still visible to viewers with precise categories like Canadian Girl Power TV Programmes or Critically acclaimed Romantic Spanish-Language Movies:

> By tracking dozens of variables in each film or show, including the level of profanity, the strength of female characters, and the ambiguity or certainty of the outcome, Netflix has assembled a sophisticated algorithmic model for describing the cultural relationships among individual film and television works, a model that fully embraces the gap between computation and culture. [...] The new thesis is not a retreat but an ambitious leap forward in expanding the calculable terrain, declaring that complex cultural concepts like lightness or darkness of a film's humor can be quantified. (Finn 2017, location 1974)

To a certain extent, genre's function has always been the capturing of dominant traits among texts, usually by ignoring others. Netflix' model, by using micro-tags, captures more subtle elements. At the same time, it is relatively reactive in the sense that genres shift and change based on the texts that are produced. Despite the creative freedom Netflix allows—at least after certain algorithmic demands are met, such as star power or conformity to the Netflix brand—it does not demand that creative staff follow a stable set of genre tags. This suggests that the system remains unstable as tags may change their meaning. Where broadcast television is complex and seems to offer almost unlimited amounts of content, the storage abilities of the internet exceed (potentially) available texts by far. This may not make the detailed differentiation of micro-genres necessary, but useful when it comes to issues of organising content. Netflix' use of genre to organise content links its organisational system to broadcast television.

Netflix' algorithm to order its content based on an individual viewer's preferences creates programmes that cater to much smaller niches than ever before. Nevertheless, the organisation of content for viewers highlights some texts and omits others. Netflix' interface can work to disguise the fact that recommendations are not only made for a singular 'you', while at the same time serving to make viewers unaware of the wealth of texts that do not conform to their individual taste structures. Yet, genre is central to Netflix' algorithm, traditionally a system based on some sort of broader social consensus: however far varying interpretations of the crime series may differ, there needs to be a broad shared idea of what the term means. In the case of Netflix, its tagging handbook and the coding of the algorithm also need to share in these definitions. This runs counter to the individualisation of Netflix' interface. Thus, Netflix' structure cannot be viewed as akin to broadcasting schedules, but also not wholly individualised. Netflix' algorithm, following the impetus to establish entrance flow, draws on both models, but ultimately uses concepts like genre to create something individualised. Thus, Netflix' recommendations to establish entrance flow follow the same logics as the various scheduling techniques of linear broadcasting.

Conclusion

This chapter dealt with Netflix' structure by relating it to the organisation of linear television, the broadcasting schedule. For linear television, the schedule has often been theorised as its most central aspect, as a way to set different broadcasters and different versions of national television apart. Though the company rhetoric of Netflix denounces it almost completely, its structure often ties in with some organising principles of the schedule. Part of this is done via the flow: television broadcasters work hard to produce a schedule that is likely to keep the attention of viewers for longer than one programming slot. Similarly, Netflix constructs an insulated flow in an attempt to keep viewers interested beyond one episode of a series. The insulated flow and its most crucial aspects, the post-play and the skip intro function similarly solicit viewers' attention beyond one episode. Though the structural unit of Netflix is season rather than individual episode, it still relies on cliffhangers and teaser trailers to get viewers to return for the next season. It poses more difficulty to establish an entrance flow. This describes the way viewers are recommended different texts, so that insulated flow can be followed. Netflix employs its recommendation algorithm to establish entrance flow. There are a number of elements to the algorithm that make it decidedly different from linear television, most importantly how it constructs an individualised experience for viewers. In this regard, the algorithm serves to set Netflix apart from the schedule and its mass media connotations. At the same time, this algorithm uses genre as central concept to recommend content to viewers based on previous choices. The choice of genre as structuring feature stands out as an element both have in common. Genre points to an underlying similarity between broadcasting schedules and Netflix recommendations: the assumption that viewers look for the repetition of generic formulas, aesthetic style or tone.

Though the schedules of linear television are significantly different from Netflix' structure, their relationship is much more complex than company language often suggests. Giving control over scheduling to viewers allows Netflix to use a central feature of binge-watching, the control to decide when to watch what, but it nevertheless strongly nudges viewers towards specific decisions. The insulated flow is strongly suggested, but so are the different options for entrance flow recommended to viewers as they navigate through the interface. Thus, Netflix is not as autonomous as often suggested, but structured and, in some ways, also scheduled, even though it is more the 'what' than the 'when' or 'how' (on what device) that is suggested. Thus, viewers have more control over choices, but Netflix has power over what choices it offers to viewers, omitting some completely.

Bibliography

Alexander, Neta. 2016. "Catered to Your Future Self: Netflix's "Predictive Personalization" and the Mathematization of Taste." In Kevin McDonald and Daniel Smith-Rowsey (eds.), *The Netflix Effect: Technology and Entertainment in the 21st Century*. New York: Bloomsbury.

Arnold, Sarah. 2016. "Netflix and the Myth of Choice/Participation/Autonomy." In Kevin McDonald and Daniel Smith-Rowsey (eds.), *The Netflix Effect: Technology and Entertainment in the 21st Century*, 49–62. New York: Bloomsbury.

Chun, Wendy Hui Kyong. 2016. *Updating to Remain the Same: Habitual New Media*. Cambridge: The MIT Press.

Cohn, J. 2019. *The Burden of Choice: Recommendations, Subversion, and Algorithmic Culture*. New Brunswick: Rutgers University Press.

Eastman, Susan Tyler, and Jeffrey Neal-Lunsford. 1993. "The RCD's Impact on Television Programming and Promotion." In Robert V. Bellamy and James R. Walker (eds.), *The Remote Control in the New Age of Television*, 189–210. London: Praeger.

Ehrenberg, Markus, and Huber, Joachim. 2015. "Deutschland '83 Endet Im Quotentief: Diese Serie Passt Nicht Ins Deutsche Fernsehen." *Tagesspiegel*. Available online http://www.tagesspiegel.de/medien/deutschland-83-endet-mit-quotentief-diese-serie-passt-nicht-ins-deutsche-fernsehen/12701524.html. Accessed: 06.08.2017.

Ellis, John. 1992. *Visible Fictions Cinema: Television: Video*. Hoboken: Taylor and Francis.

———. 2000a. *Seeing Things: Television in the Age of Uncertainty*. London: I.B. Tauris.

———. 2000b. "Scheduling: The Last Creative Act in Television?" *Media Culture and Society* 22: 25–38.

Finn, Ed. 2017. *What Algorithms Want: Imagination in the Age of Computing*. Cambridge: MIT Press.

Fiske, John. 1987. *Television Culture*. London: Methuen.

Flitterman, S. 1985. "Thighs and Whiskers: The Fascination of 'Magnum, P.i.'." *Screen* 26 (2): 42–59.

Gaw, F. 2022. "Algorithmic Logics and the Construction of Cultural Taste of the Netflix Recommender System." *Media, Culture & Society* 44 (4): 706–25.

Gillan, Jennifer. 2015. *Television Brandcasting: The Return of the Content-Promotion Hybrid*. New York; London: Routledge.

Grandinetti, Justin. 2017. "From Primetime to Anytime: Streaming Video, Temporality and the Future of Communal Television." In Cory Barker and Myc Wiatrowski (eds.), *The Age of Netflix: Critical Essays on Streaming Media, Digital Delivery and Instant Access*, 11–30. Jefferson: McFarland.

Graves, Michael. 2015. "Binge-Watching and Fan/Critic Antagonism." In Kristin M. Barton (ed.), *A State of Arrested Development: Critical Essays on the Innovative Television Comedy*, location 4219–4467. Jefferson, NC: McFarland. Kindle.

Jacobs, Jason. 2011. "Television, Interrupted: Pollution or Aesthetic?" In James Bennett and Niki Strange, *Television as Digital Media*, location 3065–3399. Durham, NC: Duke University Press. Kindle.

Johnson, Derek. 2018. "Introduction." In Derek Johnson (ed.), *From Networks to Netflix: A Guide to Changing Channels*, 1–22. London: Routledge.

Lotz, Amanda D. 2014. *The Television Will Be Revolutionized*. 2nd ed. New York: New York University Press.

———. 2017. *Portals*. Michigan: Maize Books.

Madrigal, Alexis C. 2014. "How Netflix Reverse Engineered Hollywood." *The Atlantic*. Available online https://www.theatlantic.com/technology/archive/2014/01/how-netflix-reverse-engineered-hollywood/282679/. Accessed: 16.08.2017.

Newman, Michael Z., and Elana Levine. 2012. *Legitimating Television: Media Convergence and Cultural Status*. Abingdon: Routledge.

Perks, Lisa Glebatis. 2015. *Media Marathoning: Immersions in Morality*. Lanham, MD: Lexington Books.

Salecl, Renata. 2010. *The Tyranny of Choice*. London: Profile Books.

Setoodeh, Ramin. 2017. "Has Netflix's Ted Sarandos Rescued (Or Ruined) Hollywood?" *Variety*. Available online http://variety.com/2017/digital/features/ted-sarandos-netflix-original-movies-shonda-rhimes-1202527321/. Accessed: 08.08.2017.

Silverstone, Roger. 1994. *Television and Everyday Life*. London: Routledge.
Uricchio, William. 2017. "Data, Culture and the Ambivalence of Algorithms." In Karin Van Es and Mirko Tobias Schäfer (eds.), *The Datafied Society*, 125–38. Amsterdam: Amsterdam University Press.
Williams, Raymond. 1974. *Television. Technology and Cultural Form*. Glasgow: Fontana.

Television

Alarm für Cobra 11 (1996–), D: RTL.
Arrested Development (2003–6, 2013–19), USA: Fox, Netflix.
Breaking Bad (2008–13), USA: AMC.
Cagney and Lacey (1981–8), USA: CBS.
Deutschland '83 (2015), D: RTL.
Girlboss (2017), USA: Netflix.
House of Cards (2013–18), USA: Netflix.
Kate & Allie (1984–9), USA: CBS.
Magnum, P.I. (1980–8), USA: CBS.
Newhart (1982–90), USA: CBS.
Orange Is the New Black (2013–19), USA: Netflix.
Scarecrow and Mrs King (1983–7), USA: CBS.

Film

Heckerling, A. (1995) *Clueless*, USA: Paramount Pictures.
Waters, M. (2004) *Mean Girls*, USA: Paramount Pictures.

CHAPTER 9

'Quality' and the Netflix Brand

The organisational structure of insulated flow is also reflected in the textual politics of Netflix' in-house productions. Narrative structures and aesthetics do not tend to differ much from the American 'quality' TV texts of TV III and Netflix also draws heavily on the cultural politics of this era of the 'legitimation' of television (see Newman and Levine 2012). Yet, this reliance on the structures of 'quality' TV creates problems when Netflix moves into more 'popular' genres. Netflix draws heavily on existing links between 'quality' TV and binge-watching as structuring forces. However, since 2015, Netflix has increasingly moved towards more popular tastes with films produced by and starring Adam Sandler and sitcoms like *Fuller House*. This shift is even more pronounced with its moves into reality TV successes *Queer Eye* and *Selling Sunset* and the increasingly exploitative tone of its True Crime documentaries. This can be linked to Netflix' transnational expansion and the broader spectrum of audience tastes it caters to (see Part III). As Netflix gains more subscribers and more algorithmic data becomes available, it is hardly surprising that the kind of content Netflix invests in changes, though this data is now often 'spread' between platforms. Finn argues,

> Part of the work of the Netflix culture machine is to continually course-correct between that narrow aesthetic littoral and the vast ocean of abstraction behind it, populated by billions of data points and probabilistic inferences that are much more difficult to read. (2017, location 2283)

M. Jenner, *Netflix and the Re-invention of Television*,
https://doi.org/10.1007/978-3-031-39237-5_9

Thus, the move towards more popular tastes is likely linked to an ever-growing transnational audience and the algorithmic data collected as a result. What emerges in the current cultural moment is an emphasis on diversity to build a transnational brand (see Chapters 10 and 12). At the same time, the use of relatively 'traditional' sitcoms challenges the centrality of 'quality' television to its branding, expressed in its early years as producer of original programming with *House of Cards*, *Orange Is the New Black*, *Hemlock Grove* or season 4 of *Arrested Development*. Thus, Netflix' comedy strand offers a way to analyse and understand the negotiation of cultural politics on the platform as it expands globally.

This chapter discusses Netflix' cultural politics by first discussing its investment into 'quality' television and its links to binge-watching as a strategy through which Netflix originally positioned itself as producer of original television. It will then move on to discuss issues of 'quality' and 'the popular' in relation to the comedy genre on Netflix. In a last step, it will consider how binge-watching, 'quality' and more popular versions of comedy, in the form of the sitcom genre, navigate the cultural politics of Netflix, often via opening credits. These often rather 'cinematic' opening credits often mark what I call an aesthetic rupture between them and the three-camera set up of the text. The 'aesthetic rupture' in these early series remains important as it bridges Netflix' move from addressing what Josef Straubhaar (2007) terms a 'cosmopolitan elite' to a transnational mass audience, as explored in Part III. The sitcoms discussed here are the first handful that were on Netflix as self-produced Originals. At the time of writing the Second Edition, many more sitcoms are available, often with less elaborate opening credits.

Binging 'Quality' TV

When Netflix started publishing its own original content in 2013, it highlighted two aspects to a similar extent in marketing campaigns: binge-watching and 'quality' TV (see Chapter 10 for a more detailed discussion of Netflix' marketing). This linkage, though heavily exploited by Netflix, was not established by it. The rise of DVD box sets correlated with HBO-style 'quality' TV and what Newman and Levine term the 'legitimation' of television (2012). In fact, much 'quality' television, such as the exceptionally narratively complex *The Wire* (HBO, 2002–8), was likely helped by DVD box sets as an alternative means of viewing. This points to more than a correlation, but a complex relationship between DVD box sets, the associated viewing practice of binge-watching and 'quality' TV. Particularly HBO managed to take advantage of this new revenue stream, both, in selling DVD box sets, but also in creative processes: the complex narrative of a series like *The Wire* virtually invites viewers to rewatch the series on DVD to understand how the different seasons and storylines relate to each other:

> TV on DVD was also essential for the promotion of HBO programming and of HBO subscription, functioning as a new kind of rerun for non-subscribers who had missed the first season or two of *The Sopranos* and wanted to catch up in time for subsequent instalments. In this sense, the commercial-free experience of TV on DVD was central to its positioning in the cultural marketplace – its commercial appeal. (Newman and Levine 2012, 136)

It is also worth noting that DVD box sets allowed HBO to explore international markets, even if their programmes were not broadcast in these countries or did not do well in national broadcasting schedules. The available space on DVDs also allows for viewing in the original language or with subtitles, which made it common practice for some viewers to watch in English, likely the same who would later subscribe to an early Netflix with few translation options. Maybe it was exactly this feature (with English being a common language to be spoken as second language), combined with the dominance of American exports that established a link between 'American TV' and 'quality' TV globally. The associations between American 'quality' TV of the late 1990s and DVD box sets are, thus, strong. DVD box sets, offering 'pure' texts and control over programming, are commonly associated with binge-watching (see Brunsdon 2010). This close relationship was specifically sought by broadcasters like HBO to secure an alternative revenue stream (see Newman and Levine 2012, 135–36). Lotz uses the term 'prized content' to describe "programming that *people seek out and specifically desire*. It is not a matter of watching 'what is on'; prized content is deliberately pursued" (2014, location 426, italics in the original). This deliberation does not automatically imply DVD box sets, but strongly suggests them as a medium to watch prized content on. Klinger explores how DVDs of film were often explicitly packaged and marketed to appeal to collectors and fans in 'special editions' and with new director's cuts (2006, 62–74). In a similar manner, prized content, specifically packaged and placed on a shelf to publicly display, emphasises the cultural value of DVD box sets for collectors.

Whereas the object of a DVD is relatively easy to define based on technological parameters and the content included (at least so far), the term 'quality' TV is difficult to unpack. As Jane Feuer notes: "The judgement of quality is always situated. That is to say, somebody makes the judgement from some aesthetic or political or moral position" (2007, 145). This 'somebody' is usually an interpretative community of 'gatekeepers', invested with what Bourdieu calls 'cultural capital' (2010). The interpretative community that decides on the 'quality' status of television series is most commonly journalists, often with a readership that can be classed as a 'quality demographic'. A 'quality demographic' can be defined as urban, middle-class, well-educated with disposable income (Seiter and Wilson 2008, 140). This 'quality demographic' is traditionally sought by advertisers, as this demographic has disposable income to spend on advertised products. However, in the case of DVD box sets, the dynamics shift a little: what this audience seeks is an ad-free, autonomously controlled media experience:

> This new, good television, in contrast to old, bad, addictive television is not broadcast network television, but television which one either pays to see, or watches on DVD. Instead of being associated with housebound women, this new television is young, smart, and on the move, downloaded or purchased to watch at will. (Brunsdon 2010, 65)

The disposable income (and leisure time) is invested into the ability to self-schedule rather than to reward advertisers. Though Kompare argues that DVDs were affordably priced, at least compared to sell-through VHS, DVD box sets usually were still a significant expense, particularly in its heyday between 2003 and (roughly) 2006 (2005, 208). Many of these series were shown on premium cable (such as HBO) in their original run in the US (where it could also be recorded on DVRs), which also implied a significant expense. This establishes a kind of exclusivity to binge-watching as self-scheduled viewing. Thus, 'quality' TV is not only set apart through textual features that are in line with 'quality' standards set by an interpretive community, but also through an economic expense. This suggests a real separation between 'quality' and 'non-quality' content (and, by extension, its viewers) along economic lines.

'Quality' television of the TV III era tends to be stylistically innovative in terms of aesthetics and narrative structure. Newman and Levine discuss the 'cinematization' of television. This happens on a number of levels. First of all, the technology improved to allow a television image of higher quality. Aesthetically, HBO-style television series would emulate strategies of cinema to create imagery which these new television sets would be able to do justice to. Furthermore,

> The modes of access of TV on DVD also cinematize television. When TV shows are shelved alongside films in a retailer or video rental shop, when 'television' is a category alongside genres of cinema on Amazon.com and Best Buy, when Netflix mail rental service delivers discs of films and shows in the same red envelopes (or streams them online in the same browser window), the distinctions viewers make between film and television as media become thinner and thinner. (2012, 136)

This 'quality' TV puts an emphasis on narrative complexity as a way to take full advantage of the serial form afforded by television.

Lotz (2017) highlights that episode length is often determined by advertisers' requirements. This point is important in the sense that time (meaning episode length) and notions of 'quality' are linked. Largely, it indicates how 'commercial' a text is by how much time it allows for advertising messages. HBO started to develop series that could take full advantage of the hour of television they were given, comedy episodes were 30 minutes in length, not the 43 or 22 minutes common for a network series. This format remains common on Netflix, but series like *The OA* (Netflix, 2016–19) or more conventional dramas like *Mindhunter* (Netflix, 2017–19) take advantage of the freedom to operate without the time constraints of the schedule by varying episode length significantly. Aside from episode length, the structural unit of television, with the success of DVD box sets, quickly became the season, rather than the episode (see, for example, Rose 2008). This makes it worthwhile for viewers to watch complete seasons rather than individual episodes on a weekly basis. For example, each season of *Dexter* (Showtime, 2006–13) is guided by the hunt for a new villain who is caught at the end of the season, rather than an episode, as had traditionally been the case for American television crime dramas (see Jenner 2015). Box sets can shorten the wait for such a 'payoff' at the end of a season. Though not all 'quality' TV texts adopt these textual politics, as some are still confined by the limitations of network TV, the shift in structural units is notable. Binge-watching becomes associated with viewing several episodes in a row of this kind of formally accomplished television.

Overall, the discursive link between 'quality' TV, DVD box sets and binge-watching is due to a number of factors. The assumptions about audiences' relationship to advertising and the history of technologies that gave viewers control over their programming, as discussed in Part I, are relevant: DVDs allowed for increased control over scheduling but did not threaten revenue streams of the television industry to the same extent VCRs did. DVDs also allowed for a supposed textual purity of aesthetically accomplished and narratively complex texts. This led to a strong linkage between DVD box sets, 'quality' TV and binge-watching. In fact, this relationship became so naturalised that Netflix employed it to position itself within the crowded marketplace of 'quality' television, as discussed in Chapter 10.

Genre, 'Quality' and the Popular

As Newman and Levine argue:

> Inherently, [the legitimation of television through 'quality' TV] depends upon a delegitimated 'other' television – that of the past but also that of the contemporary genres, production modes, technologies, and practices that do not receive the stamp of legitimacy. Certainly, some instances of television [...] continue to be sites of disparagement, just as some modes of experiencing television (such as live over-the-air viewing, commercials, and all) continue to be painted as inferior. (2012, 13)

These 'othered' genres are traditionally those considered highly formulaic with relatively stable social settings and aesthetics, with strong linkages to the history and social connotations of television. It is, thus, important to explore how Netflix negotiates issues of 'quality' and sub-genres more associated with 'popular' taste. Netflix' emphasis on comedy is particularly suited to explore the tensions between 'quality' television and more 'low brow' formulaic sitcoms, largely due to the variance in which cultural capital is bestowed on the genre. Netflix had been invested in producing 'quality' sitcoms that abandoned the three-camera setup, laugh-track or reliance on punch lines usually associated with the genre (see Hartley 2015). Examples of this are season 4 of *Arrested*

Development, *Unbreakable Kimmy Schmidt* (Netflix, 2015–19), or *Grace and Frankie*. Yet, Netflix also committed to more generic sitcoms soon after: the re-boot of *Full House* (ABC, 1987–95), *Fuller House* (Netflix 2016–20), was published and quickly followed by Ashton Kutcher-led *The Ranch* (Netflix, 2016–20) and the re-boot *One Day at a Time* (Netflix, 2017–20). All three series fulfil Netflix' emphasis on diversity (see Chapter 10): two are female-led and focus on the broad range of experiences accompanying single motherhood with one focussing on Cuban-American characters with Latina actresses in central roles. Meanwhile, *The Ranch* emphasises white, working-class male experiences. Yet, the series also conform to the expectations of a genre usually associated with popular tastes.

Of course, there are many sitcoms associated with 'quality' TV. Series like *The Mary Tylor Moore Show* (CBS, 1970–7), *The Cosby Show* (NBC, 1984–92) or *Roseanne* have successfully pushed boundaries of the representational norms governing television in the past. Brett Mills (2009) discusses the inconsistencies and complexities of the sitcom genre in much detail. It is not the purpose of this chapter to explore the genre's complex history. Instead, what is important for the discussion of the genre on Netflix is a cultural distinction within the genre that was established during the TV III era. At its most simplistic, the main distinction made here is that between the formulaic, aesthetically stable sitcom and the 'quality' comedy that deliberately abandons the aesthetic and narrative norms of the genre. To conceptualise this for the purpose of this chapter, it may be easiest to look at the cultural politics of the genre via John Frow's (2006) systemic approach. This approach highlights structural aspects of genre texts and organises them into a system of genre. An emphasis is on texts, though the idea of a 'system of genre' proves to be flexible and able to allow for sub-genres, micro-genres and hybridization. As Jason Mittell (2004) highlights, genre is a discursive formation constructed out of discourses of, for example, audience, industry and text. In different genres, different discourses need to be emphasised. Building on Netflix' use of genre, as outlined in Chapter 8, a focus here is on textual features, which Netflix employs to build recommendations and communicate with its audience. What Frow's approach allows for is the idea of a system of genre, which organises the comedy genre into a variety of sub-genres (such as Late Night, sketch comedy, horror comedy, some reality TV formats, sitcom, dramedy, etc.) and their national specificities and histories that invest it with regionally specific humour (see Hartley

2015). Though the aim is to produce laughter as affect in audiences, a comedy is recognisable even if viewers do not perceive it to be funny, as long as the intent can be identified. This suggests the importance of textual features in defining the genre. In this system, aesthetic distinction would be part of constituting sub-genres. The umbrella genre of comedy only implies one stable factor: the aim of the genre is to tell jokes that follow stylistic and culturally specific conventions. The division into sub-genres is necessary to do justice to the breadth of texts included in the umbrella genres. The two sub-genres discussed here are American versions of the sitcom and the 'quality' comedy, often differentiated into multi-camera or single-camera styles. The focus on US versions of the genre is due to the dominance of American comedies on Netflix. What is termed here 'quality' comedy is termed 'comedy drama' in Mills' book-length study of the genre and also often described as 'dramedy'. The terminology of 'quality' comedy is used here in parts in reference to Newman and Levine's conceptualisation of it as part of a broader legitimation of television itself and in parts in reference to the cultural politics Netflix engages with (see Elkins 2021).

In referring to 'quality' comedies here, the term 'quality' is tied to the aesthetic and narrative expectations of 'quality' television more than a judgement of what 'quality' is or is not. Though popular discourse often differentiates between multi-camera (or three-camera) and single-camera sitcoms, the difference lies largely in the rather static set-up of the previous form and the more 'cinematic' aesthetic of the latter. Hartley (2015) points to the surprising aesthetic stability that has dominated the comedy genre since its inception, with only few outliers. The sitcom is an intensely televisual genre that has dominated American television since it's very early years. An example would be the stable aesthetic forms from *I Love Lucy* (CBS, 1951–7) to *The Mary Tyler Moore Show* to *Friends* (NBC, 1994–2004). The indie-film aesthetics of *Arrested Development* would be perceived as 'quality' comedy in opposition to this. Of course, these sub-genres are distinct from each other in more ways than the camera setup or lighting. The sitcom, for example, uses a laugh track to indicate punchlines where 'quality' comedies do not, focussing on more complex jokes that build over several episodes instead. An important feature is also the use of signature catch phrases for specific characters in sitcoms. Examples of this are Joey's (Matt Le Blanc) "How are you doin'?" on *Friends* or Sheldon's (Jim Parsons) "Bazinga!" on *The Big*

Bang Theory (CBS, 2007–19). 'Quality' sitcoms like *Arrested Development* may have recurring jokes, such as Tobias' (David Cross) generous use of euphemisms for homosexual sex. However, there is little repetition of punch-lines and, instead, a repetition of sentiment, which usually amounts to character construction, difficult to compare to a catch phrase. Overall:

> The single-camera sitcom [...] appears to be a more narrowcast format compared with traditional sitcoms of the network era and into the early 2000s, which appealed as widely as possible, functioning as a common popular culture. The largest audiences do not follow the new comedy style, but critics and affluent viewers – those most likely to be viewing using DVRs, DVDs, iTunes, and other new convergence technologies – elevate them above the old-fashioned multi-cam style aesthetically by identifying them as having sophisticated and cinematic qualities. (Newman and Levine 2012, 73)

Newman and Levine make clear the class distinctions inherent in the positioning of 'quality' comedy and the sitcom formula. One functions as entertainment for 'quality' demographics with high cultural and financial capital and watched on expensive devices, the other is directed at 'the masses' with all its class connotations (see Chapter 14). The laugh track functions as an essential signifier in this distinction. These contextual discourses illuminate why Netflix' comedy strand has been focussed on 'quality' comedies rather than the sitcom formula associated with commercial network television. As Mills points out, the more traditional sitcom format around the 2000s was more suitable to reach mass audience with series like *Two and a Half Men* (CBS, 2003–15) or *Will & Grace* (NBC, 1998–2008) whereas *Arrested Development* or *30 Rock* (NBC, 2006–13) received poor ratings.[1] Nevertheless, the associations between the sitcom's links with commercial television, signified largely through length, are strong and serve to position it as 'low brow'. 'Quality' sitcoms may also run on commercial networks, such as *Arrested Development* or *30 Rock*, and be commercially successful, as *Scrubs* (NBC, 2001–8;

[1] This is hardly a binary system: *Scrubs* is arguably a 'quality' sitcom and received stellar ratings for several years. Similarly, plenty of sitcoms failed to replicate the success of the previous decade, which saw ratings hits *Friends*, *Frasier* (NBC, 1993–2004) or *Everybody Loves Raymond* (CBS, 1996–2005).

ABC, 2008–10) or *The Office* (NBC, 2005–13). However, their aesthetic features usually locate them at different points within a cultural hierarchy.

Netflix Comedies: Aesthetic Ruptures and the Negotiation of Taste

In the case of Netflix, the distinction between texts at different points of a negotiation of cultural value is marked. Continuing *Arrested Development* was an important move for Netflix to position itself in relation to 'quality' television. The increased narrative complexity of season 4 of *Arrested Development* in relation to its previous seasons drives this point home. In its comedy line-up, *Arrested Development* was followed by series like *Unbreakable Kimmy Schmidt*, Tina Fey's follow-up project to *30 Rock* with a decidedly feminist outlook (see also Havas and Horeck 2022). *Grace and Frankie*, with stars Lily Tomlin and Jane Fonda, known for their liberal politics, deals with two women in their 70s who bond after their husbands have left them to marry each other following a 20-year affair. This strand is overtly committed to issues of gender, age and sexuality, often with an emphasis on intersectionality. Aside from 'quality' characteristics explored above, such as complex, ongoing narratives, or aesthetic originality, these comedies also feature a general avoidance of sitcom staples like laugh tracks or catch phrases. Netflix' regulatory status also allows for a generous use of swearing and adult themes.

Netflix' shift towards sitcoms took place in 2016, a year when Netflix completed a vast expansion project into 120 countries. Possibly because of the wider outlook and breadth of data available on global viewing practices and after having obtained the rights to stream *Friends* from January 2015 in many countries, Netflix started to introduce more sitcoms. While Netflix focussed on 'quality' television, including 'quality' comedy by auteurs for the first two years of producing its own self-produced Originals, 2016 saw the publication of *Fuller House* and *The Ranch*, both series conforming more closely to the sitcom formula and, thus, embracing more televisual conventions. They conform to the 22-minute time constraints of network sitcoms, as well as aesthetics and narrative structure. Both also stand out for their lack of racial diversity or overt commitment to political projects like feminism.

In 2015, Netflix announced a re-boot of the popular 1980s and 1990s sitcom *Full House* as its first generic sitcom. *Full House* was a sitcom dealing with two young bachelors moving in with their widowed friend to help care for his three daughters. First broadcast in the same year as the Hollywood remake *3 Men and a Baby* (Nimoy, 1987) was released, *Full House* ties in with discourses surrounding gender equality and child-care responsibility. Other than in the film or contemporary series like *Blossom* (NBC, 1990–5), the absence of the mother is due to death rather than wilful abandonment of care responsibilities, aligning the series with the Reaganist ideology of family values. Nevertheless, the sitcom questions the gender essentialism of the era, which presumes an innate inability for men to care for children, especially female children, and often invites queer readings. In comparison, *Fuller House*'s gender swap is much tamer: after oldest daughter DJ (Candace Cameron Bure) is left widowed with three small sons, her younger sister Stephanie (Jodie Sweetin) and friend Kimmy Gibbler (Andrea Barber), herself a recently separated single mother of one daughter, move in to share childcare responsibilities. The series is riddled with cameos, particularly from the three stars of the former series, Bob Saget, John Stamos and Dave Coulier. It is also linked to the old series through visual signifiers, most importantly the setting. Yet, where three single men caring for three small children may question gender essentialism, it is difficult to find a similar politics in three single women caring for four children. The female bonding between all three is far away from the emotional bonds displayed in *G.L.O.W*. or *Grace and Frankie*. The politics of sex and dating are relatively conservative, with Kimmy usually concerned with unresolved romantic issues with her husband and DJ often unsure or undecided about dating. Unlike its 'quality' comedy cousins on Netflix, *Fuller House* refrains from discussing sex in explicit terms, particularly outside of marriage. The only character where an active sex life is suggested is Kimmy, who is still married to her partner. As much as this may go against the liberal politics usually expressed by Netflix, *Fuller House* seems to suggest a move towards some sort of middle ground between the often radical politics of its 'quality' comedies and viewers more comfortable with network sitcoms.

In her work on *Fuller House*, Kathleen Loock (2018) emphasises the centrality of family entertainment, and nostalgia for it, for Netflix, which becomes visible in its programming of *Fuller House*. This reconfiguration of Netflix as a service for the whole family suggests a strategy to address a broader audience. This needs to be understood as not only an inter-generational audience, but also a transnational audience and one that cuts across different world views and taste structures. The decision to revive *Full House* may be best understood in connection with the decision to produce Adam Sandler films: likely to appeal to a transnational popular taste, rather than the liberal cultural project Netflix usually invests in (see Elkins 2021). Thus, *Fuller House* is a deliberate move away from niche marketing and an emphasis on 'quality' comedies. In fact, it fully embraces its televisual roots. Strategies in the early 2020s have only served to emphasise this point more, as Netflix more obviously specialises in middlebrow television and is less likely to bow to pressures from viewers who enjoy more politically progressive content (see also Chapter 10).

The Ranch continues this emphasis on popular taste through the casting of its star, Ashton Kutcher. Most recently, Kutcher has been associated with popular comedy films and television programmes like *Punk'd* (MTV, 2003–15). He also filled in for Charlie Sheen on *Two and a Half Men* after the star had been fired due to derogatory and violent treatment of women as well as anti-Semitic comments about the series' co-creator Chuck Lorre. Kutcher is, thus, linked to more popular fare, but also positioned as 'tame' alternative to Sheen. *The Ranch* deals with Colt Bennet (Kutcher) who returns to his mid-Western family ranch after a failed career in professional football. The ranch is in a crisis as the agriculture business has become dominated by larger corporations and climate change leaves a visible mark. The series features largely white men, with many of the female characters conforming to relatively normative ideas of attractiveness as blonde-haired women with costumes emphasising their chest. The only exception to this tend to be post-menopausal women, such as the mother of the central family, Maggie, played by Debra Winger. Yet, other than *Fuller House*, there are several aspects that conform to the more liberal aspects of 'quality' TV: from the pilot onwards, patriarch Beau (Sam Elliott) frequently expresses his scepticism of climate change, which functions as a punchline, rather than a serious concern. His comments on the absence of climate change even as his living is seriously threatened by it, are usually followed by a laugh track, suggesting that audiences are meant to join into the laughter. In a US context, where scepticism about climate change is more acceptable than in transnational contexts, this implies a positioning within a political spectrum on the side of liberal elites.[2] Maggie's and Beau's complicated relationship, sexually

[2] Climate change is, of course, a less contentious issue in transnational contexts, meaning that the liberal politics implied in these jokes would not be perceived the same way outside of the US. Thus, the mocking of climate change denial can also be read as a concession to the transnational nature of Netflix.

fulfilling even after their separation, links the series to *Grace and Frankie*. Along with this, Sam Elliott plays Grace's (Jane Fonda) love interest in season 2, further linking the texts. A sense of loss of the 'American dream' is dominant within the series, though this is usually dealt with in a humorous manner. The younger women in the series may, at first sight, conform to relatively generic beauty standards, but share in the economic struggles of their surroundings. Additionally, the series deals with the extra burden these working-class women carry as (often single) mothers. The series also features a generous amount of swearing, indicating that, unlike *Fuller House* or *One Day at a Time*, it is not intended for cross-generational viewing. Nevertheless, the series embraces conventions of popular television in its aesthetics, themes and narrative mode over Netflix' links with 'quality' television.

One Day at a Time also conforms to the aesthetic and narrative norms of the sitcom. Yet, it merges this with some themes that conform to Netflix' branding strategy of diversity (see Chapter 10). The series deals with single mother Penelope Alvarez, played by Justina Machado of *Six Feet Under* fame. Penelope used to be a nurse in the US Army and was deployed in Afghanistan. She raises two teenagers together with her mother Lydia, played by Rita Moreno. The sitcom deals with the physical and psychological trauma of Army Vets, but also the specifics of Cuban American culture, issues regarding immigration, the broader Latinx community in the US, racism and Penelope's teenage daughter Elena's (Isabella Gomez) struggles with her sexual identity. Elena also expresses strong opinions regarding environmental politics and feminism, which leads to a number of discussions within the family context. The family discusses issues ranging from the alienation of immigrants in the age of Trump and in its historical context, how to deal with affirmative action programmes, or racial stereotyping. The series almost routinely uses and explains terms like 'mansplaining', micro-aggressions or mental health issues veterans face. In line with Netflix' commitment to diversity, the cast consists in large parts of Hispanic women, with Machado appearing in almost every scene and with the majority of spoken lines. The female characters are also commonly given the punchlines as well as being the centre of more dramatic scenes. Yet, the series conforms to the sitcom formula: the aesthetics and the extreme reliance on punchlines and laugh track make the series less associated with 'quality' TV. As such, *One Day at a Time* balances Netflix' emphasis on diversity with the generic formula of the sitcom. This also aligns it with *Fuller House* in the sense that its politics are often relatively conservative, particularly in terms of the expressed patriotism or sexual politics. It also is a sitcom that features a multi-generational cast, much like *Fuller House*. As Sarandos explicitly states about *Fuller House*, the sitcom is part of a strategy to encourage family viewing. *One Day at a Time* is clearly part of this strategy.

For a discussion of Netflix' sitcom branch, the opening credit sequence is incredibly pertinent, as it reveals tensions between televisuality, cultural value and binge-watching. In comparison to later Netflix sitcoms, *Fuller House* features a relatively conventional opening credit sequence, which serves well to consider its role on Netflix. The sequence draws heavily on *Full House* and, like the former series, uses imagery of the Golden Gate bridge and other San Francisco landmarks. Main characters are introduced with images of them as children that were used in the credit sequence of the former series. The music is a cover version of the song used for the old sequence. This strict linking with *Full House* that runs through the entire series also builds a consistency between opening credits and text that is not found in Netflix' other sitcoms. This is in line with the role of the credits in the TV II era. TV II credits showed images from the series to indicate plot and themes as well as images of the characters to indicate their role in the plot and actor's names. Accompanying music would indicate tone of the series and features, such as genre, aesthetics, actors and other factors that might 'hook' a grazing viewer. Monika Bednarek lists the following functions of the television title sequence (TTS):

- The TTS signals the beginning of another programme (on television) and/or separates elements such as recaps and scenes from the 'start proper' of the television episode;
- The TTS creates continuity between different episodes;
- The TTS identifies or names a television series (and sometimes its actors and creators);
- The TTS introduces the characters, settings, storylines, and socio-cultural context of a television series;
- The TTS aims to attract or 'grab' viewers so that they watch a television series;
- The TTS establishes a particular emotional mood for a television series and potentially produces an emotional reaction in viewers;
- The TTS creates a particular aesthetics for a television series;
- The TTS predicts the genre of the television series, creating genre expectations in viewers, and thereby also leads viewers to expect a particular relationship with the television series;

– The TTS 'types' or 'brands' a particular television series. (2014, 127–28)

Thus, it is worth looking at the title sequences of Netflix' sitcoms in more detail to understand how Netflix, with its reliance on insulated flow, deals with a textual feature of a genre so inherently rooted in network television. Additionally, Annette Davison's research on audience's relationship to title sequences notes the difference between network television and premium cable series in the TV III era, where opening credits of 'quality' television can function almost as short films unto themselves (2013, 16). In contemporary network series, opening credits are often shortened to a few seconds. This can be linked to the time constraints of linear network television, but also indicates a shift from the TV II model for the TV III era.

The Ranch's opening credits are Western-style shots of American mid-Western scenery with majestic mountains. The theme song is a cover version of Willie Nelson's 'Mamas Don't Let Your Babies Grow Up to be Cowboys'. The credits show the mountains and landscape of the American mid-west, overlaid with images signifying American patriotism and the 'American dream': the American flag, American-manufactured trucks, American football players, cowboy boots. The images then fade into family pictures of the central family when they were much younger, signifying the historical links of the family with their land and linking them with the myths of 'the American west'. The credits indicate a nostalgia that is not always present within the text itself, even though the family clearly struggles with the decline of the American dream and the freedom promised by the cowboy myth. More importantly, the credit sequence is much more stylistically accomplished than usually associated with formulaic sitcoms, such as the *Fuller House* credits. The opening credits of *The Ranch* is reminiscent of title sequences for 'quality' Western dramas *Deadwood* (HBO, 2004–6) or *Hell on Wheels* (AMC, 2011–16). Particularly in view of the reinvention of the genre in recent 'quality' TV texts, the credits suggest something different than the aesthetics or tone of the series deliver. *One Day at a Time*'s credits also suggest something different from what is offered: they feature images specific to main character Penelope's life, including her own childhood and associations with Cuban-American culture, nursing and the US army to indicate her previous profession. The accompanying music is an adaptation of the song 'This is It', performed by Gloria Estefan, using influences from Latin American pop music. Though the opening credits are edited to emulate family photo albums, its aesthetic realism suggests something other than a multi-camera sitcom. There is a marked aesthetic rupture between opening credits and text. *The Ranch* and *One Day at a Time*, the aesthetic rupture is marked and points towards bigger issues in relation to televisual genres and binge-watching.

Returning to Bednarek's list of the function of the credit sequence, it needs to be considered how many of these points are still relevant within an insulated flow. At the beginning of an entrance flow, the sequence might still fulfil similar functions as in the TV II era: it is meant to grab viewers' attention and establish the themes of the series. It even works to 'brand' the programme and the platform. For returning viewers, it may establish a continuity, an opportunity for reintroduction. Yet, Netflix' sitcom opening credits do little to introduce viewers to the programmes, offering an aesthetic rupture instead. Further, establishing consistency between episodes via the credits is unnecessary within an insulated flow. In fact, many criteria Bednarek lists are specific to linear television where different programmes need to distinguish themselves as stand-alone segments or 'items'. Thus, it is worth asking why title sequences are included at all, when the aesthetic rupture means a departure from their function, even in an entrance flow. As Djoymi Baker notes:

> For a full-season epic experience, a long, repeated title sequence each episode would seem largely redundant, as the viewer does not need to be reminded that their series is starting, and may simply skip the opening sequence. (2017, 44)

Baker makes this argument in relation to 'quality' TV and Netflix programming, in particular, but it seems heightened in relation to the insulated flow of much shorter comedy programmes. The lack of time constraints on Netflix explains why the title sequences for sitcoms can be so elaborate and why there is never a reason to shorten the opening sequence. No definition of the sitcom positions the opening credit sequence as important to the genre, so it is easily skipped. The aesthetic rupture can be read as a consequence of the binge model and the general expectation of sequential viewing. In this context, opening credits lose the function to introduce viewers to central characters and aesthetic style via scenes that feature in the text. In the case of Netflix, viewers will not graze channels until they can locate a programme they are interested in but make more deliberate choices. The interface makes sequential viewing much easier than non-sequential viewing and Netflix' skip intro function often removes opening credits altogether to make binge-watching easier. In fact, Davison finds that her participants are more likely to skip credit sequences when binge-watching:

> The practice of skipping title sequences when binge viewing serials (most often via DVD box sets) is common among some participants, as is the pleasurable sense of satisfaction that results from the ability to exit fast-forwarding and return to normal speed at exactly the right moment at the very end of the main title sequence, with visual markers used to enable successful skipping. (2013, 15)

Because binge-watching makes opening sequences (at least partially) redundant, the function of the opening credits of Netflix' sitcoms is predominantly aesthetic. Yet, Max Dosser (2022) argues that mirroring linear television's techniques for opening credits is Netflix' way of participating in broader broadcast traditions (again, positioning itself *as* television) while also reinforcing the viewer control streaming offers. This is an intriguing argument as it suggests that, even in 2022, Netflix still seeks associations with broadcast TV. Thus, it makes sense that Netflix adopts the style of 'quality' television for the opening credits of its sitcom branch: if the credits of 'quality' TV are consumed like distinct short films rather than as introductions to the text, it makes sense to produce more stylistically elaborate title sequences, even if they are out of synch with the rest of the text. Nevertheless, the aesthetic rupture between opening credits and texts also reveals the uncomfortable positioning of Netflix' sitcom strand as popular genre, and 'quality' television. The way the texts negotiate elements of 'quality' and 'the popular' or middlebrow (as explored in more detail in the next chapter) adds to this.

Netflix' comedy branch is an expression of the complicated cultural politics at stake in the genre overall, but, more importantly, of Netflix as it positions itself culturally. An additional layer of complexity is introduced through the aesthetic tension between the opening credits and the texts of Netflix' sitcoms. This aesthetic rupture can be understood as a consequence of insulated flow and its importance to the organisational structure of Netflix. Nevertheless, the creation of title sequences more reminiscent of 'quality' TV for the often derided sitcom also speaks to the uneasiness with which more popular genres are constructed for Netflix.

Conclusion

Netflix' negotiation of cultural value like 'quality' or 'non-quality' programming was explored in this chapter via Netflix' comedies as the genre offers a framework for issues like cultural distinction through aesthetic signifiers. Sitcoms are not the only genre Netflix uses to explore more popular genres: Netflix celebrates its reality TV strand with hits like *Queer Eye* (Netflix, 2018–) and *Selling Sunset* (Netflix, 2019–) and it is currently expanding its reality TV branch further. A current emphasis is also true crime documentaries, which have little journalistic ambition, but emphasise the spectacular. The discussion of Netflix' sitcoms also exemplifies some of the problems that emerge in Netflix' broadening scope and direction towards more popular, televisual genres. It is important to emphasise that terms like 'quality' have been used throughout this chapter to denote a place within the cultural hierarchies Netflix engages with and has set up for itself, rather than a value judgement.

The link between 'quality' television and binge-watching as synonymous with autonomous scheduling indicates the kind of control given to viewers. Netflix heightens this control even further than previous ancillary technologies, such as DVD, did. Yet, the link between binge-watching and 'quality' television also informs its negotiations of cultural value. This becomes particularly important in Netflix' comedy strand, but the sitcom, as genre strongly tied to broadcast television, illuminates the tensions between binge-watching and more popular television genres. This becomes obvious in the relationship between sitcoms and opening credit sequences, where the tensions between 'quality' television and popular genres, particularly more televisual genres indebted to the traditions of linear television and insulated flow, become particularly pronounced. The control viewers have over the texts makes it easy to ignore credit sequences, which lose their main function as introducing viewers to the text and to 'hook' grazing viewers. Yet, the opening credits for Netflix' sitcom branch indicate an uncomfortable positioning of the Netflix sitcom between cultural associations of the genre and 'quality' expectations of Netflix. As little more than a remnant of linear television, they highlight the mechanics of insulated flow. Binge-watching and the changed role of opening credits in an insulated flow is central to this tension.

Since the first edition of this book was published, Netflix has grown more comfortable with the sitcoms and is producing a range of self-produced Originals, often with more 'traditional' opening credits. As such, the strand works to associate the streamer closely with the 'mundanity' and 'normality' of middlebrow culture in linear television, as explored more extensively in the next chapter. While what I describe as an aesthetic rupture between opening credits and text has been eliminated, this phenomenon remains an important testament to the way Netflix negotiates tensions between its initial reliance on 'quality' TV and linear television.

Bibliography

Baker, Djoymi. 2017. "Terms of Excess: Binge-Viewing as Epic-Viewing in the Netflix Era." In Cory Barker and Myc Wiatrowski (eds.), *The Age of Netflix*, 31–54. Jefferson: McFarland.

Bednarek, Monika. 2014. "'And They All Look Just the Same'? A Quantitative Survey of Television Title Sequences." *Visual Communication* 13 (2): 125–45.

Bourdieu, Pierre. 2010. *Distinction: A Social Critique of the Judgement of Taste*. London: Routledge.

Brunsdon, Charlotte. 1981. "'Crossroads': Notes on Soap Opera." *Screen* 22 (4): 32–37.

———. 2010. "Bingeing on Box-Sets: the National and the Digital in Television Crime Drama". In Jostein Gripsrud (ed.), *Relocating Television: Television in the Digital Context*, 61–75. London: Routledge.

Davison, Annette. 2013. "The Show Starts Here: Viewers' Interactions with Recent Television Serials' Main Title Sequences." *SoundEffects. an Interdisciplinary Journal of Sound and Sound Experience* 3 (1+2): 7–22.

Dosser, M. 2022. "Streming's Skip Intro Function as a Contradictory Refuge for Television Title Sequences." *The Velvet Light Trap* 90 (Fall): 38–50.

Elkins, E., 2021. "Streaming Diplomacy: Netflix's Domestic Politics and Foreign Policy." In D. Y. Jin (ed.), *The Routledge Handbook of Digital Media and Globalization*, 150–157. London: Routledge.

Feuer, Jane. 2007. "HBO and the Concept of Quality TV." In Kim Akass and Janet McCabe (eds.), *Quality TV Contemporary American Television and Beyond*, 145–57. London: I.B.Tauris.

Finn, Ed. 2017. *What Algorithms Want: Imagination in the Age of Computing*. Cambridge: MIT Press.

Frow, John. 2006. *Genre*. London: Routledge.

Hartley, John. 2015. "Situation Comedy, Part 1." In Glen Creeber (ed.), *The Television Genre Book*, 96–98. London: BFI

Havas, J. & Horeck, T. 2022, "Netflix Feminism: Binge-Watching Rape Culture." In M. Jenner (ed.), *Binge-Watching and Contemporary Television Studies*, 250–73.

Jenner, Mareike. 2015. *American TV Detective Dramas: Serial Investigations*. Basingstoke: Palgrave Macmillan.

Klinger, Barbara. 2006. *Beyond the Multiplex Cinema, New Technologies, and the Home*. Berkeley: University of California Press.

Kompare, Derek. 2005. *Rerun Nation: How Repeats Invented American Television*. New York, N.Y: Routledge.

Lotz, Amanda D. 2014. *The Television Will Be Revolutionized*. 2nd ed. New York: New York University Press.

———. 2017. *Portals*. Michigan: Maize Books.

Mills, Brett. 2009. *The Sitcom*. Edinburgh: Edinburgh University Press.

———. 2015. "Contemporary Sitcom: Sitcom Vérité." In Glen Creeber (ed.), *The Television Genre Book*, 106–7. London: BFI.

Mittell, Jason. 2004. *Genre and Television: From Cop shows to Cartoons in American Culture*. London: Routledge

———. 2015. *Complex TV: The Poetics of Contemporary Television Storytelling*. New York: New York University Press.

Modleski, Tania. 1979. "The Search for Tomorrow in Today's Soap Operas: Notes on a Feminine Narrative Form." *Film Quarterly* 33 (1): 12–21.

Newman, Michael Z., and Elana Levine. 2012. *Legitimating Television: Media Convergence and Cultural Status*. Abingdon: Routledge.

Rose, Brian G. 2008. "The Wire." In Gary R. Edgerton and Jeffrey P. Jones (eds.) *The Essential HBO Reader*, 81–92. Kentucky: University Press of Kentucky.

Rose, Lacey. 2015. "Netflix's Ted Sarandos Opens Up about 'Arrested Development,' 'Fuller House' and Adam Sandler." *The Hollywood Reporter*. Available online https://www.hollywoodreporter.com/live-feed/netflixs-ted-sarandos-opens-up-811445. Accessed: 01.01.2018.

Seiter, Ellen, and Mary Jeanne Wilson. 2008. "Soap Opera Survival Tactics." In Gary R. Edgerton and Brian G. Rose (eds.), *Thinking Outside the Box: A Contemporary Television Genre Reader*, 136–55. Lexington: University Press of Kentucky.

Straubhaar, J.D. 2007. *World Television: From Global to Local*. Thousand Oaks, CA: Sage Publications.

Television

30 Rock (2006–13), USA: NBC.

Arrested Development (2003–6, 2013–19), USA: Fox, Netflix.

Big Bang Theory, The (2007–19), USA: CBS.

Blossom (1990–5), USA: NBC.
Cosby Show, The (1984–92), USA: NBC.
Deadwood (2004–6), USA: HBO.
Dexter (2006–13), USA: Showtime.
Everybody Loves Raymond (1996–2005), USA: CBS.
Frasier (1993–2004), USA: NBC.
Friends (1994–2004), USA: NBC.
Full House (1987–95), USA: ABC.
Fuller House (2016–19), USA: Netflix.
G.L.O.W. (2017–19), USA: Netflix.
Grace and Frankie (2015–22), USA: Netflix.
Hell on Wheels (2011–6), USA: AMC.
Hemlock Grove (2013–15), USA: Netflix.
House of Cards (2013–18), USA: Netflix.
I Love Lucy (1951–7), USA: CBS
Mary Tyler Moore Show, The (1970–7), USA: CBS.
Mindhunter (2017–19), USA: Netflix.
OA, The (2016–19), USA: Netflix.
Office, The (2005–13), USA: NBC.
One Day at a Time (2017–20), USA: Netflix.
Orange Is the New Black (2013–19), USA: Netflix.
Punk'd (2003–15), USA: MTV.
Ranch, The (2016–19), USA: Netflix.
Queer Eye (2018–), USA: Netflix.
Roseanne (1988–97), USA: ABC.
Scrubs (2001–10), USA: NBC, ABC.
Selling Sunset (2019–), USA: Netflix.
Six Feet Under (2001–5), USA: HBO.
Sopranos, The (1999–2007), USA: HBO.
Two and a Half Men (2003–15), USA: CBS.
Unbreakable Kimmy Schmidt (2015–20), USA: Netflix.
Will & Grace (1998–2008), USA: NBC.
Wire, The (2002–8), USA: HBO.

Film

Nimoy, L. (1987) *3 Men and a Baby*, USA: Touchstone Pictures.

CHAPTER 10

Diversity, Netflix and the Binge

A central aspect of the way Netflix has positioned itself within a market of increased media options is the legitimation of binge-watching through 'quality' TV. Early marketing of Netflix' in-house productions heavily focussed on exploiting the links between 'quality' television and binge-watching outlined in Chapter 9. There is a strong linkage between binge-watching and the overall mainstreaming of fan practices (Jenner 2017). Binge-watching, as practice more than as concept, was associated with fans, who would often perform it as a version of repetitive viewing. Hills and Garde-Hansen (2017) outline the audio recording or *Doctor Who* (BBC, 1963–89, 2005–) episodes by fans in the 1960s, suggesting that strategies of repetitive 'viewing' of episodes at a viewer's own pace has been common among fans since any kind of recording technology was available. In line with this, Stevens (2021) points to the use of the term 'binge' in fanzines surrounding the *Starsky and Hutch* fandom, as far back as 1985. Binge-watching is rooted in fan practices, though other viewers have embraced it once DVD box sets and streaming have made it easier. Yet, as this chapter will argue, it was particularly Netflix that worked to 'mainstream' the practice as a way to watch it. Though it is possible to leave the insulated flow of a Netflix text, the interface is not structured in a way that makes it easy for viewers to leave this flow. The front page constantly reminds viewers which texts have been left unfinished. Thus, the insulated flow remains a preferred mode of watching

M. Jenner, *Netflix and the Re-invention of Television*,
https://doi.org/10.1007/978-3-031-39237-5_10

Netflix. In the communication of what Netflix is, the emphasis on binge-watching as insulated flow has been dominant in marketing messages, largely because it emphasises that viewers can remain inside *a* flow (even if it is not the same flow as that of a broadcasting schedule) without being overwhelmed by an abundance of choice every time an episode ends. This chapter will focus particularly on the role binge-watching has played in Netflix' marketing. Timothy Havens points to an interview with Allen Sepinwall in which Ted Sarandos explains that, rather than being 'branded' via specific programming output, Netflix' brand is the individualised schedule (2018, 321). Yet, as Havens goes on to explain, Netflix continues to promote itself via its programming. Particularly in its early years of producing original content, Netflix has relied strongly on 'flagship' programmes like *House of Cards*, *Orange Is the New Black*, *Hemlock Grove* or *Arrested Development*, even though some would prove to be more programmatic than others. Even now, Netflix continues to rely on broad thematic concepts to frame its output.

This chapter starts out by discussing the role binge-watching has played in marketing Netflix' original content in late 2012 and early 2013, shortly before the publication of *House of Cards* on 01 February 2013. This chapter focusses particularly on Kevin Spacey's role in the marketing of the first season of *House of Cards* and Mitch Hurwitz' use of the term in the marketing of season 4 of *Arrested Development* a few months later. Hurwitz' explanations are particularly instructive as he is much more prescriptive than Spacey in outlining how to watch Netflix. Yet, season 4 of *Arrested Development* was also met with some backlash regarding the use of the binge model. Even though this is never explicitly acknowledged, this backlash seems to have led to a change in programming strategies for Netflix. The role of binge-watching in the marketing of these series and the way Spacey and Hurwitz explain and emphasise binge-watching as mode of viewing for 'quality' television is explored here. This aspect remains important to trace how the terms binge-watching and Netflix came to be synonymous, how the marketing for these texts became exercises in explaining binge-watching, and thus, Netflix. This process, taken together with Netflix' current emphasis on middlebrow television and continuity with linear television, is important in considering not only Netflix' positioning in the streaming wars, but also the use of binge-watching as 'normalised' (see Jenner 2019).

Secondly, this chapter discusses how mainstream American print and online publications increasingly used the term binge-watching throughout 2013, essentially mainstreaming the terminology and establishing itself as synonymous. This chapter then looks at how Netflix has zoomed in on the linkage between 'quality' television and the concept of diversity to position itself within an American and a transnational television landscape. Considering the vast changes in strategy when it comes to the way 'diversity' is packaged as part of the 'normalisation' of Netflix, the last section focusses on these changes and the way Netflix aims to position itself more as part of the middlebrow. The company has visibly moved towards a more middlebrow version of diversity, which includes strategies of colourblind casting to promote the visual signifiers of diversity without considering broader political projects. The emphasis on diversity is often emphasised by Sarandos, though the concept is situated within a specifically American cultural politics. For many transnational viewers, engaging with this specific version of diversity is not new, given the prevalence of American exports in the international market. However, given the diversity of the US audience, many themes also tie in with more transnational debates, as discussed in more detail in Chapters 13 and 14.[1] The focus here is on programming and how it is used to promote the platform and normalise it.

Marketing the Binge

In line with a contemporary fascination with the CEOs of Silicon Valley, Reed Hastings and Netflix' Chief Content Officer Ted Sarandos have taken a visible role in marketing Netflix and its programming. However, when Netflix started publishing its own in-house productions in 2013, the most prominent marketer of binge-watching was possibly an enthusiastic Kevin Spacey.[2] As Finn points out, Netflix bought the rights to *House of Cards* for $100 million and immediately ordered two seasons, without

[1] As Havens' (2018) detailed study of Netflix' branding, or Ward's (2016) or Christian Stiegler's (2016) analyses of Netflix' national campaigns show, there are different approaches to take in a transnational media landscape.

[2] Spacey's role at Netflix would take an abrupt end in the face of sexual assault allegations by (at the time of the assault) underage boys as well as members of the *House of Cards* crew in 2017. Until then, however, Spacey had taken on a key role in promoting Netflix as producer of 'quality' TV. Spacey's prominent role likely informed Netflix' swift reaction, particularly as its response to allegations of brutal rape against Danny Masterson, who played Kutcher's brother on *The Ranch* and took a less prominent role in promoting the series, took several weeks.

seeing a pilot first. This made *House of Cards* "the most expensive drama on television" (2017, location 2083) at the time. The high price was the result of a highly competitive bidding war. Finn also outlines that Netflix' decision to bid for *House of Cards* was motivated by an algorithmic analysis that predicted success for a project that involved Spacey and director David Fincher. Spacey generally presented the decision to go with Netflix as a choice made by producers because it did not ask for a pilot before ordering two full seasons. This framing positioned Netflix apart from the 'old media' television industry and as a younger company that recognised what viewers wanted and willing to take on the financial risks, rather than the company ready to pay the highest price. Another aspect Spacey generally omitted was the decision-making based on algorithms. Though the system may be more sophisticated on a technological level than the 'old media' practice of looking at box office figures (which, of course, is also automated today), in the short promotional interviews Spacey gives he commonly presents himself as relatively illiterate in technological details. This suggests he would be unable to explain the algorithm and its difference to 'old media' systems. Yet, he proclaims to be a firm believer in binge-watching as publication model and viewing practice.

During the marketing campaign for the first season of *House of Cards* in late 2012 and throughout 2013, Spacey went on a number of late-night talk shows to highlight the control given to viewers through binge-watching. At the time, Spacey was largely known as Oscar-winning star of *American Beauty* (Mendes, 1999) or his performances in *The Usual Suspects* (Singer, 1995), *Se7en* (Fincher, 1995) or *L.A. Confidential* (Hanson, 1997). More recent films were often unsuccessful, but his fame from the mid-to-late 1990s sustained his reputation as outstanding character actor, particularly as these films have remained favourites in a culture of repetitive viewing. In the years before his appearance in *House of Cards* and his subsequent firing due to sexual assault allegations in 2017, Spacey had largely appeared in stage productions, usually with the Old Vic theatre in London. In his interviews, Spacey was careful to position *House of Cards* as 'quality' TV, highlighting his own theatre background, in an interview with Wolf Blitzer and Kate Bouldan on *The Situation Room* (CNN, 2005–) on 01 February 2013 and on the *Late Show with David Letterman* (CBS, 1993–2015) on the same day. Having just finished a tour playing the title role in Shakespeare's *Richard III* on stage, he was filled with anecdotes on how to counter audiences who looked at their phones while enjoying his performance. In an interview with *The*

New York Times: TimesTalks, an audiovisual online addition to the newspaper, Spacey is joined by co-star Robin Wright and writer/creator Beau Willimon. Journalist Mark Leibovich notes that this is the first time he heard the term 'binge-viewing'. Spacey immediately counters, arguing that the practice is well established with series like *Dexter* or *Breaking Bad* (AMC, 2008–13). One aspect he particularly highlights is that audiences are in control, as they are in control when they read novels. In his interview with Letterman, Spacey also emphasises that audiences can watch at their own pace. Going further than this, he emphasises that such a measure may also prevent piracy:

> I think that it's giving the film and television industry an opportunity to learn the lesson the music industry didn't learn: give the people what they want, when they want it in the form they want it in at a reasonable price and they'll buy it and they won't steal it.

In a red carpet interview with *Yahoo!* at the 2013 Emmys, he also emphasises that "the audience has evolved", giving particular agency to viewers. In the context of the prestigious James MacTaggart Memorial Lecture at the Edinburgh International Television Festival, Spacey goes into more detail on the production process, highlighting that Netflix diverts from traditionally used industry models by not asking to see a pilot first.

In these interviews Spacey manages to address various, likely overlapping, audience segments at once: he speaks to an 'evolved' audience used to binge-watching, a 'quality' TV or film audience familiar with Spacey's acting portfolio in film and on stage and an audience that may be sceptical of the technology of Netflix. He also taps into the way television's ancillary technologies have always highlighted control by emphasising that (once again) the audience is in control—though he discusses the control associated with high-culture (novels) over the control linked to RCDs, VCRs or digital television discussed in Part I. Spacey, in many ways, explains Netflix to these viewers, formulating who Netflix is for. But it also explains how Netflix should be watched: the highlighting of binge-watching as a means to watch *House of Cards* may give viewers permission to binge-watch, but, more importantly, those not used to the practice are given an explanation of *how to* binge-watch. As the insulated flow is crucial to Netflix' structure, this instruction is of particular relevance to new viewers who may be uncertain about how to use Netflix.

Another marketer and 'explainer' of Netflix is *Arrested Development* creator Mitch Hurwitz. In this case, binge-watching takes on a different, perhaps more complicated, role. Season 4 of *Arrested Development* was released on 26 May 2013, the Sunday of Memorial Day weekend in the US. It was accompanied by a marketing campaign that relied heavily on its cast, which usually emphasised how glad they were for the chance to reunite. The interviews often highlighted disappointment with original broadcaster Fox, which had cancelled the series after three seasons in 2006, positioning Netflix as 'saviour' of 'cult' TV. However, Mitch Hurwitz, as the *auteur* figure, was well positioned to speak to the creative process and the concept of binge-watching. Whereas *House of Cards* writer/creator Beau Willimon was comparatively unknown, Hurwitz reappeared as a familiar figure. *Arrested Development*'s cult appeal, only heightened by its premature cancellation, ensured Hurwitz' presence on the pages of newspapers and magazines that aimed to reach a young adult, middle-class audience interested in 'cult' TV. Season 4 of the series was heavily anticipated by the 'gatekeepers' of 'quality' TV: *The Atlantic*, for example, accumulates five reviews by different authors and most reviewers highlight their love for the original series (Barkhorn and Kornhaber 2013; Abrams 2013; Orr 2013; Kornhaber 2013; Ching 2013). Though the series' original three seasons are certainly an innovation to the sitcom genre, aesthetically and in its narrative structure, it still follows conventions of broadcast television by accounting for ad time and assuming viewing in weekly instalments. Yet, its fourth season was produced and aired by Netflix and published through the 'binge model'. The series' narrative structure has been compared to *Rashômon* (Kurosawa, 1950) (see Hale 2013; Goodman 2013; Orr 2013): episodes focus on individual characters whose stories intersect with those of other characters at specific moments. Many jokes and narrative enigmas only become clear in later episodes, drawing the season tightly together. The shift in narrative structure as the series moves from network TV to Netflix makes clear how the writing has changed. The season remains a significant example in the way texts can take advantage of the binge model as publication model by introducing an increased level of narrative complexity.

Hurwitz discusses the idea of binge-watching more than the cast, though it is a marginal topic in many interviews and is usually framed in terms of the creative process (see, for example, Greene 2013). An article in *The New York Times*, published online on 23.05.2013 and in print on 26.05.2013 (the day the season was published) includes the quote by Hurwitz: "this is a new media where you get to see all the episodes at once. Maybe they should all happen at the same time". and goes on to point out: "That's what the new season became: a sequence of overlapping stories that seem independent at first, but are actually tightly connected" (Stelter 2013). In an interview with *Wired*, Hurwitz mentions the notion of 'modified binge-watching':

> I think that people do sit down and watch it all at once. Personally, I think [that] will be very fatiguing and will lose some of the fun of being able to mull on it. But I think that with the majority of binge watchers, it's a modified binge watching, just like the majority of novel readers. You know, you don't read it all at once. But you are in control of when you feel like going back to it... I personally hope people don't sit and watch it for, you know, 500 minutes or longer. (Paskin 2013)

Thus, Hurwitz emphasises similar points as Spacey: he uses the term control and likens binge-watching to novel reading. Yet, he is also much more prescriptive than Spacey, possibly anticipating some of the problems mentioned in later reviews. Central to this is a review in *The New York Times*: Mike Hale's review starts off as follows:

> Chalk one up for the Internet: It has killed "Arrested Development." The actual execution was carried out by the producers of the show's fourth season, posted on Sunday morning on Netflix, seven years after the original television series was canceled by Fox. But watching 8 of the 15 new episodes — the biggest binge I could manage before deadline — it seemed likely that the on-demand, all-at-once possibilities of online streaming had helped lead this groundbreaking comedy's creator, Mitch Hurwitz, and his colleagues down a bad path. (2013)

The author's annoyance at having to binge the series is palpable. In the mainstream US press, the general tendency of reviews was along the lines that the text itself did not disappoint, but the 'binge model' was problematic. Dan Zak's review in *The Washington Post* is titled "A Chore to Watch and a Delight to Decrypt" (2013), an opinion that is often shared by other reviewers. Particularly for those reviewers working in the American mainstream press, the most common complaint is that they felt compelled to watch the series very quickly to produce the review by their deadline.[3] As Michael Graves (2015) outlines, fan debates on Twitter also noted this and promoted a decidedly more positive view of the season itself. Graves also observes television journalists joining the debate to discuss how to review television released through the binge model. The general disparity between the pace at which 'official' reviewers watch the season and viewers would is rarely as obvious as in the comments and reviews of season 4 of *Arrested Development*. Thus, it is not surprising that Hurwitz' post-release interviews tend to focus on reviewers' misunderstanding of binge-watching:

> We put the new series out at midnight so it was on at 3am on the east coast. I was trying to say: "Hey, don't watch this all at once, it's just an 8½-hour thing." But the New York Times reviewer really started us off on the wrong foot and created the impression that we got bad reviews when he wrote: "I watched six episodes. The shows are too slow, too long." I was like: "Yeah, it's 3am, you're watching until 9am, you're pissed off, it's memorial weekend, you don't get to have brunch with your family – I get it." (Freeman 2013)

It is important to note just how much his response focusses on Hale's supposed misunderstanding of binge-watching. As Grandinetti (2017) outlines, the print press has also adjusted models on how to report on Netflix series.

Though Spacey does not mention DVD box sets, he highlights the historicity of binge-watching by discussing piracy. Spacey also uses words like control, which emphasises links with television's ancillary technologies. Hurwitz' paradoxical notion of 'modified binge-watching' also emphasises control and links it with self-discipline, even though the terminology of the binge suggests something different. Reviews of season 4 of *Arrested Development*, particularly Hale's review, speak to a complete

[3] This general impression of mixed and sometimes negative reviews may, at least partially, account for the fact that the season was generally seen as disappointing. Nevertheless, both 'official' reviews and audience ratings on Rotten Tomatoes are currently at 76% for season 4 (original cut) (as of 28.12.2022), suggesting an overall more positive reception. Unused to Netflix' silence on viewing numbers or any measure of 'failure' or 'success', business insiders took *Arrested Development*'s failure to attract many new subscribers as failure of the series and Netflix' stock briefly plummeted.

lack of control—even if this seems more determined by publishing deadlines than an inability to stop watching. Unlike with *House of Cards*, which received largely positive reviews, the case of *Arrested Development* is compelling in the way it allowed for an extended debate on what binge-watching actually is. Maybe most importantly, it highlights that binge-watching is not a 'natural' progression for 'quality' television from DVD box sets, but a protocol that is marketed and in need of explanation.

Mainstreaming the Binge

Throughout 2013, a number of mainstream news publications started to use the term binge-watching or binge-viewing more routinely. Even the word 'binge' by itself started to be used to mean binge-watching rather than other forms of binges, such as alcohol or food. Dictionary.com named binge-watching its 'word to watch' in 2013. Of course, as argued in the previous chapters, binge-watching is hardly a phenomenon invented by Netflix. A number of articles in major publications have also discussed it in those terms or in principle before: in July 2011, Emily Nussbaum described her *Breaking Bad* 'bender' in *New York Magazine*; in 2012, a number of television critics in *Slate* (Pagels 2012), *Time Magazine* (Poniewozik 2012) or the *Los Angeles Times* (McNamara 2012) discussed the various pros and cons of binge-watching; in academia, Newman wrote a piece on binge-watching for *Flow* in 2009 and Perks conducted her study on media marathoning in 2012. This is hardly surprising, as sales for DVD box sets had spiked significantly in the mid-2000s (see Chapters 5, 6 or 7). Yet, the fact that television critics and academics, as 'professional' television watchers, routinely binge-watched TV series long before Netflix popularised the term further is hardly an indication of a 'mainstream' activity. One thing notable in all of the analyses above is the consistent parallel to novels, often the literature of Dickens, some of whose novels were originally published in serial form. This suggests how much binge-watching is understood in relation to another medium rather than on the terms of television, for example by invoking the marathon or the common practice of spending several hours watching broadcast television. There also is no sense that binge-watching may be part of a reconception of television. An exception to this line of argument is John Jurgensen of *The Wall Street Journal* who already notes in July 2012 that:

> Binge viewing is transforming the way people watch television and changing the economics of the industry. […] The industry ramifications are bigger than the occasional weekend lost to "Lost." Bingeing breaks habits that have long supported the TV business, built on advertising and syndicated reruns. TV executives are torn by the development: gratified that people are gorging on their product, frustrated because it's a TV party that all-important advertisers aren't invited to. For middlemen like Amazon Instant Video, Hulu Plus and Netflix, it's a godsend, boosting their quest to attract and retain subscribers. Writers and producers are just starting to confront the challenges of creating TV for an audience that may digest an entire season in one sitting.

The outlook of the publication clearly marks this emphasis, though it is instructive in the way the article includes the television industry in the debate on binge-watching. Meanwhile, other debates are also instructive to understand the well-established link between binge-watching and 'quality' television: *Breaking Bad*—at the time still ongoing—features most prominently in articles in the mainstream press, but *Six Feet Under* or *Friday Night Lights* (NBC, 2006–11) are also discussed. The parallel to literature tends to be common in discussions of 'quality' television, highlighting the link between binge-watching and 'quality' television.

What Netflix managed to do was to conceptualise binge-watching as a terminology more specifically linked to television and its own brand. As cited by James Hibberd in *Entertainment Weekly*, Reed Hastings states that "Netflix's brand for TV shows is really about binge viewing" (2013). Rather than relying on a comparison to other media, the terms on which binge-watching was discussed throughout 2013 were increasingly those of an 'evolved audience' (as Spacey puts it) of television. Surrounding the publication of *House of Cards* through the binge model, a number of US television critics engaged in debates on the validity of the business model (Wallenstein 2013) and Dorothy Pomerantz of *Forbes* even argues that 'Binge-Watching Is Our Future' (2013). The fact that industry publications and financial publications like *Forbes* or *The Wall Street Journal* engage in this is indicative of the disruption Netflix' binge model caused at the time—whether it posed a significant threat to existing business models or television itself. At the very least, it was interpreted as something that investors would need to consider.

December 2013 saw the publication of Netflix' Harris Interactive study, which was widely covered with headlines like 'Netflix Survey: Binge-Watching Is Not Weird or Unusual' (Spangler 2013) or its own press release title: 'Netflix Declares Binge Watching is the New Normal' (https://media.netflix.com/en/press-releases/netflix-declares-binge-watching-is-the-new-normal-migration-1). Netflix certainly did not invent binge-watching, but the way the series and its business model was debated, often in the context of its release strategy for *House of Cards* and season 4 of *Arrested Development* has made it a phenomenon more easily observed and talked about. Inserting the term into discourses around contemporary television legitimised the practice and, along with it, Netflix as relatively affordable delivery system. Netflix' exploitation of the link between 'quality' television and binge-watching in the form of *House of Cards* and *Arrested Development* and the (at the time) less talked about *Orange Is the New Black* or the less successful *Hemlock Grove*, created by Eli Roth, led to a brand heavily informed by this relationship.

Binging Diversity

As argued in Part III, Netflix features different content in different countries and, as argued by Axelle Asmar et al. (2022), diversity plays a central role in its transnational positioning, as discussed further in Chapter 12. Thus, as much as it is of interest to marketers of Netflix to reduce its branding to a single key term like binge-watching or personalization, the actual brand is much more complex. Asmar et al. point to the way Netflix markets itself through an emphasis on diversity and a report published to prove its commitment. What is notable, however, is that Netflix seeks to quantify diversity, thus relying on sheer numbers of actors and writers from backgrounds that don't conform to hegemonic gender ideologies and whiteness. Obviously, quantitative data is important, but can only ever capture part of a problem. After all, Netflix has more recently faced massive backlash over the transphobic comedy special *The Closer* (Netflix, 2021) by Dave Chapelle. This points to one of the problems that arise when only quantitative data is looked at without acknowledging the qualitative: counting 'diverse' character on screen acknowledges Chapelle's Blackness, but disregards the story he tells, even if it marginalises trans people. Over the years, Netflix has moved closer to a model of diversity that, instead of telling stories of marginalisation, seeks to reduce 'diversity' to images on screen, rather than stories that highlight how marginalisation occurs. This shift in strategy allows Netflix to continue marketing itself as furthering diversity without actively telling its stories.

Since 2013, Netflix has published a large number of self-produced Originals, immensely widening its interpretations of 'quality' television. Most of the comedy series discussed in Chapter 9, for example, were published from 2015 onwards. The popularity of *House of Cards* indicates how important the version of quality it conforms to is: authorship, Hollywood stars with an emphasis on dramatic roles, complex narrative structures, 'serious' subject matter, accomplished aesthetics, etc. This version of Netflix remains important, but surprise hit *Orange Is the New Black* may be more instructive in understanding Netflix' long-term strategy in developing a specific brand of 'quality'. With a lack of Oscar-winning actors and producers, the series' marketing campaign was not conducted on the same scale as that of *House of Cards* or season 4 of *Arrested Development*. Yet, with a cast of well-known indie film and 'quality' TV actresses (Natasha Lyonne, Tyler Schilling, Taryn Manning, Laura Prepon) and Jenji Kohan as showrunner, the series managed to gain traction on social media. What sets *Orange Is the New Black* apart, as a text, is its focus on women as morally complex characters and its racial and linguistic diversity. Netflix' lesson from the success of *Orange Is the New Black* appears to be a broader definition of diversity. This definition includes not only a stronger emphasis on non-white identities, a questioning of heteronormativity, and a broad variety of series with (often white) female leads, but also multilingualism. The emphasis on diversity is hardly accidental but builds on features in the 'quality' TV of the late 1990s and 2000s: this includes striving towards acceptance of identities that are traditionally inscribed as 'other' to white, straight, cis male, middle-class, middle-age, able-bodied American. American director Ava DuVernay argues that diversity is an essential part of how Netflix can position itself against established media conglomerates:

> That's the way it was; we weren't seeing enough inclusion. Now there are more options. Inclusion is a necessity for survival. It's ignorance to think you can continue to operate in the same way as an industry and shut out a country that is largely made of people who are not white men. If you're going to be holding onto that, you're going to keep having companies that can read the tea leaves, like Netflix, come in and snatch your wig. (Setoodeh 2017b)

Yet, this does not come without precedent or in a vacuum. More recent years have seen more African American female leads on US television, as in *How to Get Away with Murder* (ABC, 2014–20), *Empire* (Fox, 2015–20) or *Greenleaf* (OWN, 2016–20). As more gaps in representation become apparent within white mainstream society and become part of public debate, a broader variety of representations of marginalised groups becomes available. Yet, what this diversity represents is often an inclusion of those viewed as 'other' by American society. Versions of racism these characters may experience are also heavily influenced by the cultural and historical conditions of the US. Considering America's dominance as exporter of television, international audiences may readily accept this. Yet, where American programmes that are later exported to transnational markets view the US market (and US identities) as primary market and viewership, Netflix increasingly addresses a transnational viewership (see Part III). Thus, for Netflix, the focus on diversity becomes more important due to its transnational reach and its precise niche marketing. The multilingualism becomes particularly important here: for example, *Narcos* employs Spanish to represent Colombian culture as well as linguistic realism. A consequence of this is its popularity in Latin American markets. Thus, Netflix' drive towards diversity is closely linked with its transnational expansion project. Yet, this also makes problems in understanding diversity, and lack thereof, as specifically American more marked: though oppression of Black communities in the US is tied to a specific history of slavery, this is not the case in most countries where Netflix is available. Yet, this does not mean that racism towards Black communities, especially in majority White countries, is less of a problem. Though, as argued in Chapter 12, some aspects of Netflix' insistence on diversity may work universally, its understanding of diversity as tied to a specific cultural context also automatically excludes other avenues of thought for a project of inclusion. In many respects, this negotiation of diversity as culturally specific, but Netflix' focus on the transnational has forced it to increasingly formulate a 'universal' kind of diversity.

As part of Netflix' emphasis on diversity and, particularly, quantitative data that reflects diversity, its tagging system becomes relevant as it includes tags on any non-normative identities. Arnold argues that a dominant indicator of this version of diversity is constructed through Netflix' recommendation system:

> Its use of identity classifications is apparent in its reference to recommend categories and tagged sub-genres such as the suffix 'with a strong female lead'. Here, Netflix infers from previous user interactions that viewer

> behaviour has been determined by gender. In other words, if a user watches a television program that happens to have an assertive female protagonist, the PRS [Personalized Recommendation System] takes this to mean that the user identifies with or engages with the program because of gender (of the user or the protagonist). [...] Netflix's PRS creates distinctions between such classifications and, like Amazon, insists on articulating only those identities culturally coded through 'difference'. Its use of tags as a means of generating subgenres works to map taste onto demographic categories, but only for those 'non-normative' identities. Users are addressed through their difference. (2016, 57)

Thus, Netflix' recommendation algorithm and tagging system, and therefore the way it understands and quantifies personalisation is heavily influenced by cultural assumptions (see also Cohn 2019). There is no male equivalent to terminology like 'strong female lead'. This kind of normative thinking is also reflected in the American self-produced Originals, though non-American ones follow their own cultural assumptions. Netflix' diversity still sets white, male, able-bodied, middle-aged, middle-class and heterosexual as 'the norm' while everybody else is 'diverse'.

I argue here that Netflix has historically relied on diversity as part of its brand, but has shifted strategies to articulate this to a 'visibility politics' that neglects a view of the structural problems that create barriers, which are usually culturally specific. I want to start here by highlighting the strategy of colourblind casting as a way to further an agenda of visibility over representation. I understand visibility here as highlighting the visual signifier of race while I understand representation as a discussion of the structural barriers that various minorities face. To put it simply, in representation, the barriers people face shape the identity of a person. In visibility politics, however, barriers were never considered in the writing of the character, so clearly do not shape it. In fact, as texts do not consider barriers, the current status quo is affirmed as, supposedly, having removed barriers. I discuss different marginalised groups together here, not because I understand them as 'the same', but they are rendered 'the same' through an emphasis on visibility over analysis. I want to briefly consider here the strategy of colourblind casting and the representation of the American underclass as examples of how Netflix changed from a strategy of representation up until around 2019 to visibility politics in its more recent texts.

The projects of African American director Ava DuVernay focus on the analysis of structural problems that still influence how Black Americans operate is the US today. This is done through projects like the limited series *When They See Us* (Netflix, 2019), which deals with the so-called 'Central Park 5', a group of five children and teens arrested and unjustly convicted for the rape of a White woman in New York in 1989. The limited series shows how racial marginalisation and bias influences the legal processes and public perception of the case. The series does focus on a specifically American story of the intersections of race and class in the legal system in the late 1980s and draws parallels to today and, thus, is an example of a strategy that seeks to address the US market more than seeking the transnational one. However, it is also emblematic of the avenues for social criticism of the US, in particular.

Netflix' later cooperation with Shondaland and producer Shonda Rhimes, however, shows a different approach and strategy widely adopted across the platform: colourblind casting. Shonda Rhimes is the producer of a range of series for US network channel ABC, including the long-running *Grey's Anatomy* (ABC, 2005–), *Scandal* (ABC, 2012–18) and *How to Get Away with Murder*. Shondaland now produces Netflix hit show *Bridgerton*. The Shondaland series kick-started careers of actresses like Sandra Oh or Carrie Washington and Ellen Pompeo, US television's best-paid actress. The production company is particularly well known for the way it creates feminist roles for its female cast and its creation of racial diversity through colourblind casting. Kristen J. Warner offers an important critique of colourblind casting in her book *The Cultural Politics of Colorblind TV Casting* (2015) by positioning it as follows:

> Discussions of post-raciality in this 21st -century moment force us to think beyond the more traditional notions of stereotype because of how race has been transformed into a marker of visual difference rather than a cultural one. (2015, 2)

She goes on to say:

> My argument is that racial colorblindness [...] is the underpinning of all contemporary rationales for universality in terms of casting primetime television programs. Because the casting process inherently produces infinite representations of a character (an actor has many ways to represent a role), casting lends itself to discussions of representation because it opens up a

> space for the ideology of colorblindness to emerge and take hold. Colorblindness is inherently seductive in a well-intentioned society full of liberal guilt, one that can then avail itself of certain legal discourses, for instance justice is blind and thus objective and fair. (Ibid., 4)

In other words, rendering race a visual (quantifiable) fact rather than a social one, shaped by the barriers that constitute marginalisation, ensures universality. This 'universal' visual fact of race is particularly suited to Netflix' version of transnationalism (see Chapter 12) as it minimises the national specificity of projects like *When They See Us*. Colourblindness emerges as a strategy to ensure racial visibility and, thus, supports claims and commitments to diversity, while not addressing more structural problems that made the policy necessary in the first place.

Bridgerton is based on a series of romance novels set in the British Regency era that tell the story of the eight Bridgerton siblings and their fulfilment in heterosexual romance and sex. The Netflix series follows a similar pattern, but employs strategies of colourblind casting, though these principles are not taken so far as to include familial relations. Hence, all members of the central Bridgerton family (and thus, current and future main characters of the series) are White, even though the romantic co-leads in the first two seasons are not. A range of problems arise, in parts due to the series' nods to historical accuracy (especially the reign of King George III) while building a deliberately historically inaccurate 'fantasy' history. The nods to real history introduce some logical problems that cannot be entirely dispensed with through allowances to suspension of disbelief. After all, the British aristocracy largely generated income by enslaving Black people in the Caribbean and other places, which can make the colourblind casting appear cynical. This becomes even more obvious in the Netflix adaptation of *Persuasion* (Cracknell, 2022), a Jane Austen novel which largely deals with characters who served as British Navy Officers in the Napoleonic wars. Here, characters who are understood (by their profession) to have actively supported slave trade and labour are often re-cast as Black, posing even more problems than *Bridgerton* does. However, as common for costume drama, especially adaptations of British nineteenth century novels, the story focusses on heterosexual romance between two White characters instead (see also Nelson 2015, 52–53). It is worth highlighting that *Persuasion* is not a Shondaland adaptation, but instead signals a broader shift by Netflix that understands diversity as quantifiable. Thus, Netflix' use of colourblind casting works more as a surface-level visibility politics rather than an exploration of more structural problems as in *Orange Is the New Black* or *When They See Us* and its analyses of the US legal system. When the first edition of this book came out, representation of various marginalised groups, such as disability and body diversity, racial diversity or representation of women and the LGBTQIA+ community on Netflix usually included discussion of the structural problems that cause marginalisation. Series like *One Day at a Time* or *Dear White People* specifically narrativize barriers through the use of comedy, for example. Similar narrative strategies are used to explore ageism in *Grace & Frankie* or barriers created through autism in *Atypical* (Netflix, 2017–21). However, this was usually set in a US context, as many non-US productions are designed for more 'universal' appeal (see Chapter 13). Thus, they showed an investment in the various political projects associated with marginalisation.

The change in content strategies also becomes obvious in a brief comparison of the White, American working class in the first seasons of 2015 hit docu-series *Making a Murderer* and 2020 hit *Tiger King*. As Tanya Horeck (2021) argues:

> If the true crime documentary blockbuster has become a sure and steady staple of Netflix's original offering since the release of *Making a Murderer* in 2015, then *Tiger King* arguably represents the 'decadent' stage of the subgenre, the point at which its conventions become fully baroque and parodic. (2021, 55)

This shift in tone is not only important in terms of genre development, but also tells us something about a shift in the narrativizing of class barriers. *Making a Murderer* focusses on Steven Avery who was found guilty in the murder of Theresa Halbach in 2007. Avery was wrongfully convicted in the 1980s for rape and served 18 years in prison, only to be exculpated by DNA evidence in 2003. The documentary makes the case that Avery and his nephew Brendon Dassey were framed for Halbach's murder by the county police as retaliation. Natalia Vedric and Janine Little summarise that:

> … structural inequality lays the narrative foundation for particularly classed selves' challenges to institutional authority via the US criminal justice system. (2022, 1)

In other words, Avery's class marginalises and stigmatises him:

> By treating Avery as a victim of class prejudice while exploring the consequences of a false conviction, the series positions his innocence in a larger context of systemic unfairness in the US criminal justice system. *Making a Murderer*'s thematic investment is in a US legal system that is prejudiced towards the Avery family because of their perceived class disadvantage and their difference from the white, middle-class American ideal. (Ibid., 6)

This stigmatisation serves to drive the narrative and erases the victim in what the prosecution describes as a truly horrific murder. The documentary heavily emphasises the class status of the Avery family as 'below' the working-class farmers around them, as highlighted in Episode 1. In fact, many of the often white, male, middle-class lawyers explicitly make the link between the Avery family's class identity and the conviction and treatment by the legal system of both, Avery and Dassey. In many respects, it is less Avery who generates sympathy, than his parents, sister and nephew. Hence, Vedric and Little focus on the way representation is framed via concepts of 'motherly love' and 'sacrifice'. The documentary formulates a call to activism and ultimately succeeded in getting appeals for Dassey and Avery. The series has been criticised for ignoring evidence to create a smooth narrative of Avery's innocence. However, what I am interested in here is the representation and narrativizing of class barriers that shape Avery's and Dassey's plight in comparison to more recent offerings.

Tiger King focusses on the original and charismatic Joe Exotic and his private zoo, which centres around the attraction of tigers and other big cats, and his long-lasting fight with animal rights activist Carol Baskin. The conflict ended when Exotic hired an assassin to kill Baskin, for which he is now in prison. Overall, the story of Joe Exotic, as presented by the documentary, is complex, expansive and often bizarre. The series itself highlights the spectacle of the absurd. *Tiger King* does not formulate a specific call to action, be that on behalf of animal rights or its characters. The working-class and underclass identities of Exotic and the various employees in the zoo, or intersections with Exotic's sexual identity and whiteness, is not framed as cause for the crime or conviction, but incidental. *Tiger King* often reduces such marginalisation to the 'spectacular', and carnivalesque. As Jorie Lagerwey and Taylor Nygaard succinctly summarise:

> The show itself encourages [a] glib, gawking viewing position as most of the show's participants are rural white people stigmatized in some way: they have spent time in prison, they are poor, they are queer, they are very young or elderly, they have addictions, have experienced trauma and violence, or are disabled. Their interviews are engaging and spark empathy, but also have the flavor of a 19th-century circus freak show, heightened by the carnivalesque setting of the big cat zoo. (2020, 560)

In other words, *Tiger King* often emphasises the 'spectacle' of societies' misfits instead of explaining why they are misfits in the first place.

In the case of *Making a Murderer*, the class identity of Avery and his family is central to the construction of powerlessness that marks the alleged crime(s) and punishment. *Tiger King* reveals a range of crimes, from drug abuse and potential sexual abuse of young men and women, various crimes of animal abuse, including potential slaughter of tiger pups, and the murder-for-hire plot for which Exotic is currently imprisoned for. None of them are presented as linked to class or the powerlessness against larger forces. In fact, as Horeck (2021) argues, what was highlighted on social media was Carol Baskin's rumoured murder of her second husband, for which no evidence is presented. In fact, Lagerwey and Nygaard summarise the dynamics of affect in *Tiger King* as follows:

> Reflecting the relationship between laughing at white male grievance and its actual misogyny, the through lines given the most visibility in *Tiger King* are the sexual exploitation of vulnerable young men and women, and physical and rhetorical violence against women. Repeated so often it becomes an adage, being associated with wild animals, especially big cat cubs, lends the male zoo owners sexual attractiveness. (2020, 562)

The series mentions at various points that many employees of the park are parolees with limited options, and lived, at times, off expired and often stolen food. Thus, the subject matter does lend itself to class analysis beyond the spectacle of often disabled 'freaks'. As often simplistic as the over-emphasis on class at the root of the Avery family's powerlessness is, the de-emphasis of class in *Tiger King* leads to a creation of images of class as 'white trash' and 'freaks' without discussion of underlying structural barriers. Hence, John Finlay's teeth, marked by meth use, or Kelsi Saffery's lost hand without a prosthesis, are not discussed as symptomatic of a lack of affordable healthcare access, but visual signifiers of class. The difference in the way class is emphasised is important. *Making a Murderer* creates its affect by emphasising structural problems to the extent that they *become* affect. Meanwhile, in *Tiger King*, any structural conditions are ignored in favour of affect. This strategy is in line with visibility politics: *Tiger King* makes class and disability visible without pointing to structural problems that cause disadvantage. The series formulates no call to action, so the signifiers of class are presented without real purpose, other than the way they can be circulated on social media. However, not emphasising structural problems no doubt contributes to the transnational success of the series, as nationally specific debates (around healthcare in the US, for example) are reduced to 'universal' images of class.

The investment in a visibility politics over exploration of structural barriers is visible in the representation of many marginalised groups. Of course, this is the difference between what can be counted and rendered into quantifiable data (how many characters of a marginalised group are visible in Netflix self-produced Originals?) and what is captured by qualitative analysis (how is a story told?). The problem is not new and is also captured by Andrea Weiss' 1983 text on 'happens to be gay syndrome', or by Stuart Hall in 1974 (2021) in regard to racial representation on the BBC. More recently, Sarah Banet-Weiser (2018) has explored the problem in regard to what she calls 'popular feminism' and the emphasis on empowerment. Representation of different marginalised groups, thus, becomes a problem of visibility, the signifier of a problem without the analysis of the problem itself. Through this process, different marginalised groups are rendered 'the same', even if underlying political projects may sometimes be at odds with each other or are heterogenic themselves. For Netflix as transnational broadcaster, the emphasis on visibility, rather than representation through the exploration of structural issues, however, also works to produce programming that is never too nationally specific, as discussed in Chapter 12. Thus, various histories of gender or racial discrimination are united and supposedly remedied by the mere presence of a Black female lead.

Conclusion

This chapter explored how Netflix originally positioned itself as broadcaster of original 'quality' television with *House of Cards*. In the course of its marketing, there was also a heavy emphasis on positioning Netflix through the link between 'quality' television and binge-watching. For Spacey, in particular, a focus was also on explaining binge-watching and, thus, how to watch Netflix. The marketing campaign for season 4 of *Arrested Development* was less focussed on binge-watching, though the concept would have a significant impact on its reception. The concept became integral to Netflix, with some media outlets using the term almost synonymously with Netflix throughout 2013. In fact, Netflix' transnationally operating main competitor, Amazon, has actively tried to develop alternative models (see Carr 2013). The appropriation of the model highlights the centrality of binge-watching to Netflix. After establishing this linkage, Netflix recalibrated its brand in more concise terms as its output grew. More recent interviews with Sarandos highlight diversity, meaning racial diversity, multilingualism, representations of gender, including LGBTQIA+, and representations of disability and body diversity. Even more recently, however, the company has shifted from representation to visibility politics. In many respects, this is owed to understanding diversity as an issue that is quantifiable, in the spirit of Silicon Valley. In other words, seeking the solution to social problems in algorithms and quantifiable data. In this respect, Netflix' approach to diversity very much chimes with its emphasis on personalisation and algorithmic 'ordering' of programming.

This branding also highlights a different kind of control being exercised. Whereas the previous chapters of this book focus on the way viewers can exercise control over their experience, Netflix' branding and the use of binge-watching within it highlight the control Netflix exercises over its perception. By highlighting the control audiences exercise over their own viewing in the form of binge-watching, Netflix builds on a tradition of marketing for ancillary technologies to television. Yet, within the same parameters, it fails to acknowledge what control it may exercise over viewers. This is not to over-interpret the addiction metaphors implied in binge-watching, but what is concealed is how Netflix nudges choices about entrance flow or the kind of data it collects on viewers. Furthermore, the re-definition of the Netflix brand is linked to a neoliberal system of customer demand: appealing to a transnational audience heavily implies a gearing towards diversity. Yet, the kind of diversity represented was initially defined on American terms: hence, Black experiences tend to be an assumed universal African American experience. Identity construction focussing on sexual identity is also defined on American terms. Health issues, as related to disability, are defined with American healthcare services in mind. As the company has developed a clearer sense of its own transnationalism, it adopted strategies that don't highlight nationally specific structural barriers that shape identity. Instead, Netflix has adopted the strategies of colourblind casting and extended it to include class- and gender-blindness to render diversity a question of visual signifiers rather than identity shaped by various barriers. This strategy of what I call visibility politics over representation is part of a broader grammar of transnationalism discussed in Chapter 12. Further, the current approach to diversity is in line with Netflix' use of quantifiable data. Netflix branding is complex and consists of a variety of elements. Binge-watching and personalisation as well as Netflix' implementation of diversity in programming shape the way streaming has organised itself around these concepts, sometimes in line with and in opposition to the company.

Part II was concerned with the various ways Netflix employs binge-watching to structure itself and guide viewer experience. It focussed on the way Netflix employs insulated flow and entrance flow to structure itself in the absence of a schedule, its negotiations of cultural value and its marketing and branding. All three aspects highlight how Netflix, purportedly relinquishing control by abandoning the schedule, still guides and controls viewer choices via nudging. Thus, binge-watching does not shift power structures. Nevertheless, Netflix' use of binge-watching and its active positioning within the TV IV discourse also shows its relevance to the process of TV IV. This does not mean that binge-watching was not already an important aspect of TV III and the way broadcasters used digital technologies, but Netflix made binge-watching a central concept for TV IV by employing it for its own structures, publishing models and marketing.

Bibliography

Abrams, Lindsay. 2013. "Have You Called Anyone 'Anustart' Today?" *The Atlantic*, 06.06. https://www.theatlantic.com/entertainment/archive/2013/06/have-you-called-anyone-anustart-today/276599/.

Arnold, Sarah. 2016. "Netflix and the Myth of Choice/Participation/Autonomy." In Kevin McDonald and Daniel Smith-Rowsey (eds.), *The Netflix Effect: Technology and Entertainment in the 21st Century*, 49–62. New York: Bloomsbury.

Asmar, A., T. Raats, and L. Van Audenhove. 2022. "Streaming Difference(s): Netflix and the Branding of Diversity." *Critical Studies in Television* 18: 1–17.

Banet-Weiser, S. 2018. *Empowered Popular Feminism and Popular Misogyny*. Durham: Duke University Press.

Barkhorn, Eleanor and Spencer Kornhaber. 2013. "Arrested Development's Homophobia, Racism, and Church-Bashing: Too Far?" *The Atlantic*. Available online https://www.theatlantic.com/entertainment/archive/2013/06/-i-arrested-development-i-s-homophobia-racism-and-church-bashing-too-far/276888/. Accessed: 07.02.2018

Bjarkman, Kim. 2004. "To have and to Hold: The Video Collector's Relationship with an Ethereal Medium." *Television and New Media* 5 (3): 217–46.

Carr, D. 2013. "With 'Alpha House,' Amazon Makes Bid for Living Room Screens and Beyond." *The New York Times*. Available at: https://www.nytimes.com/2013/11/04/business/media/with-alpha-house-amazon-makes-bid-for-living-room.html?smid=tw-nytmedia&seid=auto&_r=2&pagewanted=all&. Accessed: 08.03.2023.

Chamberlain, Daniel. 2011. "Scripted Spaces: Television Interfaces and the Non-Places of Asynchronous Entertainment." In James Bennett and Niki Strange (eds.), *Television as Digital Media*, location 2457–3060. Durham, NC: Duke University Press. Kindle.

Ching, Albert. 2013. "Who Cares What Happens in the New Arrested Development Episodes?" *The Atlantic*, 23.05. https://www.theatlantic.com/entertainment/archive/2013/05/who-cares-what-happens-in-the-new-i-arrested-development-i-episodes/276177/

Cohn, Jonathan. 2019. *The Burden of Choice: Recommendations, Subversion, and Algorithmic Culture*. New Brunswick: Rutgers University Press.

Dictionary.com. "Word Watch 2013: Binge-Watch." http://www.dictionary.com/e/bingewatch/. Accessed: 07.02.2018.

Finn, Ed. 2017. *What Algorithms Want: Imagination in the Age of Computing*. Cambridge: MIT Press.

Freeman, Hadley. 2013. "Arrested Development Creator Mitch Hurwitz: 'I'm Really, Really Happy with It, for the Dumbest Reasons'." *The Guardian*. Available online https://www.theguardian.com/tv-and-radio/tvandradioblog/2013/aug/08/arrested-development-creator-mitch-hurwitz. Accessed: 01.10.2017.

Gillan, Jennifer. 2015. *Television Brandcasting: The Return of the Content-Promotion Hybrid*. New York; London: Routledge.

Goodman, Tim. 2013. "Arrested Development: TV Review." *The Hollywood Reporter*. Available online http://www.hollywoodreporter.com/review/arrested-development-tv-review-558733. Accessed: 01.10.2017.

Grandinetti, Justin. 2017. 'From Primetime to Anytime: Streaming Video, Temporality and the Future of Communal Television'. In Cory Barker and Myc Wiatrowski (eds.), *The Age of Netflix: Critical Essays on Streaming Media, Digital Delivery and Instant Access*, 11–30. Jefferson: McFarland.

Graves, Michael. 2015. "Binge-Watching and Fan/Critic Antagonism." In Kristin M. Barton (ed.), *A State of Arrested Development: Critical Essays on the Innovative Television Comedy*, location 4219–467. Jefferson, NC: McFarland. Kindle.

Greene, Andy. 2013. "'Arrested Development' Creator Mitch Hurwitz on His Two-Year Odyssey to Revive the Show." *Rolling Stone*. Available online http://www.rollingstone.com/movies/news/arrested-development-creator-mitch-hurwitz-on-his-two-year-odyssey-to-revive-the-show-20130520. Accessed: 01.10.2017.

Hale, Mike. 2013. "A Family Streamed Back to Life." *New York Times*. Available online http://www.nytimes.com/2013/05/26/business/media/arrested-development-returns-on-netflix.html. Accessed: 01.10.2017.

Hall, S. 2021. "Black Men, White Media." In P. Gilroy and R. Wilson Gilmore (eds.), *Selected Writings on Race and Difference*, 51–54. Durham: Duke University Press.

Hass, Nancy. 2013. "Is Netflix the New HBO." *GQ*. Available online http://www.gq.com/story/netflix-founder-reed-hastings-house-of-cards-arrested-development. Accessed: 06.08.2017.

Havens, Timothy. 2018. "Netflix. Streaming Channel Brands and Global Meaning Systems." In Derek Johnson (ed.), *From Networks to Netflix: A Guide to Changing Channels*, 321–32. London: Routledge.

Hibberd, James. 2013. "Netflix Touts Binge Viewing: Is Waiting Better?" *Entertainment Weekly*. Available online http://ew.com/article/2013/01/31/netflix-binge-viewing/. Accessed: 31.12.2017.

Hills, Matt, and Joanne Garde-Hansen. 2017. "Fandom's Paratextual Memory: Remembering, Reconstructing, and Repatriating "Lost" Doctor Who." *Critical Studies in Media Communication* 34 (2): 158–67.

Horeck, T. 2021. "#carolebaskin killed her husband: The Gender Politics of Tiger King Meme Culture." In J. Baron and K. Fuhs (eds.), *Tiger King: Murder, Mayhem and Madness*, 47–67. New York: Routledge.

Jenner, Mareike. 2015. *American TV Detective Dramas: Serial Investigations*. Basingstoke: Palgrave Macmillan.

———. 2017. "Binge-Watching: Video-on-Demand, Quality TV and Mainstreaming Fandom." *International Journal of Cultural Studies* 20 (3): 304–20.

———. 2019. "Control Issues: Binge-watching, channel-surfing and cultural value." *Participations. Journal of Audience & Reception Studies* 16 (2): 298–317.

Johnson, Catherine. 2012. *Branding Television*. London: Routledge.

———. 2017. "Beyond Catch-Up." *Critical Studies in Television: The International Journal of Television Studies* 12 (2): 121–38.

Jurgensen, John. 2012. "Binge Viewing: TV's Lost Weekends." *The Wall Street Journal*. Available online https://www.wsj.com/articles/SB10001424052702303740704577521300806686174. Accessed: 30.12.2017.

Kornhaber, Spencer. 2013. "Arrested Development's Crazy, Existential Message: We're all in this Together." *The Atlantic*, 29.05. https://www.theatlantic.com/entertainment/archive/2013/05/-i-arrested-development-i-s-crazy-existential-message-were-all-in-this-together/276320/.

Lagerwey, J., and T. Nygaard. 2020. "Tiger King's Meme-ification of White Grievance and the Normalization of Misogyny." *Communication, Culture & Critique* 13: 560–63.

McNamara, Mary. 2012. "Critic's Notebook: The Side Effects of Binge Television." *Los Angeles Times*. Available online http://articles.latimes.com/2012/jan/15/entertainment/la-ca-netflix-essay-20120115. Accessed: 30.12.2017.

Nelson, R. 2015, "Costume Drama." In G. Creeber (ed.),*The Television Genre Book*, 3rd ed., 52–53. London: BFI.

Newman, Michael Z. 2009. "TV Binge." *Flow*, 23.01. Available online https://www.flowjournal.org/2009/01/tv-binge-michael-z-newman-university-of-wisconsin-milwaukee/. Accessed: 30.12.2017

Nussbaum, Emily. 2011. "My "Breaking Bad" Bender." *New York Magazine*. Available online http://nymag.com/arts/tv/reviews/breaking-bad-nussbaum-review-2011-8/. Accessed: 01.01.2018.

Orr, Christopher. 2013. "The New Arrested Development Is Something Genuinely New." *The Atlantic*. Available online https://www.theatlantic.com/entertainment/archive/2013/05/the-new-i-arrested-development-i-is-something-genuinely-new/276358/. Accessed: 31.12.2017.

Pagels, Jim. 2012. "Stop Binge-Watching TV." *Slate*. Available online http://www.slate.com/blogs/browbeat/2012/07/09/binge_watching_tv_why_you_need_to_stop_.html. Accessed: 30.12.2017.

Paskin, Anna. 2013. "Arrested Development Creator on the Future of TV and Bringing Back the Bluths." *Wired*. Available online https://www.wired.com/2013/05/arrested-development-creator-mitch-hurwitz/. Accessed: 01.10.2017.

Perks, Lisa Glebatis. 2015. *Media Marathoning: Immersions in Morality*. Lanham, MD: Lexington Books.

Pomerantz, Dorothy. 2013. "Binge-Watching Is Our Future." *Forbes*. Available online https://www.forbes.com/sites/dorothypomerantz/2013/05/29/binge-watching-is-our-future/#3f0229fc15ff. Accessed: 30.12.2017.

Poniewozik, James. 2012. "Go Ahead, Binge-Watch That TV Show." *Time Magazine*. Available online http://entertainment.time.com/2012/07/10/go-ahead-binge-watch-that-tv-show/. Accessed: 30.12.2017.

Setoodeh, Ramin. 2017a. "Has Netflix's Ted Sarandos Rescued (Or Ruined) Hollywood?" *Variety*. Available online http://variety.com/2017/digital/features/ted-sarandos-netflix-original-movies-shonda-rhimes-1202527321/. Accessed: 08.08.2017.

———. 2017b. "Ava DuVernay on Why Netflix Understands Artists and Diversity." *Variety*. Available online http://variety.com/2017/film/news/ava-duvernay-netflix-diversity-1202527100/. Accessed: 30.12.2017.

Spangler, Todd. 2013. "Netflix Survey: Binge-Watching Is Not Weird or Unusual." *Variety*. Available online http://variety.com/2013/digital/news/netflix-survey-binge-watching-is-not-weird-or-unusual-1200952292/. Accessed: 23.12.2017.

Stevens, E.C. 2021, "Historical Binge-Watching: Marathon Viewing on Videotape." In M. Jenner (ed.), *Binge-Watching and Contemporary Television Studies*, 23–39. Edinburgh: Edinburgh University Press.

Stiegler, Christian. 2016. "From Online Video Stores to Global Internet TV Networks: Netflix and the Future of Home Entertainment." In Kevin McDonald and Daniel Smith-Rowsey (eds.), *The Netflix Effect: Technology and Entertainment in the 21st Century*, 235–46. New York: Bloomsbury.

Stelter, Brian. 2013. "Bananas, Anyone? The Bluths Are Back." *New York Times*. Available online http://www.nytimes.com/2013/05/26/business/media/arrested-development-returns-on-netflix.html. Accessed: 01.10.2017.

Vedric, N., and J. Little. 2022. "True Victims: Men's Privilege, Class, and Violence Against Women in Making a Murderer and The Jinx." *Feminist Media Studies* 23: 1–17.

Wallenstein, Andrew. 2013. "Analysis: Why Netflix Must Rethink Binge Viewing." *Variety*. Available online http://variety.com/2013/digital/news/analysis-why-netflix-must-rethink-binge-viewing-1118065356/. Accessed: 23.12.2017.

Ward, Sam. 2016. "Streaming Trans-Atlantic: Netflix, Imported Drama and the British Digital Television Ecology." In Kevin McDonald, and Daniel Smith-Rowsey (eds.), *The Netflix Effect: Technology and Entertainment in the 21st Century*, 219–34. New York: Bloomsbury.

Warner, K.J. 2015. *The Cultural Politics of Colorblind TV Casting*. London: Routledge.

Weiss, A. 1986. "From the Margins: New Images of Gays in the Cinema", *Cinéaste* 15 (1): 4–8.

Zak, Dan. 2013. "'Arrested Development' Season 4 Review: A Chore to Watch and a Delight to Decrypt." *The Washington Post*. Available online https://www.washingtonpost.com/entertainment/tv/arrested-development-season-4-review-a-chore-to-watch-and-a-delight-to-decrypt/2013/05/29/d0480f3e-c7cf-11e2-8da7-d274bc611a47_story.html?utm_term=.fc53e97b7e91. Accessed: 30.12.2017.

Television

Arrested Development (2003–6, 2013–16), USA: Fox, Netflix.
Breaking Bad (2008–13), USA: AMC.
Bridgerton (2020–), USA: Netflix.
Dave Chappelle: The Closer (2021), USA: Netflix.
Dear White People (2017–21), USA: Netflix.
Desperate Housewives (2004–12), USA: ABC.
Dexter (2006–13), USA: Showtime.
Doctor Who (1963–89, 2005–), UK: BBC.
Empire (2015–20), USA: Fox.
Friday Night Lights (2006–11), USA: NBC.
Greenleaf (2016–20), USA: OWN.
Grey's Anatomy (2005–), USA: ABC.
Hemlock Grove (2013–15), USA: Netflix.
House of Cards (2013–18), USA: Netflix.
How to Get Away With Murder (2014–20), USA: ABC.
Late Show with David Letterman (1993–2015), USA: CBS.
Making a Murderer (2015–18), USA: Netflix.
Narcos (2015–17), USA: Netflix.
One Day at a Time (2017–20), USA: Netflix.
Orange Is the New Black (2013–19), USA: Netflix.
Scandal (2012–18), USA: ABC.
Situation Room, The (2005–), USA: CNN.
Six Feet Under (2001–5), USA: HBO.
Starsky and Hutch (1975–9), USA: ABC.
Tiger King (2020–1), USA: Netflix.
When They See Us (2019), USA: Netflix.
Wire, The (2002–8), USA: HBO.

Film

Cracknell, C. (2022) *Persuasion*. USA: Netflix.
Fincher, D. (1995) *Se7en*. USA: New Line Cinema.
Hanson (1997) *L.A. Confidential*. USA: Warner Bros.

Kurosawa, Akira (1950) *Rashômon*. Japan: Daiei Motion Picture Company.
Mendes, S. (1999) *American Beauty*. USA: DreamWorks.
Singer, B. (1995) *The Usual Suspects*. USA: Blue Parrot.

YouTube

New York Times: TimesTalks: House of Cards, Interview. Published: 11.09.2013. The New York Times Media. Available at: https://www.youtube.com/watch?v=m7elqrPiLAo&t=7s.

Yahoo! News: House of Cards' Kevin Spacey on the 2013 Emmy red carpet. Published: 24.09.2013. Live Media Group. Available at: https://www.youtube.com/watch?v=gdpls_sl-TE.

PART III

Netflix and the Re-invention of Transnational Broadcasting

CHAPTER 11

Netflix and the Re-invention of Transnational Broadcasting

In 2014, Netflix commissioned four films starring and produced by Adam Sandler with budgets of $40–$80 million, with Sandler's salary as actor and producer being estimated at $20 million per film (see Plante 2014). The decision was met with little understanding by American media outlets and industry. Sandler's last few films for Sony had flopped at the box office in the US, still a dominant market for Hollywood films. Sandler's first film for Netflix, *The Ridiculous 6* (Coraci, 2015), was plagued by accusations of racism during the production when Native American actors walked off the set in protest (see Schilling 2015). The film received bad reviews: its reviewer rating on Rotten Tomatoes is 0% and its audience rating stands at 35%, a remarkably low number (as of 20 September 2022). Yet, Sarandos explained Netflix' decision for the Sandler deal as follows in an interview with *The Hollywood Reporter*:

> The more global we become, the more access we have to global behavior data so we can see what people are watching all around the world. In our earliest streaming days, we used to have the Sony output deal through Starz. We had almost all of Adam's movies in the first pay window in the U.S. Today, we continue to have those movies in the first pay window in Canada. And then, through various windows that follow the pay window all the way to the deep catalog, we've licensed Adam's movies in all of our territories. Very uniquely, he stands out for his global appeal to Netflix

M. Jenner, *Netflix and the Re-invention of Television*,
https://doi.org/10.1007/978-3-031-39237-5_11

> subscribers. Even movies that were soft in the U.S. [theatrically] outperformed dramatically on Netflix in the U.S. and around the world. (Kilday 2014)

Additionally, Ben Child notes in *The Guardian* that Sandler's films receive some of the highest repeat viewing figures on Netflix (2014). Justin Moyer notes in *The Washington Post* that *The Ridiculous 6* was a hit for Netflix (2016). In 2017, before the first four films were published, Netflix ordered four more films with and produced by Sandler (Mumford 2017). The deal suggests a move towards mass appeal as opposed to the niche appeal of the 'quality' TV and political documentaries Netflix entered the field of original programming between 2013 and 2016. Yet, this mass appeal is a very specific *kind* of mass appeal: it is not the appeal of 'traditional' mass media. The term 'mass' as applied to 'the masses' is most commonly applied to an audience delineated by national borders. Meanwhile, the audience Netflix addresses, particularly with its Adam Sandler films, may be massive, but can hardly be compared to the 'masses' of national mass communication. The Adam Sandler films suggest an open embracing of transnational audiences: Sandler may no longer be a popular star in the US, but his appeal remains robust in other territories. His appeal may also draw diminished crowds to the cinema, but home viewing on Netflix continues to be strong. The two deals with Sandler, spanning eight films in total, may be the most remarkable indication that Netflix aims to gear itself towards audiences that are more global in scope. As such, the box office appeal of Sandler in the US is only a secondary concern: the audience Netflix tries to appeal to may not be a national 'mass' audience, but it is, nevertheless, massive and may even be more difficult to capture due to its transnational nature. Part III of this study explores Netflix as transnational broadcaster, aiming to capture a global, rather than a national, audience.

Whereas the last two parts focussed on the control audiences exercise over their viewing, this part is about how Netflix integrates and assimilates (Ward 2016) to not only into national markets, but the transnational market it also shapes. Though national governments can intervene through policy decisions or specific arrangements with Netflix, it is still distinct from traditional broadcasting through its online delivery. Netflix' geoblocking (see Elkins 2018) and subsequent blocking of the use of proxy servers (see Lobato 2019 for closer analysis) at the behest of licensing rights holders indicates how much Netflix limits audience control while its publishing model for its own content suggests efforts to mitigate the implications of such a move. In fact, Elkins (2021) argues that:

> Netflix's relationships with powerful political actors [like the Obamas] and global encouragement of deregulation encourage platform-imperialist practices, while its cosmopolitan brand promotes the platform as responsible, progressive global actor. (2021, 150)

Part III explores Netflix' transnational scope through its textual structures and by conceptualising a transnational audience. Unlike Elkins' analysis, the focus here is more on the way Netflix constructs itself as global actor via its texts and the networks of meaning it constructs via its texts and interface. Transnational broadcasting is not a new phenomenon, but Netflix offers a new kind of transnational broadcasting through ease of access and the kind of content it delivers. In this, Netflix operates in what Couldry (2012) terms a decentred media system. Netflix' positioning as online television means that it has to integrate itself not merely as new channel, but distinct media form, within most markets.

Underpinning Part III is Couldry's (2012) assertion that media is decentred. This is largely predicated on an understanding of the vast complexity of global media streams, as asymmetrical as these relations may often be, and the recognition that globalisation also has no stable centre (Iwabuchi 2002). In a global media system, media practices, regulatory frameworks and access to different media will necessarily differ. While Netflix is an American company, it is also a global actor that operates under different conditions and with different content in each national context it enters. Roman Lobato (2019) goes as far as to suggest that the different catalogues available in each country constitute fundamentally different versions of Netflix, an assertion that can be extended to most platforms. Further, different national media systems also shape its forms. We cannot assume the US as a 'centre' for Netflix as cultural object. One of Netflix' central markers is that it is decentred, that it takes television away from its national context, appealing to global audiences rather than national ones. Yet, at the same time, it also attempts to integrate itself into national television landscapes, offering indigenous content and producing Spanish, Japanese, or French self-produced Originals. Thus, Netflix integrates into national media practices while also acting as (American) global actor. This tension is inherent in the way Netflix can be conceptualised as global actor. Sabina Mihelj argues,

> Rather than erasing boundaries between national economies and integrating them all into a seamlessly global market, the new communication technologies seem to encourage a reshuffling of established relations between states, markets and the media. (2011, 34)

Following this, Part III understands the relationship between Netflix, national media and individual nations as complex and unstable.

As Buonanno observes, in most discussions surrounding the global and the local, the view persists that both are static, oppositional poles. Yet, there is a much more dynamic relationship between different cultures:

> The proliferation of television channels takes place within television systems that, like any other complex environment, are characterized by asynchronies and by the simultaneous presence of formations at different stages of development, which require different strategies and resources. (2008, 92)

Buonanno notes that imported television programmes, particularly in Western Europe, are, indeed, predominantly American. Nevertheless, there is also a lively exchange of cultural products in and with other parts of the world. In relation to television, the exchange of telenovelas between Latin America, the Middle East, Turkey and Greece is one example of globalisation and cultural exchange that often escapes more Euro-centric views of global culture. Looking at Netflix, its licensing of Netflix Originals (or false Originals, as Petruska and Woods [2019] put it) signifies vast possibilities when it comes to the availability of texts from non-English speaking countries.

Joana Breidenbach and Uta Zukrigl (1998), arguing from an anthropological perspective, complicate the way cultures construct 'otherness'. They point to the way local cultures can perceive those from a few towns over as 'other' while not necessarily perceiving an international brand the same way. This suggests the complexity of how 'other' or 'threats' to national or regional culture can be constructed and the inconsistencies underpinning this. In their central analogy of a 'dance of cultures', Breidenbach and Zukrigl posit that people may resist otherness at some points and embrace or domesticate it at other points. Most importantly, both, national and global culture are dynamic concepts, never stable and always in a changing relationship with each other. Frank J. Lechner and John Boli offer a complex view of how culture functions by describing the dynamic relationship between the national and the transnational in terms of 'embattled' national culture:

> Insofar as the forces of globalization undermine a nation's settled forms of self-understandings [...] the magnitude of that task [of defining national identity] increases. Where the capacity of a nation to respond is in question, the salience of national identity as a project may well be even greater, especially if [...] the relevant cultural elite is deeply invested in it. Nations can show resilience precisely in becoming embattled. (2005, 151)

In other words, if the construct of a national identity is perceived as 'under threat' due to the dominance of foreign cultural products, 'the nation' will fight back (both, on a policy and ideological level). Thus, if there is a perception that, for example, too many television programmes are American imports, governments can use legislative means, audiences can resist, or the industry can introduce mechanisms of self-regulation to control this influx.

Though often forced to adapt to national culture through media policies, Netflix also actively seeks integration into national media systems to fend off accusations of cultural homogenization. This also responds well with Roland Robertson's concept of 'glocalisation', which theorises a dialectic relationship between the global and the local:

> The concept of globalization has involved the simultaneity and the interpretation of what are conventionally called the global and the local, or – in a more abstract vein – the universal and the particular. (1995, 40)

The term also encompasses the idea that 'global' and 'local' are not terms that can be understood in a binary, but only in a dialectic. Though Straubhaar (2007) notes that the term is formed in relation to Japanese culture, where local culture is particularly resilient, Chapter 13 will discuss strategies of domestication, such as translation, which are routinely employed by a number of national media systems to domesticate texts. Arjun Appadurai argues:

> The central problem of today's global interactions is the tension between cultural homogenization and cultural heterogenization. [...] What

> [homogenization] arguments fail to consider is that at least as rapidly as forces from various metropolises are brought into new societies they tend to become indigenized in one or another way: this is true of music and housing styles, as much as it is true of science and terrorism, spectacles and constitutions. (1996, 32)

Appadurai's work engages in depth with the various ironies and resistances that shape the way American popular culture is met with around the world. The use of different terminologies by different theorists to describe similar conditions indicates how complex this dialectic is and how its meanings can change in different contexts. Breidenbach and Zukrigl's dance analogy works well because of the imagery it invokes and its general 'openness' to accommodate the constant back, forth, sideways, jumping, touching, moving away, switching partners and occasional missteps, misunderstandings, imbalances and so on, that can go on, both, in dancing and in the exchange, domestication or reception of culture.

Netflix' reach may be wide, but in no way global and it is always bound by national law and historical forces that have shaped nationally specific media systems. Furthermore, access to Netflix is predicated on access to high-speed broadband, a functional computer, electricity and money to regularly pay subscriptions, further limiting its scope to the global elites. Because of this, the term transnational is used here, rather than 'global' or 'international'. Steven Vertovec defines transnationalism as follows:

> When referring to sustained linkages and ongoing exchanges among non-state actors based across national borders – business, non-government organizations, and individuals sharing the same interests (by way of criteria such as religious beliefs, common cultural and geographic origins) – we can differentiate these as 'transnational' practices and groups (referring to their links functioning across nation states). (2009, location 187–93)

This focus on non-state actors makes the description appropriate for Netflix as well as other cross-border broadcasters. Vertovec also takes cultural commonalities into account, allowing for a conceptualisation that can accommodate the exchange of cultural goods. The term transnationalism can also account for what Straubhaar calls 'cultural proximities' between nations that do not share borders or obvious cultural-historical connections, such as the popularity of Mexican telenovelas in the Middle East. Koichi Iwabuchi, focussing on relationships between different Asian countries, argues,

> The intricacies and disjunctiveness of emerging intra-Asian popular cultural flows under globalizing forces are better expressed by the term *transnational* as opposed to *international* or global for a variety of reasons. *Transnational* has a merit over *international* in that actors are not confined to the nation-state or to nationally institutionalized organizations; they may range from individuals to various (non)profitable, transnationally connected organizations and groups, and the conception of culture implied is not limited to a 'national' framework. [...] Moreover, the term *transnational* draws attention in a more locally contextualized manner to the interconnections and asymmetries that are promoted by the multidirectional flow of information and images, and by the ongoing cultural mixing and infiltration of these messages. (2002, location 365–72, italics in the original)

Thus, transnationalism also denotes the way imported programming does not always produce the same meanings in the target culture as in its culture of origin or other target cultures. In fact,

> Transnational cultural flows neither fully displace nationally delineated boundaries, thoughts and feelings, nor do they underestimate the salience of the nation-state in the process of globalization. (ibid., location 380)

Thus, the transnational encompasses some of the tensions between local and global inherent in processes of globalisation. Netflix is a company operating under the principles of American neoliberalism and transports these values through a variety of means (texts, publication models, marketing, etc.), but it is also a vehicle for cultural exchange. Transnationalism for Netflix is a complex network of practices of domestication and cultural exchange, of relationships audiences have with US imports and existing national media systems, of the internet and television, the national and the transnational. Pertierra and Turner introduce the terminology of 'zones of consumption' to describe the complex idea of 'location' in television reception. They remain deliberately open with this terminology, arguing that this 'zone' can be as small as a living room and can reach across borders. As they argue,

> ...the zone resists the notion that the appropriate location within which to examine television rests with any one formation – be it the home, the local community, or the nation state; a zone of consumption can be any one, some, or all of these. It is not helpful to categorically locate television

> within any one kind of media system either, or within any one kind of cultural, political, material or geo linguistic space. However, the boundary implied in the phrase also resists the temptation to see the location as utterly arbitrary, or without definition. (2013, 6)

These 'zones of consumption' are not as well defined as the territories outlined by Netflix, where territories are often aligned with continents. Territories are more strictly defined, largely by the areas of responsibility of those working in company branches. As Iwabuchi argues, a transnational or cross-border identity within territories can serve to construct transnational identities outside of Western concepts and constructions (2015, 100–13). Cultural proximities outside of geo-linguistic regions or even outside of countries linked by a common colonial history can be encompassed by the term. Zones of consumption serves well as a terminology to describe Netflix as transnational broadcaster, reaching audiences in most countries of the world. As Pertierra and Turner continue,

> What is important is to maintain a sense of the social, historical and cultural contingency of that zone, rather than approach it as merely an effect of technology, geography, politics or the market. (2013, 8)

Shaped by specific zones—whether within specific households, different social spheres, cultural contexts, or media systems or across them—Netflix cannot be viewed as the same, consistent, coherent 'thing' wherever it is. It is barely the same from one viewer to the next, as discussed in Chapter 8, but different national contexts also determine available content.

As Iwabuchi (2015) summarises, the transnational often works to re-assert the national. Castells notes,

> The age of globalization is also the age of nationalist resurgence, expressed both in the challenge to established nation-states and in the widespread (re)construction of identity on the basis of nationality, always affirmed against the alien. (2009, 30)

Thus, Netflix needs to be understood as both: national and transnational at the same time, one never being able to work without the other. Straubhaar (2007) develops an idea of transnational media by drawing on complexity theory, pointing to the various histories, dependencies, linguistic, national or regional conditions of national media that forbid broad assumptions. He differentiates between structural and cultural factors. In Straubhaar's model, Netflix is largely structural as a new technology to broadcast and receive Netflix. Yet, it is also cultural as it also features nationally or regionally produced content and offers strategies to domesticate content, as discussed in Chapter 12. Unlike Straubhaar's analysis, this study is focussed on Netflix, which somewhat limits its scope and leads to some generalisations, as it remains unspecific about national media systems and the strategies of other streamers. This study remains focussed on Netflix' self-produced Originals: not only is Netflix poised to extend its own productions and decrease dependency on international rights holders of content, it also uses these productions to market itself internationally (see Ward 2016; Stiegler 2016; Havens 2018). Furthermore, these productions remain a stable commonality between Netflix in different markets.[1]

Part III of this book ties together different theories to conceptualise Netflix as a global actor. In the first edition of this book, Part III started out with a chapter to locate Netflix within discourses of 'the nation', as ideological system more than as geographical location, national media systems as well as transnational broadcasting. However, for the Second Edition, I wanted to focus more on the way Netflix negotiates the tension between the global and the local, the national and transnational and the ways this is specific to Netflix. One factor that sets different streamers apart within the streaming wars is the way they seek to negotiate this tension on a textual level and through the network of meanings they create between different texts. Disney, as the studio with the most significant experience in transnational media and media systems, models a different kind of what I call 'grammar of transnationalism' and diegetic universes for Disney+ (see also Hunting and Gray 2023) than Amazon does. Much of this is linked to the different goals platforms have (as also discussed in the Introduction to the Second Edition), but certainly visible in the construction of texts in different markets. The First Edition formulated an idea of how we can understand Netflix as transnational broadcaster by moving away from understanding it as 'American' and

[1] Series like *Grace and Frankie* are available in markets as heavily regulated and as conservative as Saudi Arabia. Further, an episode of the comedy show *Patriot Act with Hassan Minhaj* (Netflix, 2018–20) on political oppression in Saudi Arabia was removed in the territory, though it was moved to YouTube, where it remains available worldwide. Yet, it can be assumed that access would be limited to social elites in these countries.

operating in tandem with, and in opposition to, US television as cultural product and industry. While this remains an important issue, the role of Netflix in the streaming wars poses additional questions. Because of this, this Second Edition seeks to address different strategies streamers use in order to adapt established models of industry trade and building connections of meaning between texts.

To first address the ways meaning is negotiated, Chapter 12 focusses on the publication model, the binge model, and texts to understand how Netflix positions and markets itself as transnational while also placing itself within national media systems. It explores the impetus behind the publication of texts without (or only a small) 'time lag' across borders. It then discusses Netflix' self-produced Originals to understand what its specific 'grammar of transnationalism' looks like. These may be very broad principles, such as commitments to liberal humanism, multilingualism or racial diversity, but the breadth of the transnational audience does not allow for more precision. This chapter is also concerned with strategies of domestication that allow Netflix to insert itself into existing national media systems. This discussion will focus on translation, a factor often not often discussed by scholars looking at transnational media, such as Straubhaar (2007) or Jean K. Chalaby (2009 and 2023). Chapter 13 was added to the Second Edition and explores the transnational streaming franchise *Criminal*. This will also be compared with Amazon's *LOL: Last one Laughing* to understand how cross-border properties and narratives are structured and localised. Chapter 14 considers the transnational Netflix audience in more detail. This entails understanding Netflix within a broader online landscape and participatory culture, within transnational media systems and in the context of debates surrounding audience fragmentation. Drawing on Rukmini Pande's (2018) work on fandom and diversity, however, it also draws attention to the ultimately Western ideology. Overall, Part III will consider different perspectives to understand Netflix as transnational broadcaster and enable a less anglo-centric debate.

Understanding Netflix as transnational broadcaster means understanding it within a tradition of national as well as transnational broadcasting, yet also distinct due to its usage of online infrastructures and the deployment of its own in-house productions. Other than the catch-up platforms discussed in Chapter 6, Netflix is only partially bound by national media systems. Other than previous transnational broadcasters, Netflix is also not bound by national time, as it does not have a linear schedule to begin with. Its range of non-English language productions is constantly growing, even if nationally bound versions of diversity means that these programmes often do not emphasise these aspects to the same extent. Hence, Netflix is located in a tension between the national and the transnational, a 'grammar of transnationalism' and strategies of domestication or a national and a transnational audience. The guiding question for Part III is how Netflix positions itself within a decentred media system, how it integrates itself into local media systems as transnational broadcaster and how this defines a broad, transnational audience.

Bibliography

Appadurai, Arjun. 1996. *Modernity at Large: Cultural Dimensions of Globalization*. Minneapolis: University of Minnesota Press.

Böhm, Markus. 2014. "Die Großen Video-Flatrates Im Direktvergleich." *Spiegel Online*. Available online: http://www.spiegel.de/netzwelt/apps/netflix-alternative-maxdome-watchever-sky-snap-amazon-im-vergleich-a-991197.html. Accessed: 08.08.2017.

Breidenbach, Joana, and Ina Zukrigl. 1998. *Tanz Der Kulturen: Kulturelle Identität in Einer Globalisierten Welt*. München: Kunstmann.

Buonanno, Milly. 2008. *The Age of Television Experiences and Theories*. Bristol: Intellect.

Castells, Manuel. 2009. *The Power of Identity the Information Age: Economy, Society, and Culture Volume II*. 2nd ed. Hoboken: Wiley.

Chalaby, Jean K. 2005. "Towards an Understanding of Media Transnationalism." In Jean K. Chalaby (ed.), *Transnational Television Worldwide: Towards a New Media Order*, 1–13. London: I. B. Tauris.

———. 2009. *Transnational Television in Europe: Reconfiguring Global Communications Networks*. London: I.B.Tauris.

———. 2023. *Television in the Streaming Era. The Global Shift*. Cambridge: Cambridge University Press.

Child, Ben. 2014. "Adam Sandler Signs Exclusive Four Films Deal with Netflix." *The Guardian*. Available online: https://www.theguardian.com/film/2014/oct/02/adam-sandler-netflix-movie-deal. Accessed: 08.08.2017.

Couldry, Nick. 2012. *Media, Society, World: Social Theory and Digital Media Practice*. Cambridge: Polity.

Elkins, E. 2018. "Geoblocking National TV in an On-Demand Era." In D. Johnson (ed.), *From Networks to Netflix: A Guide to Changing Channels*, 1st edn, 333–42.

———. 2021, "Streaming Diplomacy: Netflix's Domestic Politics and Foreign Policy." In D.Y. Jin (ed.), *The Routledge Handbook of Digital Media and Globalization*, 150–57. London: Routledge.

Havens, Timothy. 2018. "Netflix. Streaming Channel Brands and Global Meaning Systems." In Derek Johnson (ed.), *From Networks to Netflix: A Guide to Changing Channels*, 321–32. London: Routledge.

Hunting, K., and Gray, J. 2023. "Disney+. Imagining Industrial Intertextuality." In D. Johnson (ed.), *From Networks to Netflix. A Guide to Changing Channels*, 650–67. 2nd edn. New York: Routledge.

Iwabuchi, Koichi. 2002. *Recentering Globalization: Popular Culture and Japanese Transnationalism*. Durham: Duke University Press.

———. 2015. *Resilient Borders and Cultural Diversity: Internationalism, Brand Nationalism, and Multiculturalism in Japan*. Lanham, MD: Lexington Books.

Kilday, Gregg. 2014. "Netflix's Ted Sarandos Explains Adam Sandler, 'Crouching Tiger' Deals: "Putting our Money Where Our Mouth Is"." *The Hollywood Reporter*. Available online: http://www.hollywoodreporter.com/news/netflixs-ted-sarandos-explains-adam-737840. Accessed: 08.08.2017.

Lechner, Frank J., and John Boli. 2005. *World Culture: Origins and Consequences*. Malden, MA: Blackwell Pub.

Lobato, R. 2019. *Netflix Nations: The Geography of Digital Distribution*. New York: New York University Press.

Mihelj, Sabina. 2011. *Media Nations: Communicating Belonging and Exclusion in the Modern World*. Basingstoke: Palgrave Macmillan.

Moyer, Justin. 2016. "Adam Sandler's 'Ridiculous 6' Insulted Some Native Americans. Now It's Netflix's 'No. 1' Movie." *The Washington Post*. Available online: https://www.washingtonpost.com/news/morning-mix/wp/2016/01/07/adam-sandlers-ridiculous-6-insulted-some-native-americans-now-its-netflixs-no-1-movie/?utm_term=.859ca4ebce53. Accessed: 08.08.2017.

Mumford, Gwilym. 2017. "Netflix Can't Get Enough Adam Sandler as New Four-Film Deal Signed." *The Guardian*. Available online: https://www.theguardian.com/film/2017/mar/27/adam-sandler-signs-deal-with-netflix. Accessed: 08.08.2017.

Pande, R. 2018. *Squee From the Margins. Fandom and Race*. Chicago: University of Illinois Press.

Pertierra, Anna Cristina, and Graeme Turner. 2013. *Locating Television: Zones of Consumption*. London and New York: Routledge.

Petruska, K., and F. Woods. 2019. "Traveling Without a Passport: "Original" Streaming Content in the Transatlantic Distribution Ecosystem." In H.M. Hilmes and R.E. Pearson (eds.), *Transatlantic Television Drama: Industries, Programs, & Fans*, 49–67. Oxford: Oxford University Press.

Plante, Chris. 2014. "Why Adam Sandler Is Making Four Films with Netflix." *The Verge*. Available online: http://www.theverge.com/2014/10/2/6890741/adam-sandler-netflix-make-money. Accessed: 08.08.2017.

Rankin, Jennifer. 2018. "Online Streaming Services Face '30% Made in Europe' Law." *The Guardian*, 26.04. Available online: https://www.theguardian.com/technology/2018/apr/26/eu-third-party-trader-amazon-google-ebay. Accessed: 03.05.2018.

Robertson, Roland. 1995. "Glocalization: Time-Space and Homogeneity-Heterogeneity." In Scott M. Lash, Mike Featherstone, and Roland Robertson (eds.), *Global Modernities*, 35–53. London: Sage.

Roxborough, Scott. 2016. "Why Netflix Is Now Dubbing, Subtitling Content in Poland." *The Hollywood Reporter*. Available online: http://www.hollywoodreporter.com/news/netflix-dubbing-subtitling-polish-930982. Accessed: 08.08.2017.

Schilling, Vincent. 2015. "Native Actors Walk Off Set of Adam Sandler Movie After Insults to Women, Elders." *Indian Country Today*. Available online: https://indiancountrymedianetwork.com/culture/arts-entertainment/native-actors-walk-off-set-of-adam-sandler-movie-after-insults-to-women-elders/. Accessed: 08.08.2017.

Straubhaar, Joseph D. 2007. *World Television: From Global to Local*. Thousand Oaks, CA: Sage Publications.

Stiegler, Christian. 2016. "From Online Video Stores to Global Internet TV Networks: Netflix and the Future of Home Entertainment." In Kevin McDonald and Smith-Rowsey (eds.), *The Netflix Effect: Technology and Entertainment in the 21st Century*, 235–46. New York: Bloomsbury.

Sweney, Mark. 2016. "Netflix and Amazon Must Guarantee 20% of Content Is European." *The Guardian*. Available online: https://www.theguardian.com/media/2016/may/25/netflix-and-amazon-must-guarantee-20-of-content-is-european. Accessed: 05.05.2017.

Turner, Graeme. 2009. "Television and the Nation: Does This Matter Any More?" In Jinna Tay and Graeme Turner (eds.), *Television Studies After TV: Understanding Television in the Post-Broadcast Era*, 54–63. London: Routledge.

Vertovec, Steven. 2009. *Transnationalism*. London: Routledge.

Ward, Sam. 2016. "Streaming Trans-Atlantic: Netflix, Imported Drama and the British Digital Television Ecology." In Kevin McDonald and Daniel Smith-Rowsey (eds.), *The Netflix Effect: Technology and Entertainment in the 21st Century*, 219–34. New York: Bloomsbury.

Television

Grace and Frankie (2015–22), USA: Netflix.

Film

Coraci, F. (2015) *The Ridiculous 6*. USA: Netflix.

CHAPTER 12

The Transnational and Domestication: Netflix Texts

Netflix' in-house productions, at this stage, are predominantly American. This creates an impression of cultural imperialism. At the same time, Buonanno notes that the American text has to address a broad variety of different audiences on a national level.

> The domestic US market is not only enormous, but is very much a mixture of different ethnic groups from different geographic areas and with different cultural heritages: a population essentially of immigrants. In order to speak to such a heterogeneous audience, held together though they may be by the myth of the melting pot, and in order to offer them multicultural materials and culturally appropriate programmes, it was necessary to develop a production capacity with a high degree of universalism; in other words, to pursue the 'lowest common denominator', as it is often scathingly called. The formulae, structures, themes, characters and values had to be accessible and recognizable to people from different cultures. (2008, 97)

This kind of polysemy was already noted in 1987 by John Fiske, who positions the polysemic text as a site of (possible) resistance. Buonanno's assessment of the American national audience may account, at least in parts, for the dominance of US television. Her study describes how audiences tend to bring their own national experiences to a text in the process of reception, as also suggested by Kuipers' work and even Netflix' strategy

M. Jenner, *Netflix and the Re-invention of Television*,
https://doi.org/10.1007/978-3-031-39237-5_12

of assimilation to markets. In the context of textual production, however, the importance of exports for the economy of television means that the transnational appeal needs to be coded into the text.

Mihelj notes that different media systems develop their own 'grammars of nationhood', specific aesthetic or narrative norms, but also ways to represent 'good citizenship' along lines of gender, class, ethnicity, race, education or age (2011, 70–92). To use Bourdieu's terms, the 'grammars of nationhood' may be called the representational norms of the *habitus*. Mihelj points to the very real consequences of nations. She defines nationalism as,

> ...both a particular type of discourse and a principle of legitimation. On the one hand, nationalism is an internationally contested vision and division of the world, which sees the social world as fundamentally divided and structured along national lines. On the other hand, nationalism is also a principle of legitimation, which holds that in order to achieve legitimacy, an institution needs to act as a representative of the nation and its interests. (2011, 21)

The grammars of nationhood certainly bring into focus the ways Netflix and other platforms domesticate themselves. Thus, the concept of 'grammars of nationhood' suggests that 'the nation' is something recognisable at the textual level. Yet, this also suggests that Netflix' deliberately transnational texts would feature what may be called a 'grammar of transnationalism', specific textual features that make texts viable in a reciprocal relationship across borders:

> Transnationalism describes a condition in which, despite great distances and notwithstanding the presence of international borders (and all the laws, regulations and national narratives they represent), certain kinds of relationships have been globally intensified and now take place paradoxically in a planet-spanning yet common – however virtual – arena of activity. (Vertovec 2009, location 199)

This chapter focusses specifically on Netflix and how, as transnational broadcaster, it simultaneously evades and conforms to national media systems via its publication model and its in-house productions. The focus on transnationalism as a guiding concept also implies the reciprocity in long-term relations, as Netflix is never just American, but also Japanese, French, Nigerian and so on. In *The Mediated Construction of Reality*,

Couldry and Andreas Hepp argue that they "do not take the borders of 'national societies', whatever their practical importance for various purposes, as 'natural' limits of the social world" (2017, location 730). Though national societies are determined by various social orders, their intersection and contradiction, Couldry and Hepp argue against their primary function and, instead, state that: "Media today play a key role in the proliferating complexity of social ordering, that is, in shaping the possibilities for social order" (ibid., location 737). The authors discuss all media, including social media. Yet, in relation to transnational television, their theory can frame discussions of transnational texts and reception. Couldry and Hepp define the translocal as "relations between localities [that] are intensified with mediatization and globalization" (2017, location 2315). This is similar to the transnationalism Vertovec describes and, thus, emphasises how people from different locations communicate. Nevertheless, this communication is, at least partly, enabled through media texts that illuminate commonalities through specific strategies.

This chapter explores some elements specific to Netflix' transnationalism. This does not mean that they are exclusive to Netflix, but they are structural features of how Netflix positions itself. On the one hand, Netflix' transnationalism is about accessibility and immediacy. Though access to broadband, electricity and computers remains an issue, what is meant here is the time lag between texts' availability across countries. Netflix eliminates this lag (as much as time zones permit) for its self-produced Originals, a significant aspect to make a transnational conversation about texts possible in an age of social media. Another element is the construction of texts that, beyond expressing national sensibilities, also employ strategies that may be understood as a 'grammar of transnationalism'. As argued in Chapter 10, Netflix' texts play an essential role in the way it markets itself, both within the US and across transnational markets. As more transnational streamers have entered the market, it has also become obvious that many organise their transnationalism differently on a textual level and in ways specific to company branding and goals (see, for example, Hunting and Gray 2023). A third aspect discussed here is the way Netflix actively pushes domestication of texts through translation. This is underpinned by a number of theories to conceptualise the immediacy of online publication and Netflix' linkages with social media, Couldry's conceptualisation of a decentred media system and theories of translation. This chapter is also framed by Breidenbach and Zukrigl's concept of the 'dance of cultures'. The strategies of translocal or transnational appeal and alterations made to domesticate texts discussed in the following analysis need to be understood as part of this 'dance'. As such, the transnationalism and domestication of texts are not opposing forces, but both part of Netflix' strategy for appeal across cultures.

National Time and Space: The Binge Model, Social Media and the Schedule

Mihelj notes,

> The modern media, from the early almanacs and newspapers to radio, television and the internet, were closely involved in establishing a national sense of time, and continue to play a central role in imbuing the passage of time with distinct patterns of the day. (2011, 146)

In the case of television, the study of daytime television, particularly soaps, has long pointed to its structuring to integrate into the daily routines of housewives (Modleski 1979; Brunsdon 1981). Silverstone (1994), drawing on Giddens (1991), also points to the ways television is integrated into daily routines (see Chapter 8). These routines are nationally specific in the sense that shopping hours, times when children come home from school, etc., will differ significantly. Additionally, national television schedules are timed differently. For example, prime time will start at different times in different countries, often linked to national specificities, for example when a common dinner time is or when work or school starts the next day (see also Ellis 2000). Mihelj also notes the interruptions of scheduling routines on national holidays. Bielby and Harrington observe the importance of 'middle range factors', such as scheduling, to the success of imported programming (2008, 43–44). In fact, Chalaby argues that a major challenge for transnational broadcasters is time:

> Their schedules are also less time-specific than those of terrestrial television. The programming of national stations is based on the viewing time of a specific territory, broadcasting appropriate genres for clearly defined moments such as daytime and prime time. Global broadcasters might adapt their schedules to local times, but their programming is primarily twenty-four-hour oriented, broadcasting continuous feeds of news, documentaries or music videos. (2005, 8–9)

Netflix disrupts these patterns of 'national time' with the absence of a linear schedule, though it does not do so completely: Netflix publishes new seasons of its most popular series on Fridays, encouraging viewers to binge-watch over the weekend. These Fridays often mark the beginning of national holiday weekends in the US. These are commonly not linked to religious holidays like Christmas or Yom Kippur that may be shared across borders, but often secular national holidays specific to the history of the US, such as President's Day, Memorial Day or Independence Day (or the weekend preceding these holidays).[1] The weekend timing suggests an assumption that viewers anywhere will be available, but such timing also highlights the dominance of the US market in Netflix' consideration. As Mihelj points out, the daily routines of viewers do not necessarily change just because the availability of media forms change, so many viewers may still schedule their 'Netflix time' during prime time. Yet, Netflix arguably engages in no project of 'the nation' through scheduling, at least not outside the US—and even there only in a limited manner compared to the schedules of linear television. Considerations of space and time have long been part of globalisation theory. Specifically, Giddens points to the compression of time and spatial relations through globalisation and communication technologies (1991). Couldry and Hepp argue that compression of time and space cannot necessarily be understood as divided entities. Nevertheless,

> The relative acceleration of digital information transmission means that, rather than actors relying on moving themselves or their objects across space, they may stay in the same place and access information about most things where they are. (2017, location 2784)

Though Netflix eliminates time lags as much as possible, time and place do not become unrelated concepts. Content is released at exactly the same time everywhere, but this means that it may be middle of the night in some places and morning in others (see also Bury 2021). Thus, time and place remain intertwined, simply by the geographical-temporal organisation of the world. Nevertheless, Netflix' publication schedule means

[1] As output has grown over the last few years, only the most popular series are given a release date that corresponds with national holidays. Netflix has also adopted more seasonal genres, particularly the model of Christmas movie, though it primarily produces American ones. As dominant as this genre has become in recent years, it remains an exception.

stepping outside of the structures through which national media systems, particularly television, organise time for viewers. This can be seen as a response to the way communications media, specifically social media, have reorganised time.

Possibly the most striking aspect of Netflix as transnational actor is its publication of content simultaneously worldwide. This publication model is termed the 'binge model', described after the encouraged viewing pattern associated with it (as discussed in Part II). Leaving aside licensed content, it is this aspect of instant availability of new seasons of Netflix' self-produced Originals, that enables the streaming service to challenge established publication models. Netflix seems to respond to viewer demand, even practice. In understanding Netflix' publication models, it is essential to understand how global culture, particularly global exchange on television, has been changed through social media. Non-American viewers often see spoilers on Twitter, Tumblr or other social media sites after new episodes have aired in the US. Rebecca Williams (2004) notes the role of spoilers within fan hierarchies where fans with more knowledge hold more power than those without. In line with this, Perks and Noelle McElrath-Hart (2016) also point to the importance of power within discourses of spoilers for time-shifters. Yet, little attention tends to be paid to time lags in a publication that may put viewers at a disadvantage due to geography and national media systems. In relation to Hulu's use of geoblocking (as discussed in Chapter 6), Elkins argues:

> This is a cultural issue as much as an industrial or political-economic one. Geoblocking sets conditions for who around the world can participate in viewing, sharing, and talking about global television, and which countries the media industries perceive as most valuable—and not simply in economic terms. On the viewer end, encounters with geoblocked platforms can remind us of where we exist within these global hierarchies, and they lay bare the continued salience of geographic borders in digital culture. (2018, 338)

In the case of Hulu, geoblocking works to maintain the national borders of television despite autonomous scheduling. Though this aspect is also significant for Netflix' licensed content (see Lobato 2019), its in-house productions are not geoblocked, enabling a transnational conversation. Much of this can be understood as an effect of media convergence. Henry Jenkins' concept of convergence culture is outlined by him as:

> …the flow of content across multiple media platforms, the cooperation between multiple media industries, and the migratory behaviour of media audiences who will go almost anywhere in search of the kind of entertainment experiences they want. (2006, 3)

Of course, Jenkins means less physical migration of audiences (though this is not excluded) than an ability to access different online spaces. This also means transnational accessibility of content and visibility of fan discussion, tweets, fan fiction, memes, gifs, etc., of content that is aired in other countries. Despite television's role as convergence medium (see Chapter 5), the use of the term here indicates the ways in which Netflix adapts to the requirements of a media world significantly impacted and shaped by the immediacy of social media. In fact, the argument put forth here is that Netflix' publishing model is a direct reaction to the challenges television faces in light of Twitter and other social media. Netflix is hardly the first, or only, broadcaster to recognise and react to problems arising from time lags. As Ward notes, other broadcasters, particularly in the UK, where no translation of US texts is necessary, have long recognised and aimed to work against this: Sky Atlantic has worked from 2011 to allow British viewers to watch new episodes of HBO shows almost at the same time as they aired in the US (2016, 224–6; Lotz and Landgraf 2018). Thus, the way global time lags affect media discourse and may even increase piracy have been recognised by the industry in general and even motivated the development of catch-up services discussed in Chapter 3. Netflix takes full advantage of its own technological condition as online platform, but also its corporate model where simultaneous release does not impede profit or complicate trade with transnational partners.

As discussed in Chapter 14 viewers have generally avoided Netflix' forays into building an experience akin to social media. Nevertheless, the 'binge model' clearly responds to the conditions of time for popular culture in a transnational networked society. Though social media may not be enough to fully explain the 'binge model' it serves to help understand how viewers may perceive its benefits. Nevertheless, it is only one method through which Netflix employs and promotes transnationalism.

A Grammar of Transnationalism

The 'binge model' serves to standardise time for transnational viewers by making texts available at the same time. Yet, this publication model is relatively worthless if texts cannot be shared, in a cultural sense, across borders. Of course, imported texts are hardly new to transnational audiences. Nevertheless, transnational texts—whether imported texts on linear television or Netflix' in-house productions—need to formulate some sort of transnational appeal. Bielby and Harrington discuss four strategies in which content is made more viable for export markets: constructing narratives that decentre programmes away from the nation or culture of origin, forms of storytelling, with an emphasis on serial and series storytelling, attempts to appeal to minority audiences and programming decisions that often privilege international over national revenue. Bielby and Harrington point out that, at the point of their study:

> ...while TV producers do not traditionally create programming solely for the export market, in the current economic climate they are motivated to develop programs and program concepts that speak to *both* local and global audiences. (2008, 89, italics in the original)

Yet, as transnational broadcaster, it is imperative for Netflix to produce texts with a transnational appeal. The transnational market precedes any notions of a national market or the concept of cultural exports. Though all four strategies are employed by Netflix, this study will specifically focus on the first one of these strategies, the way content is created with what Bielby and Harrington call a 'global-local' appeal. Arguably, formulating this transnational appeal is more important to Netflix than to national broadcasters, for which national audiences remain the primary market. This 'grammar of transnationalism'—to invert Mihelj's concept of 'grammars of nationhood'—is heavily influenced by an assumed 'universality' Western cultural value systems claim for themselves, even if this may be marked by Western cultural imperialism and may be understood differently in some regions. As Iwabuchi notes,

> ...the historical process of globalization has not simply produced the Westernization of the world. Its impact on the constitution of the world is much more heterogenous and contradictory. (2002, location 342)

Within these heterogeneous understandings of Western value systems, Netflix, as transnational broadcaster, has to create a transnational appeal. As Netflix' self-produced Originals play an increasingly significant role for the company, these need to successfully formulate their own 'grammar of transnationalism'. Thus, the focus here is necessarily on perceived commonalities rather than differences.

Television has often been accused of playing to 'the lowest common denominator' within a national context. This is not easily translated into a transnational landscape. All of Netflix' self-produced Originals carry traces of 'the nation', meaning the ideology of what constitutes the 'nation', whether they are American or originated elsewhere. Whether through language or cultural specificity, they remain geographically and ideologically bound. Decentred media complicates notions of 'our' history, culture, nation, ethnic group, art, food, etc. These elements remain important. At the same time, Netflix' self-produced Originals also formulate a 'grammar of transnationalism'. Unlike domestic broadcasters that seek domestic appeal first and transnational appeal second, Netflix formulates its transnationalism *from the outset*. Some strategies are considered here through which a 'grammar of transnationalism' expresses this tension between an ideological concept of 'nation' and transnationalism.

One aspect of this is genre. Though 'quality' TV often re-invents or eschews genre, Netflix reliance on algorithms of genre, as discussed in Chapter 8, means that this often does not apply to Netflix. Instead, it often employs genres associated with 'quality' or serious subject matter.[2] Examples of this are political thrillers with *House of Cards*, *Marseille* (Netflix, 2016–18) or *Ingobernable* (Netflix, 2017), that all fall into a notion of 'quality' TV. The Mexican *Club de Cuervos* is a parody of telenovelas and, at once, addresses a Mexican national audience by drawing on the national media history and a transnational audience familiar with Mexican exports. As Mexico is the most dominant exporter of cultural products in Latin America, this market is significant. It also employs a genre associated with 'low culture', but by parodying it positions itself as 'quality' comedy. Another example is the British costume drama *The Crown*, which depicts the reign of British Queen Elisabeth II and her husband Philip, Duke of Edinburgh. Aside from genre, the text also works well as an example of how Netflix disrupts the idea of history as 'ours'.

[2] The sitcoms discussed in Chapter 5 are an exception to this, though they are also more nationally bound than other genres.

The Crown was produced in Britain and features largely British actors. Some of these, such as Helena Bonham Carter or Olivia Cole enjoy international recognisability. The series is, of course, not the first film or TV series that dramatises the life of the British royal family and received international acclaim. In fact, the series' first season relies heavily on the dramatisation of the family in *The King's Speech* (Hooper, 2010), set at the eve of Britain's entry into the Second World War, in its address to a transnational audience. Netflix' decision to produce *The Crown* may also be framed in the context of the international success of *Downton Abbey* (ITV, 2010–5), another period drama that fictionalises twentieth-century British history. As the international success of *Downton Abbey* indicates, British history can sell in transnational territories where British history is not 'our' history. *The Crown* largely reduces political battles to domestic conflicts between wife and husband, sisters or mothers and children. Later seasons frame British history entirely through the perspective of the title-giving Crown, as visible in the depiction of terrorist attacks by the IRA as predominantly attacks on the central family or of Margaret Thatcher's (Gillian Anderson) republican views as threatening the family. This aligns it with D*ownton Abbey* and *The King's Speech*, which often focus on more 'private' concerns over broader political contexts. To relate this analysis back to Couldry, the 'point of origin' for *The Crown* is unclear: a British production, the series was commissioned and is distributed by Netflix. Its narrative often eschews more controversial aspects of British history (in particular in relation to colonialism) in favour of 'the personal', even 'universal'. This suggests that its main concern is not to deal with British history for the sake of the British public, but rather to address the dramatic preferences of a transnational audience that prefers British costume drama. In line with this, the series emphasises the visual spectacle of elaborate sets and costumes. Thus, the series is devised in a manner to make its 'travel' easier. By following conventions of recent British costume dramas, engaging with history without politicising it, genre functions as a central marker of the 'grammar of transnationalism'. Another example of using genre to dramatise history within a 'grammar of transnationalism' comes from the American fantasy drama *Stranger Things* (Netflix, 2016–). The fantasy elements allow the series to avoid discussing American domestic or foreign politics in the 1980s and even provide an opportunity for revisionist gender politics. The series is American and depicts a specific period in American history. Nevertheless, its version of history is decidedly postmodern and often seems more like a reworking of 1980s Hollywood films. *Stand by Me* (Reiner, 1986) or *The Goonies* (Donner, 1985) function as the most obvious reference points. *Stranger Things* presents visual signifiers of the past, particularly technology, and its fantasy and horror elements highlight the hyperreality of the text: producing signifiers without referents in the real world, as suggested by Baudrillard (1994). The text fits neatly into conceptions of postmodern texts, presenting intertextuality and referencing a readily available (Hollywood) cinema history. Through this decentring of history, Netflix neglects constructions of a specifically American history. Thus, the idea of 'our' nation or history is neglected in favour of more transnational (cinema) history, functioning as an example of decentred media. Both, *The Crown* and *Stranger Things* use genre (costume drama and fantasy) to formulate a 'transnational' version of history which often eschews more problematic aspects of each country's history within the era discussed (the end of the British Empire and Reaganism, respectively)—and their international consequences. Both use popular culture as significant reference points, thus often using signs without referents outside of popular culture.

This de-politicisation of history is also linked to the role of nostalgia in Netflix' depiction of the past in a broad variety of its self-produced Originals from *Fuller House* to *Sex Education* to *Bridgerton*. Nostalgia works as a narrative element used in a variety of texts. Svetlana Boym (2001) understands it as a yearning for the past or a mythical place far away. Nostalgia can be viewed in different ways, though a dominant understanding views it as de-politicising engagement with the past and re-writing history, which can be interpreted in various different ways (Lizardi 2015). Yet, there are more positive ways to understand it. For example, as Alex Bevan (2020) understands it, a stylistic means that influences the production design. This is visible in the aesthetics of series that construct a progressive diegetic universe like *Sex Education* (see also Horeck 2021). Thus, the use of nostalgia, as also becomes obvious in Kathryn Pallister's (2019) work on streaming and nostalgia, spans a wide field from aesthetic pleasures (*Sex Education*, *Queen's Gambit* [Netflix, 2020–]) to deliberately a-historical (*Bridgerton*, *The Crown*) and often a-political means of constructing a text (Jenner 2021). The change in the depiction of diversity and the visibility politics discussed in Chapter 10 also work to de-emphasise national history and specificity and support constructing a supposedly 'universal' image of diversity. B. G.-Stolz (2021) also makes this argument in her elaboration of transcultural and Netflix.

In the previous edition of this book, one of the elements of Netflix' grammar of transnationalism discussed were its 'quality' TV aesthetics, influenced by American developments. As Netflix has developed more strategies, one linked issue stands out: the creation of easily identifiable visual signifiers, especially in non-English-language programmes, such as the Korean *Squid Game* and the Spanish *Money Heist*, of which a Korean version also exists, as discussed in the next chapter. The red jumpsuits and Dalí masks of *Money Heist* play an important role here, as do the turquoise jump suits, combined with the often pink background of *Squid Game*. In both cases, it is especially the bold colour schemes that serve as a tool of visual transnational communication. In both cases, visual signifiers of the series can easily be replicated in Halloween costumes, shared on social media and merchandise. In fact, *Squid Game* caused a transnational moral panic when some US schools banned specific games and Halloween Costumes, as reported and the British *BBC* or *The Indian Express*. The German *Spiegel* also reported children playing the games and punishing losers with slaps. Warning letters were sent out to parents across the country. As most of these children will not have seen the series, which is directed at an audience over 18, the visual signifiers of the shows take on new meaning.

Another strategy for a number of Netflix' in-house productions is to appeal to transnational value systems, such as those formulated by the UN in the Human Rights Convention. One of Netflix' earliest in-house dramas, *Orange is the New Black* is an example of this transnational appeal. Set in an American women's prison, the series is often preoccupied with a critique of the US penal system. Another emphasis is how the female characters relate to one another, socially and sexually. The series depicts an all-female community of different ethnicities and cultural backgrounds, largely controlled by male guards, without displaying a female utopia. Considering how invested *Orange is the New Black* is in local issues—from the American penal system to the Black Lives Matter protests—it can be difficult to see why or how this is relevant in a transnational context. Furthermore, its use of expletives and relatively graphic depiction of homosexuality is likely to offend sensibilities in various regions. Nevertheless, the series is invested in a broader project of liberal values—anti-sexist, anti-racist, anti-homophobic—that can resonate in other cultures. Breidenbach and Zukrigl (1998) describe this as a global reference system of values, such as democracy, human rights or feminism, which mark a global culture. Arguably, as the authors further note, none of these terms are unproblematic and mean the same thing everywhere, but they are values that mark Western culture, which attempts to impose them worldwide through a range of supra-national institutions, such as the UN. Elkins argues: "As a tech and entertainment hybrid, Netflix is an avatar for this blend of liberal-but-not-radical cultural politics and deregulatory (neo)liberal economic policies" (2021, 152). The value system is depicted in series like *Orange is the New Black*, but also other series like *Grace and Frankie*, *Chicas Del Cable* (*Cable Girls*, Netflix, 2017–) or *G.L.O.W*. All feature female leads and operate under broadly feminist frameworks. This broad framework also accounts for the importance of cultural differences within texts. As Mihelj notes:

> Global standardization and homogenization, therefore, does not imply an obliteration of difference. To the contrary, [...] globalization requires – and in fact thrives on – differences, but constructs and organizes them in uniform ways. (2011, 29)

Her observation is made in a different context but is nevertheless instructive for the way we can analyse Netflix texts as committed to values that acknowledge and celebrate differences in the context of a value system of liberal humanism.

All of Netflix' texts are simultaneously committed to ideological projects of 'the nation' and transnationalism. While all of these series remain committed to the very broad values of liberal humanism, they also play to nationally specific taste structures of genre, humour, performance style, choice of actors and other elements. These are only a few examples and do not even go near the wide offering on documentaries or US stand-up comedy specials that feature a broad diversity of comedy styles and artists. The series discussed here illuminate the broad variety of strategies used to create Netflix' specific transnational appeal: genre, a version of history that relies heavily on postmodernism, nostalgia, aesthetics, a commitment to liberal humanism feature prominently as part of the 'grammar of transnationalism'. This does not mean that there cannot be differences in cultural understanding on the side of audiences from various backgrounds. Yet, what emerges are individual elements of a 'grammar of transnationalism'. Admittedly, the aspects discussed here are often very broad, but the nature of transnationalism does not allow for more specificity. Thus Netflix' grammar of transnationalism is predominantly concerned with creating a 'universality' that comes at the expense of more explicit political positioning, as also explored in Chapter 10.

Strategies of Domestication

Language is the most common hindrance to any 'grammar of transnationalism'. In linear television, translation often serves as a central strategy for domestication of television and integration of foreign programmes into national media systems. It can also delay broadcasts, as it is one of the alterations to take place before texts can be integrated into national schedules. For Netflix, translation needs to take place before original broadcast, as part of its strategy to be transnational from the outset. Though often ignored in television studies, translation is a central strategy that allows for the easy transport of cultural artefacts across borders and the domestication of texts. Yet, translation studies and television studies are very different fields, the former often concerned with the minute details of language and challenges of providing 'accurate' translation while the latter is preoccupied with the cultural role and broader context of language used in specific texts. The topic is discussed here to highlight its relevance for Netflix as transnational actor. In her study of Italian dubbing, Chiara Francesca Ferrari describes dubbing as 'cultural ventriloquism', suggesting that dubbing is not only translation, but fulfils the function of adaptation into the target culture (2011).

For a transnational broadcaster like Netflix, this 'cultural ventriloquism' becomes highly relevant. Until August 2017, the only dubbing languages available on the platform (in Europe) were Spanish, French, Brazilian Portuguese and Polish with subtitles provided in traditional Chinese and Arabic as well. Dubbing into English for more recent non-English-language texts like *3%*, *Ingobernable* or *Chicas del Cable* were also provided early in 2017. As Netflix had already expanded into many countries in the world, translation programme Hermes was implemented to build a broader client base and offer more languages for dubbing and subtitles. Netflix launched its Hermes programme in early 2017, an open call for translators where anyone can take a translation test and become a freelance translator for Netflix. Steve Dent (2017) uses as a subheading for his article on the website engadget.com: "The 'Hermes' exam ensures 'Yo Mama' isn't translated to 'Yo-Yo Ma.'", pointing to mistakes sometimes made by professional translators in subtitling or captioning software. What is implied is that media fans and their understanding of language could offer more 'accurate' translation. Abhimanyu Ghoshal (2017) points out on thenextweb.com that Netflix is also responding to a lack of registered translators in some of its territories, which would suggest less a desire to standardise production than a response to a lack of qualified personnel. In Kuipers' study, France and the Netherlands emerge as two countries where holding specific qualifications (sometimes state-funded) is more important than in the other two countries she studies. The cited online articles suggest that Netflix relies on amateur translators, but the Hermes test suggests high expectations in terms of translation abilities and skilled use of industry-standard software as well as the ability to work under time pressure. The lack of coverage in more mainstream publications also suggests that Netflix' call for translators was more targeted than a broad call to fans. As such, the translators employed by Netflix cannot be considered amateurs. The Hermes programme may subvert some of the established cultural, industrial and technological norms of various translation cultures but it hardly calls for translators who are not shaped by local translation norms. Kuipers' transnational comparison of different translation industries suggests that norms and conventions are so entrenched within industries and viewing practices that it would hardly be possible to subvert them. For example, Kuipers notes the difference between 'neutral' translation, as common in France and the Netherlands, and the editing in translation to respond to cultural sensibilities, as common in Italy and Poland. In these countries, translation is guided by more regulations than in France and Netherlands:

> The limited autonomy of translation, and more generally the media system, reflect institutional and national trajectories. Both countries have a history of totalitarian rule. In both countries, non-democratic governments [the Mussolini regime and the Soviet regime, respectively] introduced screen translation systems that would allow them to control content. Today, the combined forces of politics, the Catholic Church, and—especially in Italy —the economic field exert a strong influence on media and screen translation. (2015, 1005)

It is difficult to tell how much Netflix could overrule such existing norms, particularly if they are dictated by the state and religious authorities. The 'truly Polish service' and the translation provided in this context suggests some kind of cooperation between the Polish translation industry, the authorities that shape them through formal or informal regulation, and Netflix. This is supported by the fact that Polish was one of the earliest dubbing languages (through voiceover), suggesting that authorities might wish for the kind of censorship that can be provided via translation. Other translation languages available at the time covered vast, often transnational, zones of consumption (such as Spanish or Brazilian Portuguese), so Polish stands out in the absence of dubbing for markets of similar, or larger, size (such as Russian or French).

The process of translation is never straightforward: some words from the source language do not have a direct equivalent in the target language and some culturally specific concepts may not exist in different cultures. Furthermore, translation can be hampered by the technological requirements of dubbing or subtitling. Jan Pedersen also points to the severe restrictions for subtitles set by the assumed reading speeds of viewers:

> As an extreme example, the character Vicky Pollard [Matt Lucas] in the sitcom *Little Britain* [BBC, 2003-6] produced an utterance consisting (when transcribed) of 216 characters in 5 seconds, which was then subtitled using only 58 characters, a condensation of 73%. This is quite clearly exceptionally high, but a condensation rate of about a third is well attested. (2010, 70)

Pedersen goes on to point to the need to balance these constraints with possible interventions in cases where more explanation of cultural specificities is required. As also argued by Kuipers (2015), translators work with an assumption of audiences' cultural knowledge of the source texts' country of origin. It may be easier to make these assumptions about cultural literacy if audiences are more likely to watch a lot of content from this country. Considering the dominance of American texts in Western markets, there may be less need to intervene than in Chinese texts. Though translators may receive feedback from audiences, this profession seems to make a lot of assumptions about the need for 'cultural translation' guided by norms and regulations of the industry in different countries (Kuipers 2015). Audiences are also likely to be 'shaped' by these practices insofar as their expectations of which cultural specificities need translation and which do not will be based on their experiences of translations of other texts.

Netflix currently dubs its in-house productions into a number of languages. Rucío Baños argues that,

> ...due to the specific constraints and characteristics of dubbing, we will never be able to bring the language of dubbing to the same level as that of domestic products or spontaneous conversation. Nevertheless, audiovisual translators working in the dubbing industry should be familiar with the complex nature of fictional dialogue and the principals governing scriptwriting. They should therefore understand that the orality of original dialogues is pretended or false and that, due to many factors that govern the dubbing process, the orality of dubbed dialogues will be more artificial. (2014, 91)

Baños argues that dubbing adds a layer of artificiality to an already fictional or 'artificial' text. Yet, dubbing as an adaptive practice where a layer of 'artificiality' is added does not necessarily problematise the artistic integrity of a text. Most audio-visual media are products of communal processes, and it can be argued that no 'pure' version of a text can exist. This is particularly true for television texts and the flow of the linear television schedule or even the insulated flow on streaming platforms, as discussed in Part II. In some instances of dubbing, the artistic integrity of a script can even be re-established, for example in cases where performances may be lacking. For example, Kevin Costner's and Christian Slater's inaccurate British accents in *Robin Hood: Prince of Thieves* (Reynolds, 1991) can be 'neutralised' by dubbing where differences in accents can be resolved quite easily. Irene Ranzanto (2010) points to the issues translators are faced with when confronting accents. Dubbing can either 'naturalise' accents by changing them to something less associated with class or specific national culture of the source culture, or it can find an accent in the translation language that carries similar associations. The problems inherent in both are obvious, one failing to acknowledge specific cultural characteristics of the source culture, the other meaning that translators reinforce prejudices and stereotypes that exist in their own culture. Ferrari argues that, on Italian television in the 1990s, general tendencies for whitewashing also manifested themselves in dubbing and translation "in the modification or complete erasure of ethnic differences, which are usually domesticated or reconstructed according to stereotypical and familiar national narratives" (2011, 19). Ferrari's study of Italian dubbing practices offers a detailed overview of strategies of domestication at play within a specific national context. Baños is particularly focussed on screenwriting and the task of writing 'natural' dialogue and dubbing performances may do greater justice to the written text in the script than performances in the source text. Emilio Audissino notes how in the Italian dubbing of Marilyn Monroe in her post-1956 films:

> ...Marilyn's tender lisp and breathy voice were replaced by Rosetta Calavetta's blaring high-pitched tone and over-excited performance. In Italy, Marilyn's characters sound giddier than they actually are. In the Italian version of *Let's Make Love* (Cukor, 1960), Marilyn's character is even given a lower level of education. (2014, 105)

As much as Audissino problematises this intervention, questions can be raised about norms of 'attractiveness' in women in Italy in the 1950s and 60s, which might inform such an intervention. Kuipers observes that translation practices in the Italian dubbing industry do not aim for an exact translation but follow the principle of 'dubbing from the heart', as one of the dubbing actors calls it (2015, 998). In this, the Italian system differs from the French and Dutch systems, which aim to offer more 'neutral' translation. Kuipers also notes that dubbing in French or Italian often means that translators change jokes where they do not translate, either linguistically or culturally. In other words, the cultural ventriloquism Ferrari mentions is routinely performed. These interventions may also add a different layer of 'artificiality', but ultimately work to domesticate a text. Thus, the process of domestication may go far beyond written text to include cultural norms and (often problematic) *habitus*. Thus, texts are not only adapted to a target language, but also to a target culture. This becomes a problem in discussing Netflix as its translation is more directed towards broad zones of consumption of Spanish or French-speaking nations, rather than nation-states. In other words, Colombia and Spain or France and Haiti may share an official language, but not the same national culture. Yet, it also needs to be emphasised that dubbing is an expensive process that requires the hiring of additional voice actors. Dubbing has traditionally even been a reason for lags in distribution in different markets, as time needs to be made for translation and dubbing. Dubbing provides a way for Netflix to be domesticated into national cultures through its quality of cultural ventriloquism, which is heightened in comparison to subtitles. The changes made to original texts through dubbing carry markers of how much Netflix texts are changed as it integrates into national media systems. In the course of this integration, Netflix tends to imitate and adopt power structures inherent in global media systems as well as within 'the nation'.

For Netflix to expand its transnational subscriber base, it is essential to provide options to domesticate texts. Translation is an essential aspect to it, particularly as linear television imports, such as HBO, provide this. Translation as a strategy to domesticate texts is an important element of the 'dance of cultures' where texts are modified to fit target cultures. The struggles, cultural norms, policies and regulations in place to govern and shape translation play a significant role in the resistances and integration at play in cultural exchange.

Conclusion

This chapter explored how Netflix negotiates its position as transnational broadcaster within national media systems through texts. A central aspect of this is Netflix' role within a decentred media system. Thus, this chapter conceptualised Netflix in the context of its publication model and its reduction of a time lag in transnational publication of its texts. This aspect is important as it deals with the way texts are presented in its transnational context. The chapter then moved on to consider how Netflix texts negotiate the transnational and the national. Thus, it considered the idea of a broad 'grammar of transnationalism' and domestication, which Netflix provides through translation. Transnationalism and the domestication of texts or their integration into national media systems are not contradictory, or even opposing, strategies. A text that employs a 'grammar of transnationalism' can be translated and integrated into existing cultural conditions of a national media system. Netflix' ability to integrate into these systems rather than overhaul them, adapt some of their strategies while neglecting others, indicates that it does not directly challenge existing power structures within these systems. Its compliance with regulations and norms of media systems also indicates its inability to wrestle control away from existing media systems.

Netflix should be viewed through the concept of a decentred media system. Where, traditionally, texts were produced for domestic markets and then altered for broadcast as imports, Netflix' self-produced Originals are produced with a desired transnational appeal in mind. Thus, they are thought of as transnational from the outset. This leads to an adoption of a 'grammar of transnationalism'. This transnational appeal can lie predominantly within a specific territory or beyond this. Yet, no texts are predominantly devised for a specific national context. This does not mean that 'the nation' is not invoked. It is impossible to escape the ideology that shapes 'the nation'. Furthermore, texts are domesticated in national media systems. In other words, translation can provide a way for Netflix to integrate into national media systems—or at least the most dominant cultures among those with a shared language (Spain, Germany, France, etc.). What this makes visible is also the 'dance of cultures' performed by media texts.

Bibliography

Audissino, Emilio. 2014. "Dubbing as Formal Interference: Reflections and Examples." In Dror Abend-David (ed.), *Media and Translation: An Interdisciplinary Approach*, 97–118. New York: Bloomsbury.

Baños, Rucío. 2014. "Insights into the False Orality of Dubbed Fictional Dialogue and the Fiction of Dubbing." In Dror Abend-David (ed.), *Media and Translation: An Interdisciplinary Approach*, 75–96. New York: Bloomsbury.

Baudrillard, Jean. 1994. *Simulacra and Simulation*. Ann Arbor: University of Michigan Press.

BBC News. 2021. "Netflix Squid Game Schools Warning Sent to Parents." BBC News. Available at: https://www.bbc.com/news/uk-england-beds-bucks-herts-58958698. Accessed: 03.03.2021.

Bevan, A. 2020. *The Aesthetics of Nostalgia TV: Production Design and the Boomer Era*. New York: Bloomsbury Academic.

Bielby, Denise D., and C. Lee Harrington. 2008. *Global TV: Exporting Television and Culture in the World Market*. New York: New York University Press.

Boym, S. 2001. *The Future of Nostalgia*. New York: Basic Books.

Breidenbach, Joana, and Ina Zukrigl. 1998. *Tanz Der Kulturen: Kulturelle Identität in Einer Globalisierten Welt*. München: Kunstmann.

Brunsdon, Charlotte. 1981. "'Crossroads': Notes on Soap Opera." *Screen* 22 (4): 32–37.

Buonanno, Milly. 2008. *The Age of Television Experiences and Theories*. Bristol: Intellect.

Bury, R. 2021, "'A Small Christmas to Me': A Study of Binge-Watching and Fa Engagement on Reddit." In M. Jenner (ed.), *Binge-Watching and Contemporary Television Studies*, 40–58. Edinburgh: Edinburgh University Press.

Chalaby, Jean K. 2005. "Towards an Understanding of Media Transnationalism." In Jean K. Chalaby (ed.), *Transnational Television Worldwide: Towards a New Media Order*, 1–13. London: I. B. Tauris.

———. 2009. *Transnational Television in Europe: Reconfiguring Global Communications Networks*. London: I.B.Tauris.

Couldry, Nick. 2012. *Media, Society, World: Social Theory and Digital Media Practice*. Cambridge: Polity.

——— and Andreas Hepp. 2017. *The Mediated Construction of Reality*. Cambridge, UK and Malden, MA: Polity Press.

Creeber, Glen. 2015. "Killing Us Softly: Investigating the Aesthetics, Philosophy and Influence of Nordic Noir Television." *Journal of Popular Television* 3 (1): 21–35.

Dent, Steve. 2017. "Netflix Has a New Translation Test to Avoid Subtitle Fails." *Engadget.Com*. Available online: https://www.engadget.com/2017/03/31/netflix-has-a-new-translation-test-to-avoid-subtitle-fails/. Accessed: 08.08.2017.

Ellis, John. 2000. *Seeing Things: Television in the Age of Uncertainty*. London: I.B. Tauris.

Elkins, Evans. 2018. "Geoblocking National TV in an on-Demand Era." In Derek Johnson (ed.), *From Networks to Netflix: A Guide to Changing Channels*, 333–42. London: Routledge.

Elkins, E. 2021. "Streaming Diplomacy: Netflix's Domestic Politics and Foreign Policy." In D.Y. Jin (ed.), *The Routledge Handbook of Digital Media and Globalization*, 150–7. London: Routledge.

Explained Desk. 2021. "Explained: Why Several New York Schools Are Banning Squid Game-Themed Halloween Costumes." *The Indian Express*. Available at: https://indianexpress.com/article/explained/why-new-york-schools-are-banning-squid-game-themed-halloween-costumes-7599126/. Accessed: 03.03.2023.

Ferrari, Chiara. 2011. *Since When Is Fran Drescher Jewish?: Dubbing Stereotypes in the Nanny, the Simpsons, and the Sopranos*. Austin: University of Texas Press.

Fiske, John. 1987. *Television Culture*. London: Methuen.

G.-Stolz, B. 2021. "National, Transnational, Transcultural Media: Netflix—The Culture-Binge." In M. Jenner (ed.), *Binge-Watching and Contemporary Television Studies*, 145–61. Edinburgh: Edinburgh University Press.

Ghoshal, Abhimanyu. 2017. "Netflix Wants to Pay You to Translate Subtitles." *Thenextweb.Com*. Available online: https://thenextweb.com/apps/2017/03/31/netflix-wants-to-pay-you-to-translate-subtitles/. Accessed: 08.08.2017.

Giddens, Anthony. 1991. *Modernity and Self-Identity: Self and Society in the Late Modern Age*. Cambridge: Polity.

Horeck, T. 2021. "Better Worlds: Queer Pedagogy and Utopia in Sex Education and Schitt's Creek." *Jump Cut* 60.

Hunting, K., and J. Gray. 2023. "Disney+. Imagining Industrial Intertextuality." In D. Johnson (ed.), *From Networks to Netflix. A Guide to Changing Channels. Second Edition*, 650–67. New York: Routledge.

Iwabuchi, Koichi. 2002. *Recentering Globalization: Popular Culture and Japanese Transnationalism*. Durham: Duke University Press.

———. 2015. *Resilient Borders and Cultural Diversity: Internationalism, Brand Nationalism, and Multiculturalism in Japan*. Lanham, MD: Lexington Books.

Jenkins, Henry. 2006. *Convergence Culture: Where Old and New Media Collide*. New York: New York University Press.

Jenner, M. 2021. "Netflix, Nostalgia and Transnational Television." *Journal of Popular Television* 9 (3): 301–5.

Kuipers, Gieselinde. 2015. "How National Institutions Mediate the Global: Screen Translation, Institutional Interdependencies, and the Production of National Difference in Four European Countries." *American Sociological Review* 80 (5): 985–1013.

Lizardi, R. 2015. *Mediated Nostalgia: Individual Memory and Contemporary Mass Media*. London: Lexington Books.

Lobato, R. 2019. *Netflix Nations: The Geography of Digital Distribution*. New York: New York University Press.

Lotz, A. D. and Landgraf, J. 2018. *We now Disrupt this Broadcast: How Cable Transformed Television and the Internet Revolutionized it All*. Cambridge, Massachusetts: The MIT Press.

Mihelj, Sabina. 2011. *Media Nations: Communicating Belonging and Exclusion in the Modern World*. Basingstoke: Palgrave Macmillan.

Modleski, Tania. 1979. "The Search for Tomorrow in Today's Soap Operas: Notes on a Feminine Narrative Form." *Film Quarterly* 33 (1): 12–21.

Pallister, K. 2019. *Netflix Nostalgia: Streaming the Past on Demand*. Lanham: Lexington Books.

Pedersen, Jan. 2010. "When do You Go for Benevolent Intervention? How Subtitlers Determine the Need for Cultural Mediation." In Anna Matamala, Joselia Neves, and Jose Diaz Cintas (eds.), *New Insights into Audiovisual Translation and Media Accessibility Media for All 2*, 67–80. Amsterdam: Editions Rodopi.

Perks, Lisa Glebatis, and N. McElrath-Hart. 2016. "Spoiler Definitions and Behaviors in the Post-Network Era." *Convergence: The International Journal of Research into New Media Technologies* 1–15.

Ranzanto, Irene. 2010. "Localising Cockney: Translating Dialogue into Italian." In Anna Matamala, Joselia Neves, and Jose Diaz Cintas (eds.), *New Insights into Audiovisual Translation and Media Accessibility Media for All 2*, 109–22. Amsterdam: Editions Rodopi.

Spiegel Online. 2021. *Ohrfeigen statt Schüsse: »Squid Game« auf deutschen Pausenhöfen.* Available at: https://www.spiegel.de/panorama/bildung/squid-game-schuelerinnen-und-schueler-ahmen-spiele-aus-netflix-serie-nach-und-ohrfeigen-sich-a-de7013bb-d2ec-4304-8fbb-2d3519732234. Accessed: 03.03.2023.

Silverstone, Roger. 1994. *Television and Everyday Life*. London: Routledge.

Vertovec, Steven. 2009. *Transnationalism.* London: Routledge.

Ward, Sam. 2016. "Streaming Trans-Atlantic: Netflix, Imported Drama and the British Digital Television Ecology." In Kevin McDonald and Daniel Smith-Rowsey (eds.), *The Netflix Effect: Technology and Entertainment in the 21st Century*, 219–34. New York: Bloomsbury.

Williams, Rebecca. 2004. "It's About Power': Spoilers and Fan Hierarchy in On-Line Buffy Fandom." *Slayage: The On-Line International Journal of Buffy Studies*: 11–12.

Television

3% (2016–), BR: Netflix.
Bridgerton (2019–), USA: Netflix.
Chicas Del Cable (Cable Girls, 2017-), ES: Netflix.
Club de Cuervos (2015–), MX: Netflix.
Crown, The (2016–), UK: Netflix.
Doctor Who (1963–89, 2005–), UK: BBC.
Downton Abbey (2010–5), UK: ITV.
GLOW (2017–), USA: Netflix.
Grace and Frankie (2015–), USA: Netflix.
House of Cards (2013–), USA: Netflix.
Ingobernable (2017–), MX: Netflix.
Little Britain (2003–6), UK: BBC.
Mad Men (2007–14), USA: AMC.
Marseille (2016–), FR: Netflix.
Queen's Gambit (2020–), USA: Netflix.
OA, The (2016–), USA: Netflix.
Ozark (2017–), USA: Netflix.
Sex Education (2019–), UK: Netflix.
Squid Game (2021–), KR: Netflix.
Stranger Things (2016–), USA: Netflix.

Film

Cukor, G. (1960) *Let's Make Love*. USA: Jerry Wald Productions.
Donner, R. (1985) *The Goonies*. USA: Warner Bros.
Hooper, T. (2010) *The King's Speech*. UK: SeeSaw Films.
Reiner, R. (1986) *Stand By Me*. USA: Columbia Picture.
Reynolds, K. (1991) *Robin Hood: Prince of Thieves*. USA: Warner Bros.
Ritchie, G. (2011) *Sherlock Holmes: A Game of Shadows*. USA: Warner Bros.

CHAPTER 13

Transnationalising the Franchise

This chapter follows on from the discussion of textual strategies of transnationalism and domestication in the last chapter to conceptualise the way transnational streaming draws on and confuses concepts like franchises, formats and adaptations. Especially format and franchise are industry terms and concepts that organise trade, but, on a different level, they also establish connections for viewers between different texts. These connections can be both, transnational or national, but importantly, different characters, functions or storylines are recognisable beyond channels, production companies and/or borders. This chapter aims to explore these ties between Netflix texts. Further, this chapter looks at how these networks of meaning function in the broader transnational Netflix ecosystem. Though the focus stays on Netflix, it is worth looking outward and placing the platform in context and relationship with other streamers and the way they understand and build on established systems of transnational television. Thus, the chapter emphasises Netflix' *Criminal* and *Money Heist*, as well as Amazon's *LOL: Last One Laughing*. The example of *LOL* serves on the one hand, to offer a comparison, and on the other, to elucidate how different streaming services have different organisational strategies to integrate themselves into national media systems both, on a textual, and industry level. It is important to note that Disney+ especially, seeks to implement similar structures with its reliance on universe and world building. As Hunting and Gray (2023) show, this strategy has

M. Jenner, *Netflix and the Re-invention of Television*,
https://doi.org/10.1007/978-3-031-39237-5_13

a long history for Disney, especially in its children's programming. For Netflix and Amazon, which both look back at a much shorter company history, these webs of meaning are deliberately transnational with texts produced in and for specific global markets, especially in the case of *LOL*.

Criminal is a crime series set in an interrogation room, which deals with the interrogation of a suspect or witness by police. There are different versions (British, French, German and Spanish), which are adapted to different cultural contexts while still constructed to speak to a transnational audience, as explored later on. The UK version was released on 16 September 2019 and the German, Spanish and French versions on 20 September 2019, indicating they were conceived together. With *Criminal* there isn't one central series where other versions can be understood as spin-offs. The British version was only published a few days before the other series and while this indicates that it was meant to create buzz the other versions can capitalise on, the other versions cannot be viewed as transnational adaptation, as common for fictional formats. A model to conceptualise these series is provided by franchises. Franchises do operate *internal* to a TV channel or streamer. Most commonly, there is one central series, as, for example with the popular franchises *CSI* or *NCIS* and in both cases, other series in the franchise features the original title and the different setting (Miami, New York, Los Angeles, New Orleans, Hawai'i), as with all versions of *Criminal* (*Criminal: UK*, *Criminal: Spain*, *Criminal: Germany* and *Criminal: France*). *Criminal* had little success, despite featuring major national stars. Only the UK version had a second season, the German, French and Spanish versions all have only three episodes. Despite this, I want to consider this as a way to understand how Netflix aims to integrate into media systems—in this case a transnational European one—and expand on existing models.

Meanwhile, *Money Heist* and *Money Heist: Korea—Joint Economic Area* follow the traditional franchise model more closely. *Money Heist* is a Spanish series originally produced for the channel Antena 3 Televisión and then continued by Netflix in 2018. In 2022, one year after the finale of the Spanish series, *Money Heist: Korea—Joint Economic Area* was published. The series sit somewhere between franchise and adaptation as similar storylines are repeated, but the titling model is familiar from other franchises. The most marked visual signifiers, the red jumpsuits and Dalí masks featured in the original series, are repeated as well, functioning both as part of a visual grammar of transnationalism and to tie the series together.

LOL on Amazon is a competition show where some of the most famous local comedians compete not to laugh at each other, with the last person to laugh to win the competition. Humour can be deeply nationally specific and the *LOL* franchise uses this by emphasising national comedy cultures through well-established and popular comedians. At the time of writing there are a Canadian (1 season), Brazilian (1 season), Indian (1 season), Australian (1 season), Colombian (1 season), Nigerian (1 season), Dutch (1 season), Polish (1 season), Argentinian (1 season), South African (1 season), French (1season), Spanish (2 seasons), Italian (2 seasons), German (4 seasons) and Mexican (5 seasons) version, though more may come out before the book is published. Humour and the celebrity comedians that carry *LOL* are variable, finely tuned to specific cultures and cultural moments and, thus, nationally specific. Of course, viewers can watch what, to them, is a foreign version of the format, but it is not necessarily produced *for* them. This means that they often don't have the cultural knowledge (such as knowledge about career and star personas of established comedians, or the cultural reference points comedians draw on) to decode the text. For example, three seasons of the German *LOL* (Amazon, 2021–) feature Anke Engelke, a comedian and actress who has been a steady presence in German popular culture since the mid-1990s. Audiences knowledgeable about German popular culture will be familiar with her and her work with other contestants, which creates its own draw for the series and an incentive to watch. Audiences to whom she is 'foreign' in a geographic and, more importantly, cultural sense will need to find other incentives. The target audience is a deeply nationalised one, as also indicated by the lack of dubbing.

In this chapter, I first want to draw attention to the various ways streamers are adapting established models of television trade by looking at the model of the format and the franchise and in what ways they structure how different streamers act. As much as Netflix and the various versions of *Criminal* and *Money Heist* are the focus here, I also want to draw attention to the way Amazon organises transnational TV with *LOL*. This is to highlight that different streamers often act differently in transnational markets, but also in their use of existing industrial and cultural infrastructures. This should not be understood as a 'hard' line of separation. Indeed, in the transnational publication of its American series (*The Marvellous Mrs. Maisel* [Amazon 2017–], *The Boys* [Amazon, 2019–]), Amazon acts similarly to Netflix or other streamers. Yet, *LOL* acts as an important example in localisation on Amazon.

These different examples show a complex picture of transnational television and streaming, which often draws on established models of transnational television production, distribution and culture. As this chapter will show, streaming acts in many ways within the infrastructures of transnational (linear) television. And still, it can never be mapped onto these structures precisely. In other words, *LOL* is like a format, but not quite; *Criminal* and *Money Heist* in many respects act like a franchise, but not quite like it. A deciding factor that determines the 'not quite' nature of these models is access points. These are individual platforms, which, as pointed out in the Introduction to the Second Edition both, function akin to channels, but also a whole 'television', which makes them an important feature of transnational streaming infrastructures. But they are also further determined by publication dates or production cultures. I use the term 'transnational streaming franchise' here to describe Netflix's use of the franchise and to capture the 'not quite'-ness of the way streaming properties fit into this model. In conceptualising the 'transnational streaming franchise' on Netflix, this chapter first establishes different concepts in television trade. It then explores textual links and, in a last step, draws attention to the way dubbing furthers these linkages. Thus, the focus is less on the questions of how television trade functions and more on the textual networks Netflix establishes beyond systems of TV trade. This is linked to systems of domestication and transnationalism. Even though the chapter includes a comparison with Amazon, this is mostly to point to the way Netflix constructs a 'textual transnationalism' that is specific to it and activates meanings distinct to it.

Formats and Franchises

This section aims to carve out the 'not quite'-ness of the ways streamers organise linked series. While I use the industry trade terms format and franchise, I am more interested in the way these organise networks of texts to create meaning. Transnationalism in contemporary television has received much attention, mostly for linear television. In many respects, at least part of Amazon behaves in similar ways as channels like MTV or Al Jazeera (see Chalaby 2005) with different channels providing integration into national markets, offering various localised versions of the *LOL* format. While I focus here on *LOL*, Amazon organises other franchises in a similar manner, such as its *Modern Love* franchise. This is, of course, in addition to its rental service of digital video, sale or licensing of content, which remain primary functions. Over the last two decades, the format trade has dominated the business of transnational television. As Chalaby argues in 2013:

> In an age of fierce competition, TV formats enable broadcasters to offer local programming – always the audience favourite—whilst managing risk (with the knowledge that the same concept has a proven track record in other markets) and driving down costs (through the progressive refinement of the production model). (2013, 54)

Yet, importantly, he also points to some textual elements and the way local and global are mixed. At its most basic level, a format is a TV programme that can be easily boiled down to identifiable narrative and visual features. Formats provide cornerstones of the narrative, but these are likely to develop differently in each version. For example, Snookie on *Jersey Shore* (MTV, 2009–12) gets drunk in the pilot episode, similar to Holly (who would soon leave the house) on *Geordie Shore* (MTV, 2011–22). The difference, however, lies in how housemates react, the American ones leaving her to fend for herself while the British housemates, especially women, care for Holly. Thus, the global is provided by the cornerstones of the narrative (basic narrative premise, events and branding), but the local lies in the way the story develops, such as the reactions to a young drunk woman.[1] As Chalaby and Andrea Esser note:

> A format (or part of it) can be called global, not because it travels to every single country, but because its IP [Intellectual Property] definers - structure and brand attributes - will be replicated everywhere it goes. For instance, *The Great Bake Off* (2010) has only travelled to two dozen territories so far but, wherever it goes, the future local versions will all include a tent, judges with baking credentials, at least three challenges (the Signature Bake, Technical Bake, and Showstopper Bake), a star baker, and a story driven by the elimination process. (2017, 4)

In other words, while formats describe a trade 'unit', they are also marked by common textual features. Esser also summarises the history and use of the format:

[1] Legal drinking age differs between the US and the UK and Snookie in the US version was under age, meaning that there are also differences in legal framing.

> The ongoing growth and commercialization of the TV sector globally boosted the demand for formats throughout the first two decades of the new millennium. Competition for both content and audiences rose steadily. Format acquisition was cost effective and enabled speedy production as the show was already fully developed and came with detailed production guidelines. Moreover, the latter meant that buyers benefitted from knowledge transfer. This was attractive for new, popular genres like sitcoms and soap operas in the 1990s, and lifestyle and reality TV in the 2000s. (2022, 352)

Notably, formats structure transnational television and shared global television culture.

It is clear how *LOL* fits into this system: sharing names, basic narrative premise and branding (including the Amazon sites) but providing something culturally specific through local comedians. It is not even particularly extraordinary that all versions are available on the same platform, as reality TV is often featured in different regional (different US cities *The Real Housewives* format) and national versions on the same platform in times of transnational streaming. Considering Amazon's localised access points (amazon.au, amazon.fr, amazon.co.uk, etc.) and structure, a further level of localisation is added. What is different, however, is that the transnational format trade usually involves a level of localisation beyond the programme itself: the integration into local television, television schedules and national time. Amazon relies on already being integrated into national culture via its other businesses as recognisable brand name. This also foregrounds that Amazon is its own transnational company first and can only be understood as streamer second. Localisation serves to bind viewers to the brand, but also is a significant part of Amazon's business structure. Yet, if this was the only motivation, Amazon could license local content (which it already does) rather than produce local formats. Of course, the markets covered are of strategic relevance (Mexico, Australia, Brazil, etc.), in size and as producers of transnational content. Yet, despite Amazon's structure into localised access points, all versions are available on each national site, allowing viewers to consume all versions (though Amazon's algorithm does not recommend them and, indeed, different versions can be difficult to find). This is not common for format trade: in some countries, local versions may run alongside 'foreign' ones (such as *Jersey Shore* and *Geordie Shore*), but these decisions are made by national broadcasters, not the production company. Amazon as producing streamer adds a further connection between texts that produces meaning in a way that companies like Endemol, a major player in the field of format trade, do not. Of course, localisation in all forms serves Amazon's goals, but also highlights the ways in which the company has its own strategies, infrastructures and incentives as streamer. The example of *LOL* is used here, on the one hand, to clarify some of the ways streamers differ from each other, also in their transnational production. Structures and goals of Amazon determine how it integrates itself transnationally. On the other hand, it also shows how streamers adapt to established flows of transnational television.

Lobato highlights in the Conclusion to *Netflix Nations*:

> Netflix is not the same service worldwide: catalogues, language options, and platform features change when accessed from different countries. Looking forward, the general trend is toward more differentiation rather than less, because of increasing regulatory pressure for Netflix to behave differently in different countries. (2019, 184)

As I have already made clear, the Netflix platform as a common access point where border crossing is not made as clear as with Amazon, is highly relevant. Netflix has to submit to the same regulatory and legal pressures as Amazon, but the access point remains the same, while that for Amazon differs with different Amazon websites or complicated procedures to change what bought content can be accessed through the app. Further, most interface features do remain the same. As much as we have seen standardisation in production over the last few years, media policy remains a varied field, dictating different behaviours.

Money Heist is originally a Spanish series, which has also been adapted to a Korean context. In many respects, this is similar to the way *The Office* and *Ugly Betty* have 'travelled' around the world via national adaptations. The main difference, however, is that rather than being condensed to formats and sold, these franchises exist in different versions on their 'home' streaming service, meaning Netflix. At first sight, this is similar to the way transnational channels like MTV used their infrastructure to adapt formats from one market to another. The main difference, however, is that on streaming, all versions are available to a transnational audience. On Netflix, however, the access point remains the same. Unlike with Amazon, different versions are recommended to the same viewers, no matter their local preferences and the series are both domesticated via dubbing and the grammar of transnationalism, thus creating a system where the texts are tied closely together. Audiences are invited to compare versions and create new meanings, or to re-experience a familiar text in a different way, thus playing on the importance of repetition in binge-watching.

Discussing Korean media in a global media landscape, Ju Oak Kim explores the so-called 'Korean Wave', which started in the 1990s:

> I propose that the Korean Wave opened up its third phase in the late 2010s; Korean popular content, including television formats, original series, films, and K-pop, has penetrated the mainstream US media industries. During its second phase, Korean media products went beyond the Asian region with the support of online media platforms. While media scholars considered the Korean Wave as a global phenomenon during its second phase, the Korean Wave was still one of the subcultures that specific fans of various societies consumed. However, the new phase of the cultural phenomenon has been promoted by industrial practices through which US major networks and streaming services have become proactive in securing the transnational flow of Korean media content. (2021, 80)

Thus, *Money Heist: Korea—Joint Economic Area* stands in context, not only of various Korean Netflix films and the general transnational appreciation for, and mainstreaming of, Korean media, as evidenced by Bong Joon-ho's Best Film Oscar for *Parasite* (Joon-ho, 2019). For Netflix series, the context is transnationally successful series like *Squid Game* and *All of Us Are Dead* (Netflix, 2022–), both graphically violent Korean horror series. In fact, even before these series became available, Kim argues that Netflix had "accelerated changes in the landscape of the US media industry by making direct investments in Korean production companies" (2021, 79). *Money Heist: Korea—Joint Economic Area* is a relatively straightforward adaptation of the Spanish series, repeating many structural features like character names (or codenames), costumes and basic storylines. However, the Korean version is set in the near future with a reunited Korea, shortly before a joint currency is introduced. In line with Netflix' grammar of transnationalism, the series discusses localised issues in a way that build on more transnational themes. Thus, the theme of financial hardship and economic depression is already familiar from both, *Parasite* and *Squid Game*. As much as this is a futuristic setting, many story elements hark back to discussions around communism and neoliberal capitalism, which dominate transnational economic discussion frequently. Topics linked to the North Korean dictatorship are usually avoided, so that the series never becomes entrenched in nationally, historically and politically specific debates a transnational audience may not be familiar with. The anticapitalistic themes that only emerge slowly in the Spanish series, are made explicit from the start in the Korean version, largely due to the negotiation of North and South Korean ideologies. While the Korean series is an adaptation, its argument is modified and adapted to a changed cultural context, with Netflix's grammar of transnationalism in mind. Several storylines are also modified, though character functions are similar. The role of Netflix as platform and common access point also means that both series are marketed as connected: the recommendation algorithm links both series and dubbing domesticates them. The series fit into what Michelle Hilmes (2012) calls 'creative adaptations' where an original series is adapted to a different national context. Partly because the *Money Heist* property remains solidly in Netflix's hands, taken together, both series follow the franchise logic. In the same way, *CSI: Crime Scene Investigation* (CBS, 2000–15) and *CSI: Miami* (2002–12) are structurally the same, though stories are influenced by their setting, *Money Heist* and *Money Heist: Korea* are structurally similar, but stories are changed according to cultural context. But beyond the story, both texts are tied together via a branding infrastructure, algorithmic recommendation and tagging and the platform as structuring force and access point. As the Spanish version of *Money Heist* was concluded before the Korean version was published, Netflix clearly built on a long-running success, which makes the two series more akin to the CBS franchises and less to *Criminal*.

Criminal can be read as an attempt to fit into the wider infrastructures of European television but was much less successful than European coproductions via PSBs. Netflix's self-produced Originals are all transnational series, and there are many series from non-English-language markets. Its short-lived experiment with *Criminal*, however, stands out. The four series are not narratively linked or are adaptations of each other in the sense that they tell the same story. The setting in a police building is the same in all versions, though this building is located in a different European city, depending on version (London, Madrid, Paris, Berlin). Netflix' spirit of standardisation in production becomes highly visible here, as it provides a visual framework, but lets local producers fill in the rest: city, characters and architecture. *Criminal* is both, separate entities *(Criminal: Germany*; *Criminal: Spain*; *Criminal: UK* and *Criminal: France*) but also linked, as the algorithm automatically recommends another version if a viewer watches one. Additionally, dubbing is provided for all versions, with the English dubbing with a British accent. It is easy to see the different series' potential to develop storylines together, though only the British version was continued beyond a three-episode first season. At the same time, *Criminal* shows how the logic of the series franchise is mixed with the logic of the format as transnational strategy for Netflix.

Franchises are possibly best known from US broadcaster CBS's *CSI* (*CSI: Crime Scene Investigations*; *CSI: Miami*; *CSI: NY* [CBS, 2004–13]; *CSI: Cyber* [CBS, 2015–16]) and *NCIS* (*NCIS: Naval Investigative Service* [CBS, 2003–]; *NCIS: Los Angeles* [CBS, 2009–]; *NCIS: New Orleans* [2014–21]; *NCIS: Hawai'i* [CBS, 2021–]) franchises. Importantly, the franchise is an intra-channel network of series that share a range of structural features such as methods of detection, narrative structures, intertextual linkages, etc. (see also Jenner 2015). Much like company franchising, a successful original text unfolds within a network of different products, locations or texts and thereby shares or minimises risk. Both, *CSI* and *NCIS* were extraordinarily successful so repetition of the formula in different series, as well as using the series branding through titles, was relatively low risk. However, *CSI* celebrated almost immediate success and ran for two years before *CSI: Miami* was added to the franchise. In the case of *NCIS*, it took six years until *NCIS: Los Angeles* was added, due to the series' slower building of audience success. In other words, the original series 'proved' the success of the formula with audiences first. The same was not true for *Criminal*, with the UK version being published only four days before the other three. This may also serve to explain the short-lived nature of the project. Yet, the series share titles and visual signifiers. While they do not share crossover episodes, as common for the CBS series, most only have three episodes. This indicates the failure of the project, but this cannot detract from the cross-border potential of it. Additionally, it is a transnational franchise, showing the potential of transnational platforms in transnational TV production and reception. As much as *Criminal* may have failed in Netflix's experimentation with transnationalism, it is also an important way to formulate this perspective. The franchise is hardly new to television, but the way transnational streamers organise their own franchises differs greatly, negotiating a space between format and franchise. Most importantly, the access points for all of the programmes are their 'home' streaming platforms with series available in all markets. Importantly, rather than a risk reducing measure, *Criminal* was conceived as franchise without any version of the series having proven itself to be successful. Even though, as for example for CBS franchises, series have a common access point (the channel), the 'not quite'-ness of Netflix is established at the point of conception, but without first establishing a successful 'central series' for the franchise as *CSI: Crime Scene Investigation* or *NCIS: Naval Criminal Investigative Services*.

The connecting linkages of the streaming sites and their recommendation systems are an important feature of how the 'not quite'-ness of different meaning-making structures is established. To a certain extent, the trade definitions of format and franchises become irrelevant as the connecting streaming sites mean that there is no trade outside of the platform. Instead, however, interfaces and branding structures create the way series are framed and marketed to the audience.

The Textual Politics of the National/ Transnational Streaming Franchise

When looking at the way streaming services structure their own transnational streaming franchises, there are a range of factors that need to be considered: the transnational structure of the platform; the text; the relation of both to the way formats and franchises have formulated transnational television in the past. The structure of Netflix as transnational platform is explored throughout this book. As already discussed, Netflix' version of the grammar of transnationalism structures the texts. The different versions of *Criminal* use similar legal and moral frameworks, an identical mise-en-scène, and are set in the cosmopolitan European cities of Madrid, Paris, Berlin and London. The German version is, perhaps, the most obviously localised one, referring to the cities' and countries' GDR past throughout. *Criminal* is nationalised on the surface, but ultimately uses a grammar of transnationalism.

Coproduction, especially in Europe where this is an important feature of PSB, is usually studied from an industry studies or policy studies angle. These are vital and the public money and the way streamers access it in Europe remains a dominant focus. However, as Julia Hammett-Jamart et al. (2018) point out, European coproduction funds come with demands for cultural representation and, therefore, in terms of policy and industrial practice, are defined by legal and policy frameworks. Further, European film and television funds usually require licensing and copyright frameworks that are not suitable for the production models of Netflix. However, as Adeleida Afilipoaie et al. point out:

> The advent of new players has clearly impacted the traditional financing of TV fiction in Europe. Broadcasters seemingly engage more in co-productions to increase scale and retain exploitation rights and possibilities to recoup investment or are exploring large scale SVOD collaborations such as Britbox in the United Kingdom and Salto in France. OTT players are increasingly exploring domestic European productions directly or through co-financing and co-production (for example HBO, Netflix), while cable and telecommunications distributors, trying to compete with online streaming platforms, are increasingly taking part in co-productions as a means to increase or maintain their subscriber base. (2021, 307)

While coproduction in Europe is usually organised via different national broadcasters, Netflix offers a different industry formation which determines differences in the way texts are structured. National broadcasters are increasingly reasserting themselves through projects like Britbox, a streaming platform in the UK, which is a collaboration of various terrestrial TV channels. The systems are not binary, but the industry is more and more establishing itself and the way the global and local are negotiated becomes increasingly specific to different national and transnational platforms.

Legal systems differ from country to country, but TV viewers are much more used to consuming crime series from foreign countries than comedy. Crime series travel well, as the basic principle is often simply the question: Whodunit? Answering this question may be framed by different systems but this does not compromise the underlying moral and socio-political questions of the genre (see Jenner 2015). *Criminal* is a franchise that is almost completely set in interrogation rooms, though police characters move between this room, the observation room behind a two-way mirror and the lobby of the building floor. The interrogation rooms of *Criminal* all look identical, and the series never moves outside the building. Team dynamics differ, the franchise is more about interrogating suspects than the personal or professional drama of the detectives, though team dynamics often become elucidated in the course of an interrogation. The French and German series start out with crimes surrounding important historical events with influences that travel far beyond national borders: the fall of the Berlin Wall in 1989 and the terrorist attacks in Paris that involved an attack on the Bataclan night club in 2015. The

British and Spanish versions, not accidentally given the transnational reach of both languages, deal with less localised crimes. Since all series are Western European, the legal systems of the countries somewhat align as well as moral framings of the crimes. It is not until the third episode of *Criminal: Spain* until remarks to Catalan independence localise the series. In all series, the police sometimes use illegal means of interrogation, though the Spanish officers seem to have the most leeway. All series feature different storylines about the private lives of detectives. The German version also localises the team via the GDR past of one of the detectives. The framing of an interrogation means that the question of Whodunit? is somewhat changed. Episodes start at the moment the interrogation has already started or is about to start and viewers are only rarely informed of what the person to be interrogated is supposed to have done.

As argued in previous chapters, content on transnational platforms has to strike a balance between domestication and transnationalisation via a grammar of transnationalism. This looks different for each platform. While there are commonalities for all transnational circulation and the grammar of transnationalism outlined in the last chapter is deliberately held general, Netflix' push towards uniformity in production processes certainly becomes visible on screen in its use of mise-en-scène in *Criminal*. The gesturing towards recent national history in versions of *Criminal* is certainly part of the negotiation between the national and the transnational.

LOL, in contrast, is extremely nationalised by relying on local comedy talent, usually those that are well known on national TV. This is mixed with the format logic of competition reality TV. Amazon's algorithm is adjusted more to the recommendation of products than programmes, so viewers of one *LOL* are not necessarily recommended other versions. Discussing a different sub-genre of comedy, the sitcom, Harrington and Bielby argue that "situation comedies are often too culturally specific and as a result do not transport well across borders" (2008, 53). Further, comparing it to a genre that does well in transnational television trade:

> … while soap opera is based upon widely shared assumptions about the elements comprising human social bonds, the premise of situation comedy often resides in the temporary social rupturing of those bonds. Because cultures vary in their tolerance of the social contrasts exposed by humor and in solution to these contrasts, the resolution proposed in comedic narrative itself is very localized. (2008, 53–54)

Some sitcoms travel well on streaming ([NBC, 2005–13], *Friends*, the Canadian *Schitts Creek* [CBC, 2015–20], *Ted Lasso* [AppleTV, 2020–]), often marketed as 'comfort' or repeat viewing on a platform that relies on autonomous scheduling. Yet, it is worth remembering that the transnational Netflix audience is often a cosmopolitan audience, as discussed in the next chapter. Perhaps this is why Afilipoaie et al., in their analysis of Netflix investment strategies in Europe find:

> Although these genres were well-represented in our dataset, the investment in European comedy was rather surprising, due to the popular belief that comedy is a culturally specific genre, which does not appeal to foreign audiences (Raats et al.,[2018]). It is worth mentioning, however, that the comedy series in the dataset were primarily hybrid genres, such as comedy-drama or comedy-romance. (2021, 319)

Both, Bielby and Harrington and Afilipoaie et al., show how insufficient the category of comedy is in the context of transnational television, as the many forms, formats and sub-genres of comedy offer different degrees of cultural specificity. Nevertheless, the reality TV format offers an important template of how highly localised forms of humour, embodied by local comedians, serves to further an understanding of what *LOL* is.

Importantly, it can be argued that, where Netflix produces for the transnational market, the different versions of *LOL* are produced for national audiences. As such, the programmes somewhat copy strategies of national television. Amazon, as company, has adopted a strategy of nationalisation where a number of different national websites exist, often reflecting (in its audio-visual content) different licensing deals or (in its shopping business) different taxes on products. However, as *LOL* is self-produced, all different versions are available in all of its markets, as all of its self-produced originals, but not promoted or recommended in the same way Netflix does for *Criminal*. Much like other streamers, Amazon does not freely share viewing figures, though these may not be as relevant to a company which largely aims to tie viewers to a 'consumption universe' of Kindle, Echo, Audible, Amazon Music, etc. Petruska notes:

> In these diversified corporate contexts, the value of entertainment media derives less from aesthetics, narrative complexity, or pleasure, and more from how media helps attract and hold the attention of consumers for all sorts of products and services. (2022, 427)

As local content continues to be highly successful, the investment of Amazon into nationalised formats lines up with its goals in a way that simply adopting Netflix' strategies would not. *LOL* is organised through the structure of Amazon and its reliance on local entities. This differs from the way national versions of Netflix exist (Lobato 2019), as Amazon has different access points.

It is especially *Money Heist* and *Money Heist: Korea—Joint Economic Area* that positions the political transnational dimensions of the text. Both identify poverty as common themes, though there are limits to the way this is explored, partly due to Netflix positioning as, in the words of Elkins, "responsible, progressive global actor" (2021, 150). Of course, the economic histories and pressures of Spain and Korea are different, though the grammar of transnationalism enables a nationally unspecific discussion of the theme. The argument has a specific political thrust, which is not necessarily reflected in the companies' own behaviours, but never goes as far as naming a perpetrator or cause for poverty other than a vague notion of 'the rich'. As such, the series enable transnational discussion without identifying the nationally specific debates.

Dubbing Politics and the Transnational Streaming Franchise Logic

When the first edition of this book came out, Netflix dubbing into English was done with an American accent. For some series, such as the French series *Plan Coeur* (Netflix, 2018–22) or the German series *How to Sell Drugs Online (Fast)* (Netflix, 2019–21), first seasons were dubbed by the cast. This strategy may be highly reliant on the cast's ability to speak English (though it is hardly likely this can be repeated in other dubbing languages) but can also lend a certain 'authenticity' to the series. In 2020, the English-language versions were re-dubbed. In the French series, dubbing was replaced by voice actors with an American accent and for the German series by voice actors with a British accent. As this shows, the British accent is not necessarily used to connote 'Europeanness', but it evidences the experimentation with dubbing and accents for self-produced Originals. However, I have previously explored linkages between the British series *Sex Education* (Netflix, 2019–) and *How to Sell Drugs Online (Fast)*, which may account for the British accents. Similar generic linkages are established for the Korean series *Squid Game* and *All of Us Are Dead*, both dubbed with an American accent. These would serve to link both series, in addition to genre, visual style and categories within the recommendation algorithm (see Jenner 2021).

Both versions of *Money Heist* are dubbed with American accents and all versions of *Criminal* with British accents. *Criminal: UK*, however, was published a few days before the other versions. Thus, the British accents serve to link the franchise together and, to a certain extent, position the British series as the 'central' text, as does the publication date a few days before the others. However, while this furthers the perception of the British version as the 'central' series, this is entirely artificially constructed through what Harrison and Bielby (2008) term mid-range factors. Language settings remain across the app, so if a viewer only watches English-language content, series are automatically played with dubbing (viewers can change this setting, if desired). Thus, the dubbing serves to create a further linkage. In the case of *Criminal*, this is in addition to title and identical mise-en-scène. The dubbing, thus, should not be neglected as structural feature.

The American and British dubbing also has different connotations. As argued above, the dubbing with British accents does not necessarily connote Europenness as such, but it is significant that this is applied to establish linkages between the different texts of this intra-European streaming franchise. Similarly, the linkage between *Sex Education* and *How to Sell Drugs Online (Fast)*, though primarily via genre, not franchise, is intensified through this. As much as not all European productions are dubbed with a British accent, the dubbing serves to localise series and tie them to a (small) continent and political union. As argued in the previous chapter, the dubbing of accents is difficult, as it can reveal classist, sexist and racist assumptions. However, Netflix actually imposes different readings on its own terms through its experiments with dubbing. As such, a significant layer of meaning is added in the different accents used for dubbing, which in English are relatively generic versions of 'American' and 'British'. These meanings can tie various texts together as franchise or via genre. The dubbing does not establish these linkages but can serve to reinforce ties that already exist.

French and Spanish are both languages with a wider transnational reach, due to different histories of colonialism. Though far from what Lydia Hayes describes as "devoid of culturally weighted connotations" (2020, 3), the American accent aligns with the language of the majority of self-produced Originals on Netflix and connotes familiarity to US audiences, who remain the majority of Netflix's audience share (as much as the company has made significant inroads transnationally). The American dubbing works to establish a kind of 'universality' of *Money Heist*, signifying the reach of Spanish-language series, especially in Latin America. This is later extended to the Korean version. As such, the franchise spans several continents, united by the American dubbing. Yet, these are hardly the only options. *Call My Agent!* (France 2, 2015–20) is a French series that has proven successful through distribution via Netflix, especially in the UK. The Indian version, *Call My Agent Bollywood* (Netflix, 2021–), is a Netflix self-produced Original. This is originally in Hindi. Dubbing in English, however, is done with an Indian accent. Thus, Netflix, which acts only as distributor in some markets, not producer of the original series, foregoes the establishing of connections via dubbing in this case in favour of domestication.

Importantly, *LOL* is not dubbed, heightening the sense of localisation and an intent to produce for a national audience, rather than a transnational one. The series are available subtitled, but the distinction from the way Netflix organises translation is sharp.

As dubbing is hardly a neutral practice, it is worth observing the connections Netflix forges between different series of a franchise, between series of the same genre, but also where Netflix denies such connection.[2] It can serve to tie a transnational streaming franchise together as structural feature and heavily inform its character and how it is marketed. In fact, if the recommendation algorithm functions akin to scheduling (see Chapter 8), then dubbing functions as additional means to create webs of meaning. Importantly, Netflix also changes dubbing practices and strategies. The audio tracks of the cast dubbing of *Plan Coeur* or *How to Sell Drugs Online (Fast)* are no longer available.[3] As Hayes (2020) argues, these are very early days for English-language dubbing and Netflix has long dominated the market and shaped practices for it. Much of this stands in opposition to Amazon's highly localised *LOL* and its resistance towards dubbing.

[2] This is only the connection through dubbing, as *Call My Agent: Bollywood* is clearly linked to the French series through title.

[3] Both instances also rely on my observation, as this was a research focus at the time, but this likely also affects other series. At the same time, tracks may be made available in the future.

Conclusion

This chapter has dealt with the way Netflix has established its own franchising logic by investing in what I call transnational streaming franchises. I understand this more as a way to tie networks of texts together and generate meaning, rather than an economic unit that structures trade. Netflix' strategy here is significantly different from that of Amazon and its investment in reality TV formats and the localisation this offers. To a certain extent, this shows how transnational streamers employ different strategies to match different goals. However, it also helps understand how streamers adapt strategies common to linear TV and the television industry. *LOL* and *Money Heist* are relatively straightforward in this way, mostly creating new networks of meaning through the access point. *Criminal* is an intriguing example of how streaming can reorganise European coproduction, though the series did not run long enough to fulfil its potential.

Both, the *Money Heist* and *Criminal* transnational streaming franchises also use dubbing to create and further established linkages between programmes. This chapter only explored English-language dubbing, but there is a need to explore the workings of dubbing in other languages. This goes beyond studying the practice of dubbing in general, but how different platforms employ it. The function of dubbing changes, but it generates transnational meanings. Streamers can run different programmes alongside each other and create new networks of meaning and reinforce old ones. Thus, this chapter set out to explore how different streamers establish textual networks, partly through industrial practices and concepts, and partly through textual practices, algorithmic recommendations and access points. These elements are important, as they inform how audiences create meaning and the ways Netflix wants to be understood as player in an increasingly diversified field.

G.-Stolz (2021) identifies the creation of the transcultural in the streaming environment, which influences how different platforms, including Netflix, structure texts. This chapter and the last highlighted ways Netflix organises texts to create, not only texts within the framework of the grammar of transnationalism, but is creating textual 'universes' or streaming franchises to further carry its transnationalism.

Bibliography

Afilipoaie, A., C. Iordache, and T. Raats. 2021. "The 'Netflix Original' and What It Means for the Production of European Television Content." *Critical Studies in Television* 16 (3): 304–25.

Bielby, D.D. 2008. *Global TV: Exporting Television and Culture in the World Market*. New York and London: New York University Press.

Chalaby, J.K. 2005. *Transnational Television Worldwide: Towards a New Media Order*. London and New York: I.B. Tauris. Distributed in the U.S. by London and New York: Palgrave Macmillan.

———. 2013. "Reflection i: Transnational TV Formats: Making the Local Visible and the Global Invisible." *Critical Studies in Television* 8 (4): 54–56.

——— and A. Esser. 2017. "The TV Format Trade and the World Media System: Change and Continuity." *International Journal of Digital Television* 8 (1): 3–7.

Elkins, E. 2021, "Streaming Diplomacy: Netflix's Domestic Policy and Foreign Policy." In D.Y. Jin (ed.), *The Routledge Handbook of Digital Media and Globalization*, 1st ed., 150–57. London: Routledge.

Esser, A. 2022. "TV Formats: Transnationalizing Television Production and Distribution." In P. McDonald (ed.), *The Routledge Companion to Media Industries*, 1st ed., 351–62. London: Routledge.

G.-Stolz, B. 2021. "National, Transnational, Transcultural Media: Netflix—The Culture-Binge." In M. Jenner (ed.), *Binge-Watching and Contemporary Television Studies*, 145–61. Edinburgh: Edinburgh University Press.

Hammett-Jamart, J., P. Mitric, and E. Novrup Redvall. 2018. "Introduction: European Film and Television Co-Production." In J. Hammett-Jamart, P. Mitric, and E.N. Redvall (eds.), *European Film and Television Co-production. Policy and Practice*, 1–26.

Hayes, L. 2020. "Netflix Disrupting Dubbing: English Dubs and British Accents." *Journal of Adiovisual Translation* 4 (1): 1–26.

Hilmes, M. 2012. "The Whole World's Unlikely Heroine: Ugly Betty as Transnational Phenomenon." In J. McCabe and K. Akass (eds.), *TV's Betty Goes Global: from Telenovela too International Phenomenon*, 26–44. London: I.B. Tauris.

Hunting, K., and J. Gray. 2023. "Disney+. Imagining Industrial Intertextuality." In D. Johnson (ed.), *From Networks to Netflix: A Guide to Changing Channels*, 650–67. 2nd edn. New York: Routledge.

Jenner, M. 2015. *American TV Detective Dramas*. Houndmills, Basingstoke, Hampshire and New York: Palgrave Macmillan.

———. 2021. "Transnationalising Genre: Netflix, Teen Drama and Textual Dimensions in Netflix Transnationalism." In M. Jenner (ed.), *Binge-Watching and Coontemporary Television Studies*, 183–200. Edinburgh: Edinburgh University Press.

Kim, J.O. 2021. "The Korean Wave and the New Global Media Economy." In D.Y. Jin (ed.), *The Routledge Handbook of Digital Media and Globalization*, 1st ed., 77–85. London: Routledge.

Lobato, R. 2019. *Netflix Nations: The Geography of Digital Distribution*. New York: New York University Press.

Petruska, K. 2022. "Amazon Prime Video Scale, Complexity, and Television as Widget." In D. Johnson (ed.), *From Networks to Netflix. A Guide to Changing Channels*, 2nd ed., 425–44. New York: Routledge.

——— and F. Woods. 2019. "Traveling Without a Passport: "Original" Streaming Content in the Transatlantic Distribution Ecosystem." In H.M. Hilmes and R.E. Pearson (eds.), *Transatlantic Television Drama: Industries, Programs, & Fans*, 49–67. Oxford: Oxford University Press.

Raats, T., I. Schooneknaep, and C. Pauwels. 2018. "Supporting Film Distribution in Europe: Why Is Overcoming National Barriers So Difficult?" In P.C. Murschetz, R. Teichmann, and M. Karmasin (eds.), *Handbook of State Aid for Film*, 193–210. Cham: Springer.

TV

All Of Us Are Dead (2022–), KR: Netflix.
Boys, The (2019–), USA: Amazon.
Call My Agent! (2015–20), FR: France 2.
Call My Agent Bollywood (2021–), IND: Netflix.
Criminal: France (2019), FR: Netflix.
Criminal: Germany (2019), DE: Netflix.
Criminal: Spain (2019), ES: Netflix.
Criminal: UK (2019–20), UK: Netflix.
CSI: Crime Scene Investigations (2000–2015), USA: CBS.
CSI: Cyber (2015–16), USA: CBS.
CSI: Miami (2002–2012), USA: CBS.
CSI: NY (2004–13), USA: CBS.
Friends (1994–2004), USA: NBC.
Geordie Shore (2011–22), UK: MTV.
How to Sell Drugs Online (Fast) (2019–21), DE: Netflix.
Jersey Shore (2009–12), USA: MTV.
LOL: last One Laughing Germany (2021–), DE: Amazon.
Marvellous Mrs. Maisel, The (2017–23), USA: Amazon.
Money Heist (2017–21), ES: Antena 3 Televisión, Netflix.
NCIS: Naval Investigative Services (2003–), USA: CBS.
NCIS: Hawai'i (2021–), USA: CBS.
NCIS: Los Angeles (2009–), USA: CBS.
NCIS: New Orleans (2014–21), USA: CBS.

Office, The (2005–13), USA: NBC.
Plan Coeur (2018–22), FR: Netflix.
Schitt's Creek (2015–20), CN: CBC.
Sex Education (2019–), UK: Netflix.
Squid Game (2021–), KR: Netflix.
Ted Lasso (2020–), USA: AppleTV.

Film

Joon-Ho, Bong (2019) *Parasite*. KR: CJ Entertainment

CHAPTER 14

The Netflix Audience

This chapter deals with conceptualising a 'Netflix audience' within this transnational structure. The term is consciously selected: the term global audience does not capture the limited accessibility due to economic concerns or infrastructure. The term transnational audience is often applied to much broader ideas of an 'internet audience' or a 'networked society', which interacts with others using communications technologies afforded by the internet (see Athique 2016, Chun 2006 and 2016, Castells 2009, Van Dijk 1999, Couldry and Hepp 2017). Mike Wayne (2022) and Wayne and Ana C. Uribe Sandoval (2021) take particular issue with Netflix' refusal to share geographical audience data, even where they (selectively) share data. They are right to point to the specific issues this presents for audience research and, on an industry level, discursive constructions of 'success', trying to establish frameworks to study this transnational audience in the absence of data from streamers. Rather than specific audience data, this chapter is concerned with how a very specific, Netflix-watching audience can be conceptualised. This audience is necessarily a transnational one that will overlap with other streamers, though these often configure their audiences in distinct ways, in line with their goals. This does link in with G.-Stolz's assertion that:

M. Jenner, *Netflix and the Re-invention of Television*,
https://doi.org/10.1007/978-3-031-39237-5_14

> Audiences are constructed groupings, shaped by industry expectations and considered when their members do not turn that dial, push that button or turn off their screens. In other words, appropriate audiences are made of consumers who keep consuming. (2021, 146)

While we, thus, actually do not know much about the global Netflix audience, it is still worth exploring ways to conceptualise it. Due to the individuation Netflix offers, we know that the Netflix audience is a highly fragmented audience. Netflix is available in 190 countries and in a world with more than 7.8bn people, 220.67 million subscribers (in Q2, 2022) hardly means that it spans the world, particularly if we consider that most subscribers will have economic stability with consistent access to electricity and broadband. According to statista.com, the majority of subscribers at the end of the second quarter of 2022 were from the North America, but this number comprised less than 50% of all subscribers (73.28 million), as Netflix has made significant inroads in transnational territories. Thus, audiences for a specific text will accumulate *across* borders rather than in one national context. It may be easiest to return to the introduction to Part III to illustrate this: it is not the US appeal of Adam Sandler films that guided the decision to invest in them. Instead, it was the star's transnational appeal, the number of viewers he can attract across the world. Following this logic, audiences must be conceptualised as dispersed, fragmented and spread across different nations. This chapter aims to offer some sort of concept, if not for transnational audiences in general, then for 'the Netflix audience' and its transnational nature. As argued in the previous chapters, Netflix needs to be understood as both, national and transnational. This chapter is not a reception study, but an attempt to conceptualise the Netflix audience within the dialectic relationship between the national and the transnational outlined in Chapters 11 and 12. The aim of this chapter is to move away from conceptualisations that presume an American audience or 'the West' as audience for Netflix and to start thinking about Netflix as a transnational decentred media operation that, as the example of Adam Sandler films shows, often makes decisions based on its global trajectory.

Audiences are traditionally understood as national audiences:

> ...prior to the advent of the World Wide Web, there was no real foundation for the idea of a transnational crowd formation. So we had a world of audiences, but no framework for an international audience in the singular tense. (Athique 2016, location 349)

This highlights that audience reception studies has most commonly understood national identity—albeit diverse national identities—as organising identity axis. Before the internet, this boundary makes sense: as noted before, broadcasting has traditionally been delineated by national borders, meaning that those from other countries could not receive it (with the exception of border regions). Turner notes,

> As the consumers of television move ever more fluidly across national boundaries—accessing programming via satellite or the internet—it seems inevitable that the nation must become a more marginal player in the future of the medium. (Turner 2009, 54)

The combination of a more fluid concept of national identity, in relation to 'the nation' and national media systems, and a more dispersed and fragmented global audience leads Adrian Athique to summarise:

> The vast transmission 'footprint' of satellite broadcasts inherently favours a new supra-national media geography, the limits of which are established somewhat less by the sovereignty of nation states and more fundamentally by the larger map of linguistic and cultural affinities of civilizations. (2016, 2593)

Athique's focus is a broad concept of media, rather than television. In an age of media convergence, it is relatively easy to conceptualise audiences as consumers of all media. However, this lack of specificity makes it almost impossible to make any statements about audiences. As much as people may use different media forms in parallel or on the same device, the way they use Skype, Facebook, the telephone or Netflix are, at least to some degree, qualitatively different. Control for audiences can be hampered by national media systems, but media form also heavily informs interaction. This is not to fall back to the technological determinism of Marshall McLuhan's 'the medium is the message'-dictum, but to acknowledge that, even in an age of media convergence, audiences do not relate to all media in the same way.

This book is rooted in television studies, which has consequences for the way audiences are understood here. In television studies, the national audience looms large. This is hardly surprising, considering how much existing national media systems have traditionally shaped television. As Pertierra and Turner note in their study on Mexican television audiences,

> Among the conclusions to come from our ethnographic research was both a confirmation of the national character of the consumption of television within this community, and a sense of the unremarkable—that is, thoroughly naturalized—status of this behaviour. The platforms used have changed, and the structure and viability of the nation state has changed, but there remains a strong, if altered, relationship between television and national identity. (2013, 52–3)

Nevertheless, their study includes another important aspect: the building of communities elsewhere, predominantly online. Their discussion is heavily influenced by a scepticism around the 'authenticity' of these communities, which ultimately serves to assign a precedence to 'the nation'. The transnational qualities of these communities and how viewers engage with them remain unmentioned. This is not particularly unusual. Reception studies, for very practical reasons, has often failed to produce transnational accounts, or a theoretical framework for the study of transnational audiences. Further, as shown in Wayne and Uribe Sandoval's work, the lack of geographical data limits the field's ability to do so. Linear broadcasting is organised and regulated via the nation-state, with scheduling, translation and content all designed to appeal to audiences that are geographically, linguistically, ethnically and culturally delineated. As Pertierra and Turner show, 'the nation', as ideological construct, is an important reference point for linear television and remains impossible to ignore. Furthermore, qualitative audience research usually only works with relatively small focus groups, often only in the context of one country. Combining or comparing data from different countries on national audiences is difficult, though, as Castro and Mikos (2021) show, hardly impossible. However, their work focusses on German and Dutch audiences, who are culturally and geographically close to one another. In general, a number of questions remain unanswered, starting with how we can compare the different alterations and changes made in the course of the domestication of texts (see Chapter 12).

This chapter will approach the Netflix audience from three perspectives: it will first outline conceptualisations of an online audience and how Netflix failed to establish itself along the lines of many-to-many networks. This informs the argument that conceptualisations of online audiences need to make distinctions between behaviours solicited by online media. As such, Netflix audiences are positioned closely to television audiences. In a second step, it will conceptualise the idea of a transnational audience. In a third step, it will discuss fragmented audiences, particularly fans, in more detail to look at how fragmented audiences organise across borders. The discussion remains focussed on how various concepts relate to a 'Netflix audience' to remain specific rather than offer broader ideas of a transnational audience. This specificity is considered central, largely because Netflix' audience is relatively small if compared to other media and the way audiences relate to it is comparatively specific.

Watching Netflix: Participatory Culture, Television and Netflix Viewing

Athique summarises that, in light of online media and media convergence, "...our conceptualisation of the media audience becomes at once radically individuated and densely interconnected" (2016, location 1429) and moves on to highlight two points highly relevant for conceptualising a Netflix audience. First, in the context of the 'active' audiences of new media, "...we can no longer assume the physical co-presence of audience members, nor their simultaneous activity in a common moment in time" (ibid.). Secondly, the "personalized control over the programming 'flow' being accessed certainly undermines any assumption of a common media experience based around the content of the medium" (ibid., location 1429–1435). Athique, in this context, discusses many-to-many networks, but this argument is highly relevant for a Netflix audience. The transnational nature of the audience combined with the individuation of media experience means that the Netflix audience is significantly different from the television audience that could be presumed to be limited by national borders. Of course, as Mikos and Castro (2021) show, communal viewing is possible. Further, over Covid-19-related lockdowns, streaming services introduced features to enable communal viewing, but these features largely presumed viewing in an already existing community (family and friends, etc.), not the communities of strangers and 'nations' linear television relies on. It is argued here that, rather than a national audience, Netflix is aiming to address exactly this audience that is fragmented across borders.

As argued in Chapter 6, the audiences of participatory media are closely linked to ideas of Web 2.0 and interactivity. The amount of control they are invested with goes beyond traditional ideas of viewership to elevate them to the level of producer (see Bruns 2007). Athique formulates a theory of transnational audiences but makes no distinctions between media forms and generally presumes audiences of participatory online media, such as social networks. Castells (2009), Van Dijk (1999), Couldry (2012) or Couldry and Hepp (2017) formulate theories of societies, but also focus more on participatory media. This is understandable as the level of supposed control users are invested with suggests high levels of 'activity'. Within the control-power nexus explored throughout this book, activity refers to choice and control rather than power. These concepts need to be understood in different ways for different media forms. However, participatory media also poses questions surrounding Netflix. Though Netflix has actively positioned itself as discursively tied to television, it is also an online medium. Yet, the kind of choices or control it demands from viewers are hardly comparable to writing tweets or status updates, never mind uploading a video to YouTube. In fact, whereas YouTube is deliberately tied to the Web 2.0 discourse, Netflix positioned itself as television, a medium that demands much less interaction and productivity. Television audiences may be 'active' in the sense that they are cognitively active, make deliberate choices (for example by changing channels or switching their set off altogether), design their own stories to explain gaps in narratives, etc. They may also be the producers who upload fan-videos to YouTube, write their own fanfiction or live-tweet, but this is done on separate platforms. In other words, Netflix itself is not participatory. In an age of media convergence, it seems somewhat forced to make this argument, but there is a difference between the kind of engagement Netflix and participatory media solicit. Wolff argues:

> Other than being delivered via IP, Netflix had almost nothing to do with the conventions of digital media—in a sense it rejected them. It is not user generated, it is not social, it is not bite size, it is not free. It is in every way,

> except for its route into people's homes—and the differences here would soon get blurry—the same as television. (2015, location 987–93)

Nevertheless, Netflix did try to position itself as participatory medium. As Alexander (2016, 86) notes, Netflix' attempts to integrate into social media have failed. Alexander refers to 'Netflix Friends', which allowed users to share viewing lists with Facebook friends. Finn summarises:

> …in 2013, Netflix unveiled the U.S version of its facebook integration system, allowing users to see recommendations based on what their friends on facebook rated highly. (2017, location 1949)

Chuck Tryon describes the problems with a Netflix app that automatically publishes users' rental records on Facebook: in the US, video-rental records are considered confidential and publishing without consent is a breach of privacy laws. According to Tryon, "many users expressed serious concern about having private information revealed to others" (2013, 134). Though this only describes the US market, the feature (or a version thereof) was available for a short period in other markets, as well. In 2012/2013, Netflix tried to build more of a 'community' experience by linking with Facebook, allowing viewers in the UK to selectively share what they are watching (rather than whole lists) and asking viewers to write reviews. Netflix has since dropped many of these features. This suggests that Netflix has been unable to mobilise the kind of engagement social media or many-to-many networks solicit. Instead, features like the 'thumbs up' or 'thumbs down' button as well as national and international Top Ten mostly serve to build a better system for personalised recommendation, not a community one. Nevertheless, on company pages, it still describes subscribers as 'members', language normally associated with club membership or social media rather than audio-visual experiences (cinema and television usually uses terms like customers or viewers). The failure to construct more of a 'community' experience for viewers indicates how much Netflix itself attempted to position itself within a framework of participatory media—despite the discursive link to television it established. Yet, it also shows that audiences chose to seek their participatory experiences elsewhere.

Netflix' 'difference' from social media, thus, allows for the conclusion that the way viewers relate to Netflix is closer to the way television is consumed rather than social media. Dawson and Tryon, in the context of a study into the use of 'connected viewing' practices of American college students, find:

> ...in focus groups and interviews, many of the students in our samples described behaviors that are at least superficially consistent with established consumption styles. For example, a number of our respondents use Netflix in a manner reminiscent of channel surfing on television. That is, rather than watching a specific program or film, they 'surf' Netflix's content categories until something catches their interest. These Netflix 'surfers' watch the beginning of a movie or program before committing to watching it in its entirety. (2014, 227)

The time periods to make decisions are significantly longer than the less than five seconds spent on channels while channel surfing (Kaye 1994, xi–xii). Dawson and Tryon give the example of a student who reported that a film had five minutes to capture his interest. Nevertheless, the parallel to viewing behaviour linked to linear television is striking. Similar to linear television, audiences make decisions about how much they want to engage with a programme. Dawson and Tryon find that several students in their study employ Netflix to provide 'background noise' or 'ambient sound' while doing other things. These parallels with linear television, in addition to an expressed desire by study subjects for an easily manageable, easily responsive interface and easy login process, suggests an audience that is active in similar ways a television audience is active. They make decisions on what they want to watch and how much attention they want to pay to content, but this is hardly the same as a skype conversation or a Facebook post. They may use social media as 'second screen' where they actively engage and communicate, but viewers do not engage *on* Netflix.

Unlike linear TV, however, decisions are also made on when, on what device, and where to access content, which sets Netflix and other streamers apart from broadcast television. Thus, viewers are invested with more control over their own viewing. As a consequence, 'watching Netflix', or streaming as a whole are qualitatively different from 'watching TV', or at least from what watching linear TV used to be, but also from produsing. Overall, the Netflix audience seems more closely linked to the television audience than online users. Nevertheless, it still has to make different decisions than a television audience. Focussing more on the practice of binge-watching rather than specific platforms, Perks finds that audiences actively schedule 'binges' or, as she terms it, media marathons, into holiday breaks or breaks from media routines (2015, location 5021). As Netflix penetrates viewers' everyday lives further, and as other streamers adopt many of its features, these individual scheduling practices might shift depending on the programme, as with Dawson and Tryon's college students who have Netflix running as ambient sound while cleaning or doing other chores. Emil Steiner and Kun Xu, in a study on binge-watching, also observe:

> Interviewees described binge-watching along a continuum of attentive viewing to inattentive viewing. Attentive binging was described as focused study of the text that was both entertaining and educational and often motivated by the need to catch up or feel narratively immersed. The less attentive binging was almost always for relaxation or distraction. The degree of attentiveness is difficult to explicate qualitatively, but it was clearly related to content genre and form. (2018, 11)

Pertierra and Turner speculate how choice is managed in media environments where viewers are confronted with an abundance of options, such as on US television. Based on conversations between Turner and his students while teaching in the US, they argue that 'playlists' are assembled of online videos (catch-up services or other time-shifting devices), chosen by following recommendations from 'taste communities' (such as their friends). Netflix' recommendation algorithm makes it easier for viewers to find content, but, as argued in Chapter 8, these recommendations are still likely to be similar among taste communities: "The paradox about the individuation of choice on this scale is that it seems you need something like a community to help you manage it" (Pertierra and Turner 2013, 76). Grandinetti traces how television journalists, viewers and Netflix worked together to shape how series released via the binge model would be talked about. In the absence of the communal viewing allowed for by television schedules, new norms of talking about television had to be devised to avoid spoilers while allowing for conversation among viewers online and permitting the press to fulfil their function as 'gatekeepers' of culture. The culture of viewing lists associated with streaming platforms makes it highly important for trusted news sources to highlight programming worth viewing to allow viewers to find texts they are interested in.

Many of the studies cited above refer to the US where Netflix has been established the longest and market penetration is high. Nevertheless, these studies allow for at least some conceptualisation of Netflix audiences, particularly regarding the similarities between 'watching TV' and 'watching Netflix'.

Transnationalising the Television Audience

Discussing postmodern and postcolonial theory, Bhabha argues,

> The move away from singularities of 'class' or 'gender' as primary conceptual and organizational categories, has resulted in an awareness of the subject positions—of race, gender, generation, institutional location, geopolitical locale, sexual orientation—that inhabit any claim to identity in the modern world. What is theoretically innovative, and politically crucial is the need to think beyond narratives of originary and initial subjectivities and focus on those moments or processes that are produced in the articulation of cultural differences. These 'in-between' spaces provide the terrain for elaborating strategies of selfhood—singular or communal—that initiate new signs of identity, and innovative sites of collaboration, and contestation, in the act of defining society itself. (Bhabha 2004, 2)

As such, it becomes easier to formulate transnational identities. As Straubhaar puts it,

> Identities [...] layer up as people migrate, acculturate to new cultures, live abroad, travel, learn languages, join or leave religions, and, although the experiences are less directly personal and less intense, perhaps as they acquire access to new forms of media. (2013, 61)

Straubhaar applies concepts of hybrid identities to ideas of media reception, arguing that complex layers of organisational structures, commercial systems and audience identities intersect. Straubhaar's research helps conceptualise how audience identity can be understood as simultaneously transnational and national.

When conceptualising the Netflix audience as transnational audience, command of a foreign language (namely, English) and familiarity with different cultures (particularly US) emerge as important aspects of the transcultural experience. Tamar Liebes and Elihu Katz' seminal 1993 study on transcultural audiences and their reading of *Dallas* (CBS, 1978–91) remains central to understand different interpretative frameworks for culturally different audiences in Israel. Transcultural is not synonymous with transnational in this context, but rather refers to different cultural identities either in the same or across national contexts. Nevertheless, as John Tomlinson notes, an important issue arises in how Liebes and Katz' data can be evaluated:

> …the cross-cultural nature of the investigation in the case of media imperialism means that another layer of difficulties is added: that of *interpreting* the empirical data. The point at stake here is whether researchers can correctly interpret responses from a different cultural context in terms of their own cultural understanding. (1991, 51, italics in the original)

More recent studies tend to account for this by forming research teams that consist of researchers from different cultural and national backgrounds, as, for example, the size of teams interpreting data in the context of *The World Hobbit Project* show. This enables researchers to pay attention to different understandings and discursive constructions of genre. For example, Vanda de Sousa and Sascha Trültzsch-Wijnen (2016) point towards the different meanings genre categorisations can have, based on etymological and cultural histories. This also points to a deeper problem where different descriptors for genre or emotions may be expressed in the same way linguistically, but be discursively framed by different constructs. The often subtly or marginally different texts (and meanings) produced through translation practices or cultural interpretative frameworks remain under-explored within audience reception studies. *The World Hobbit Project* gathered audience responses from 46 countries accompanying the release of the three films of the *Hobbit* franchise between 2012 and 2014 (see Barker and Mathijs 2016). The various data analyses released so far offer great insights into how we can understand this global audience. Aleit Veenstra et al. (2016), for example, offer insight into the 'cross-national' and 'cross-linguistic' reception of the films in France, Belgium and the Netherlands. This study is particularly valuable as Belgium is bilingual (French and Dutch): the French tradition usually uses dubbing while Dutch film works with subtitles to translate film. These studies are particularly relevant for Netflix due to publication strategies: the simultaneous release worldwide, common for major blockbusters, is linked to Netflix' strategy (see Chapter 8). The lack of linguistic unity in some countries also has consequences for the way we can understand a Netflix audience as not simply an accumulation of 'fragments' of different national audiences but organised across different zones of consumption.

Robins and Aksoy study Turkish-speaking communities in London and identify these groups clearly as transnational audiences. Their understanding is based on the fact that these bilingual communities negotiate different national and cultural allegiances:

> Transnational audiences are involved in a complex process of negotiating a position between familiar national moorings and new transnational connections. (2006, 15)

In this, Robins and Aksoy identify a 'transnational sensibility', by which they mean that "transnational experiences were often associated with new kinds of mental and imaginative spaces, and with the capacity to function and think across cultural domains" (2006, 14–15). Stuart Cunningham (2001) discusses the 'diasporic subject' as transnational subject. His research also focusses on migrant subjects and communities and he also finds complicated networks and allegiances as well as different strategies of consumption of popular culture. What the diasporic reading position may indicate is the various viewing positions that can be taken to negotiate identity, with national identity not always acting as a dominant axis. Identity, within contemporary postmodern society, is understood as a complex system where national 'belonging' hardly serves as primary axis, as noted by Bhabha above. Robins and Aksoy link this 'transnational sensibility' directly to the migrant experience, but, as Athique notes, "there is little evidence that migration alone implicates a particular viewing culture or audience" (2016, location 1797). Indeed, there is nothing to indicate that this 'transnational sensibility' is not also present when viewers from Italy watch American, Greek or Spanish imports.

Pertierra and Turner, in their study of Mexican audiences in Chetumal, observe:

> The broader geo linguistic or regional nature of the television market was clearly evident in the list of the television programmes people were watching but, for its audience in Chetumal, television strongly retained a role as a conveyor of a national popular culture, while at the same time serving as the key facilitator of people's participation in an imagined community of metropolitan cultural consumption. (2013, 49–50)

Pertierra and Turner study linear television audiences in a central Latin American market (Mexico comprises the largest audience within this market), rather than online platforms or streaming. It is also worth noting that Mexico is a strong producer of domestic programming, which has implications for how readily available programmes that shape 'the nation' are. Nevertheless, their observation has implications for a conceptualisation of transnational audiences: much like Netflix can configure itself as simultaneously national and transnational, audiences may configure themselves in the same terms. Maybe more than other broadcasters, Netflix allows viewers to take the 'national' out of the equation and relate to a 'transnational sensibility' in the same way Pertierra and Turner's viewers understand themselves simultaneously as rural and cosmopolitan. As argued above, Netflix can be an intensely national experience, but it is up to viewers to make decisions on whether they want to take advantage of nationally sourced programmes or not. Even if watching a 'truly Polish service', viewers can still choose to watch *Orange is the New Black* or *The Crown* dubbed into Spanish. These kinds of cultural and linguistic choices make it difficult to assess *how* Netflix is watched. This disrupts, maybe even subverts, control of the national media system over what viewers watch significantly, even if these systems remain intact. Though Netflix aims to embed itself into national television cultures, it is not committed to the construction of the concept of 'the nation' in the same way linear television is. The zone of consumption may be made up of regionally, nationally or locally specific criteria, but Netflix' texts and publication models guarantee a significantly transnational dimension. Though not participatory media itself, Netflix' in-house productions enable transnational communication on participatory platforms. This aspect is significant for the way Netflix configures its own audience.

Fragmented Audiences, Fans and the Netflix Audience

As this suggests, the Netflix audience cannot be grasped through national borders. Instead, it may be easier to grasp it through the concept of audience fragmentation. Pertierra and Turner summarise this as follows and link it to television's ancillary technologies and the intense personalisation of schedules that goes along with this:

> The protocols of choosing are still tailored to the demands and patterns of everyday life, but this is not necessarily a shared everyday life; indeed, what makes this regime of choices attractive is precisely its capacity to be tailored to a highly personalized practice of everyday life. (2013, 69)

In other words, greater control for viewers over their own entertainment translates into audience fragmentation. These 'niches' are transnational, though it is a relatively under-explored field. As outlined above, there are very practical reasons for this: transnational cultures are difficult to explore and require thick descriptions of a number of cultures, histories, norms and practices that shape how content is received. Nevertheless, a fragmented audience is not necessarily an isolated audience. If, as Pertierra and Turner argue, choice is managed via 'taste communities', then these communities also enable exchange. Furthermore, as much as Netflix may not be a participatory site, the internet offers plenty of spaces where audiences can share opinions and experiences. The current dominance of fan studies in audience research can be helpful in exploring transnational audiences: instead of trying to grasp an internet audience or 'users' as a whole, the focus lies on a transnational community organised around one specific fan object. As a number of fan scholars have pointed out, fans can engage with their fan object at varying intensities (see, for example, Hills 2002; Gray 2003). At their most basic levels, fan communities only share one identifiable common interest. Yet, this common interest implies that a fan community is always also a taste community, as fans exchange information about texts they perceive as similar. This community is transnational, but also fragmented: some fans may not know another person offline who shares this interest. Yet, online communities can easily organise *across* borders. As much as fan studies tends to understand fan communities as implicitly transnational, there is not much research on fan cultures as transnational formations. Bertha Chin and Lori Hitchcock Morimoto (2013) conceptualise trans-border or transnational fandom as groups that identify commonalities other than nationality to bind them together. They use a concept of 'transcultural homology' (Hills 2002a) to theorise transnational fandom:

> Writ large, this concept frees fandom from the constraints of national belonging, reinforcing our contention that fans become fans of border-crossing texts or objects not necessarily because of where they are

> produced, but because they may recognise a subjective moment of affinity regardless of origin. (Chin and Morimoto 2013, 99)

In other words, the fan subject is predominantly constructed through the fan object and seeks out those interested in the same fan object, disregarding (or at least de-emphasising) national identity. Their specific examples move on to show how fan art often draws from various cultural influences. These artworks are transcultural rather than necessarily transnational, as national identity becomes de-emphasised. Wikanda Promkhuntong (2015) also points to mashup videos on YouTube that mix trailers or teasers of Wong Kar-Wai films with more Western interpretative frameworks and music. In both cases, the fan art shows elements of cultural adaptation. These kinds of fan practices do, of course, imply a stronger engagement with texts than normally assumed for television audiences. Nevertheless, they are indicative of the 'dance of cultures' audiences are likely to engage with. What Straubhaar posits as 'layers of identity' and Pertierra and Turner also find in the relationship between rural and cosmopolitan, is that transnational, national or regional identity are never exclusive categories, but co-exist. Yet, Rukmini Pande has usefully problematised race and identity negotiations within online fan spaces, which naturally influences transcultural and transnational fan engagement. She argues, in response to Castell's more positive outlook on the potential of online networks:

> When viewed through the lens of postcolonial studies, however, these new networks continue to be ordered by historically rooted global power structures oriented by the forces of neocolonization in the interests of the Global North, even in cases where their humanitarian potentiality is foregrounded. (2018, 41)

She further argues:

> Although I agree with the broad consensus that the internet has enabled the creation of alternative public spheres, there is also a danger of this celebratory discourse eliding persistent, crucial power differentials. (ibid.)

Pande's work is crucial, not just to fan studies, but broader considerations of a 'transnational audience', social media and networked communities. This power differential, which favours whiteness and the global north, is also addressed in Evan Elkins' work on geoblocking, which highlights one means (among many), in which power is exercised to reinforce global structural biases in online culture.

Fan activities, particularly fan production, are often perceived as relatively marginal practices. Nevertheless, in an increasingly fragmented media landscape where media experiences are often shared online and across borders, fan studies has become a significant field to understand audience behaviours. A further aspect is the fact that, along with the cultural legitimation of television (see Chapter 9), it has become increasingly acceptable to share passionate reception of popular culture, legitimising fan practices. Fan practices have also been 'mainstreamed', among them the practice of binge-watching: previously associated with fan practices, Netflix has positioned binge-watching as a dominant practice (see Part II). This linkage between viewing practices promoted by Netflix and fan practices explains why fan studies is so important to understanding Netflix audiences. Yet, fan studies also manages to grasp fragmented audiences across borders in a way that most research into television audiences cannot. Along with this, however, stands research into systems of power created (among other things) by technologies like geo-blocking.

Conclusion

Based on these considerations, how can we, in fact, conceptualise a Netflix audience? Dawson and Tryon (2013) note how much media practices are shaped by social context, which suggests that national customs cannot be ignored in conceptualising a Netflix audience. In fact, learned practices associated with national media systems remain relevant, even in a media environment without schedules. Thus, the transnational audience is complex and elusive. It is hardly enough to simply grasp it by taking national identity out of the equation, as this remains an important axis in identity construction, especially as both Pande and Elkins suggest that online culture is simply not accessible in the same way for everybody. This would even go against Netflix' own efforts to assimilate and integrate into national media systems. Thus, a Netflix audience cannot be understood as a non-national or supra-national audience, as the company likes to present it (Wayne and Sandoval 2022). Yet, it is transnational. Connections with audience 'fragments' from other countries are easily established when content is published on the same day.

The conceptualisation proposed here does not aim to ignore the specificities of cultural contexts of reception. It also does not aim to homogenise the Netflix audience. Yet, it does aim to move away from concepts of a national mass media audience. It aims to conceptualise the transnational audience within a similar dialectic of national and transnational as Netflix itself. In reception processes, identity axes of national or transnational identity are contradictory and constantly shifting and changing. As fan studies has moved to become a vital field of study to understand fragmented audiences, Morimoto and Chin's call for a focus on the transcultural organisation of fan groups seems important to understanding how a Netflix audience might function. This is less because a Netflix audience is an audience of fans, but because fan studies offers the tools to understand fragmented audiences across national borders. The field often focusses on extra-textual activities and the idea of popular culture as unifying factor: for Netflix audiences, this is a vital commonality as national identity and interpretative frameworks, particularly after alteration through translation, may not be shared. Arguably, this can only be a starting point, particularly as fandom implies stronger viewer engagement than necessarily suggested by Dawson and Tryon or Steiner and Xu. Thus, the Netflix audience operates along a national-transnational dialectic, it is synched via the 'binge model' method of publication, and its main commonality is, thus, via texts. It is intensely personalised and, thus, fragmented. This fragmentation takes place across borders. This audience can assemble on participatory platforms of the internet, such as social media, but no exchange takes place on Netflix.

As the last few chapters have shown, Netflix needs to be understood as transnational broadcaster. As such, it comes with a number of complexities and contradictions that influence reception and how it is integrated into national media systems. Transnationalism also poses significant questions about power and control. The increased control of individual viewers heavily influences how media power is organised in transnational media systems, largely because Netflix can be employed to subvert national media systems. For example, national media systems cannot influence in which language Polish viewers might watch programmes like *Grace and Frankie*, so its powers to mitigate are limited. Nevertheless, Netflix does not work to interrogate systems of neoliberal capitalism. Furthermore, the fragmented nature of its audience also means that it is difficult to imagine how it can be organised in a meaningful way. Yet, this does not mean that this broader interrogation of transnational systems of power is impossible. Thus, transnationalism may allow for a different set of questions and perspectives on power, subversion, choice and control, but Netflix as transnational broadcaster does not currently challenge this in a meaningful way.

Bibliography

Aksoy, Asu, and Kevin Robins. 2005. Whoever Looks always Finds: Transnational Viewing and Knowledge-Experience. In Jean K. Chalaby (ed.), *Transnational Television Worldwide: Towards a New Media Order*, 14–42. London: I. B. Tauris.

Alexander, Neta. 2016. "Catered to Your Future Self: Netflix's "Predictive Personalization" and the Mathematization of Taste." In McDonald, Kevin and Smith-Rowsey, Daniel (eds.), *The Netflix Effect: Technology and Entertainment in the 21st Century*, 81–97. New York: Bloomsbury.

Athique, Adrian. 2016. *Transnational Audiences: Media Reception on a Global Scale*. Cambridge: Polity.

Barker, Martin, and Ernest Mathijs. 2016. Introduction: The World Hobbit Project. *Participations* 13 (2): 158–74.

Bhabha, Homi K. 2004. *The Location of Culture*. London; New York: Routledge.

Bruns, Axel. 2007. "Produsage: Towards a Broader Framework for User-Led Content Creation." ACM, . http://eprints.qut.edu.au/6623/.

Buonanno, Milly. 2008. *The Age of Television Experiences and Theories*, Bristol: Intellect.

Castells, Manuel. 2009. *The Power of Identity the Information Age: Economy, Society, and Culture Volume II*, Hoboken: Hoboken (ed.), 2nd ed: Wiley.

Chin, Bertha and Morimoto, Lori Hitchcock. 2013. "Towards a Theory of Transcultural Fandom." *Participations* 10 (1).

Chun, Wendy Hui, and Kyong. 2016. *Updating to Remain the Same: Habitual New Media*. Cambridge, MA: The MIT Press.

Chun, Wendy Hui, and Kyong. 2006. *Control and Freedom: Power and Paranoia in the Age of Fiber Optics*. Cambridge, MA: MIT Press.

Couldry, Nick. 2012. *Media, Society, World : Social Theory and Digital Media Practice*. Cambridge: Polity.

__________and Hepp, Andreas. 2017. *The Mediated Construction of Reality*. Cambridge, UK; Malden, MA: Polity Press.

Cunningham, Stuart. 2001. "Popular Media as Public 'sphericules' for Diasporic Communities." *International Journal of Cultural Studies* 4 (2): 131–47.

Dawson, Max, and Chuck Tryon. 2014. Streaming U: College Students and Connected Viewing. In Jennifer Holt and Kevin Sanson (ed.), *Connected*

Viewing: Selling, Streaming, & Sharing Media in the Digital Era, 217–33. London: Routledge.

Dijk, Van. Jan.1999. *The Network Society*. London: Sage.

Finn, Ed. 2017. *What Algorithms Want: Imagination in the Age of Computing*. Cambridge, MA: MIT Press.

G.-Stolz, B. 2021, "National, Transnational, Transcultural Media: Netflix—The Culture-Binge" In Jenner, M (ed.), *Binge-Watching and Contemporary Television Studies*, 145–61. Edinburgh University Press, Edinburgh.

Grandinetti, Justin. 2017. "From Primetime to Anytime: Streaming Video, Temporality and the Future of Communal Television." In Barker, Cory and Wiatrowski, Myc (eds.), *The Age of Netflix: Critical Essays on Streaming Media, Digital Delivery and Instant Access*. 11–30. Jefferson: McFarland & Company, Incorporated Publishers.

Gray, Jonathan. 2003. New Audiences, New Textualities. Anti-Fans and Non-Fans. *International Journal of Cultural Studies* 6 (1): 64–81.

Hills, Matt. 2002. *Fan Cultures*. London: London Routledge.

———. 2002a. "Transcultural Otaku: Japanese Representations of Fandom and Representations of Japan in Anime/Manga Fan Cultures."

Kafka, Peter. 2012. "Please Don't Tell Me what You're Watching on Netflix." *All Things D*, Available online http://allthingsd.com/20120313/please-dont-tell-me-what-youre-watching-on-netflix/. Accessed: 08.08.2017.

Katz, Elihu, and Tamar Liebes. 1993. *The Export of Meaning: Cross-Cultural Readings of Dallas*, 2nd ed. Cambridge: Polity Press.

Kaye, Barbara Kowaleski. 1994. "*Remote Control Devices: A Naturalistic Study*." Florida State University.

Mikos, L., and D. Castro. 2021. Binge-Watching and the Organisation of Everyday Life. In Jenner, M. *Binge-Watching and Coontemporary Television Studies*, (ed.), 112–30. Edinburgh: Edinburgh University Press.

Pande, R. 2018. *Squee from the Margins Fandom and Race*. Chicago: University of Iowa Press.

Perks, Lisa Glebatis. 2015. *Media Marathoning: Immersions in Morality*. Lanham, Maryland: Lexington Books.

Pertierra, Anna Cristina and Turner, Graeme. 2013. *Locating Television: Zones of Consumption*. London; New York; Abington, Oxon, UK: Routledge.

Promkhuntong, Wikanda. 2015. Cinephiles, Music Fans and Film Auteur(s): Transcultural Taste Cultures Surrounding Mashups of Wong Kar-Wai's Movies on YouTube. *Participations* 12 (2): 255–74.

Steiner, Emil and Kun Xu. 2018. "Binge-Watching Motivates Change: Uses and Gratifications of Streaming Video Viewers Challenge Traditional TV Research." *Convergence: The International Journal of Research into New Media Technologies* (OnlineFirst): 1–20.

Straubhaar, Joseph D. 2013. Sedimented, Hybrid and Multiple? the New Cultural Geography of Identities. *Matrizes (english Version via ResearchGate)* 7 (1): 59–79.

Trültzsch-Wijnen, Sascha, De., Sousa, and Wanda. 2016. Watching the Hobbit in Two European Countries: The Views of Younger Audiences and Readers in Austria and Portugal. *Participations* 13 (2): 469–495.

Tomlinson, John. 1991. *Cultural Imperialism: A Critical Introduction*. London: Continuum.

Tryon, Chuck. 2013. *On-Demand Culture—Digital Delivery and the Future of Movies New Brunswick*. New Jersey: Rutgers University Press.

Turner, Graeme. 1994. *Making it National: Nationalism and Australian Popular Culture*. St. Leonards, N.S.W.: Allen & Unwin.

———. 2009. Television and the Nation: Does this Matter any More? In Jinna Tay and Graeme Turner (ed.), *Television Studies After TV: Understanding Television in the Post- Broadcast Era*, 54–63. London: Routledge.

Wolff, Michael. 2015. *Television is the New Television*. New York: Portfolio / Penguin.

Veenstra, Aleit, Annemarie Kersten, Tonny Krijnen, Daniel Biltereyst, and Philippe Meers. 2016. Understanding the Hobbit: The Cross-National and Cross-Linguistic Reception of a Global Media Product in Belgium, France and the Netherlands. *Participations*. 13 (2): 496–518.

Wayne, M. 2022, "Netflix Audience Data, Streaming Industry Discourse, and the Emerging Realities of 'Popular' Television," *Media, Culture & Society*, 44 (2): 193–209.

Wayne, M. & Uribe Sandoval, A.C. 2021, "Netflix Original Series, Global Audiences and Discourses of Streaming Success," *Critical Studies in Television*, 1–20.

Television

Dallas (1978–91), USA: CBS

CHAPTER 15

Conclusion: The More Things Change…

I approached writing the second edition of this book with hesitance, mostly because the streaming landscape looks so different to what it was only five years ago. Yet, looking at my argument, I was surprised to find how much the different elements analysed here remain important aspects of the streaming landscape. Leaving aside industrial influences and structures, Netflix clearly influenced the way online viewing is organised for self-scheduled viewing, auto-play of the next episode, so binge-watching and sequential viewing is privileged. Disney+, Amazon or AppleTV may rely on a different kind of transnationalism that is embedded in their own company history, but follow the structures developed by Netflix. Thus, as Netflix' economic fortunes shift, it's positioning as streaming 'normality' is important, not only when we consider content, but also in thinking about how streaming, in general, structures our media consumption.

Netflix and the Re-invention of Television was guided by two thematic strands: how does Netflix change what television is in the context of larger shifts and how does this relate to concepts of control and power? To explore these questions, Part I outlined how control and power have been negotiated through television's ancillary technologies in the TV II and TV III era. Part II moved on to analyse Netflix and the centrality of the concept of binge-watching in more detail. Part III took a different perspective by looking at how Netflix positioned itself as transnational broadcaster within national media systems. These three perspectives of

M. Jenner, *Netflix and the Re-invention of Television*,
https://doi.org/10.1007/978-3-031-39237-5_15

analysing Netflix allow for a broad understanding of Netflix' position within a TV IV context. Netflix' re-invention of television is linked to its use of the concept of control in relation to binge-watching and its reconceptualisation of transnational broadcasting by reinterpreting how time and international release schedules work online.

Television history can be understood from a number of perspectives: it can be understood through television texts or the various genre histories; it can be understood via policy and how various state actors shape and understand the medium; it can be approached via a technological or a cultural history. Part I of this book approached it via the concept of control and the various technologies of control that have shaped a cultural understanding of television. Control remains a surprisingly stable concept for the marketing of television's ancillary technologies, usually meaning the control viewers can exercise over their television set. Nevertheless, the kind of control that can be exercised can vary. While early remote controls, for example, were introduced as a means to allow US viewers to mute advertising, remote controls later enabled viewers to graze through the choices vastly extended by cable television. This had the potential to threaten the underlying structure of commercial television in the US—an assumption based on fears that viewers would change channels during ad breaks. Though changes were made to the content of individual spots, the system in itself was not changed and the threat proved to be less substantial than feared. Yet, as Chapter 4's discussion also shows, the remote control also became a powerful symbol within gender and class discourses or the continuing anxieties surrounding television in the TV II era. Chapter 5 discussed time-shifting technologies as a second technology to allow viewers increased control. The VCR, in particular, gave viewers options to move to pre-recorded tapes or time-shift broadcast television, even zip through ad breaks. Though the communication enabled by the RCD is not particularly direct, VCRs allow viewers to move completely out of reach of broadcasters and advertisers. Thus, it became particularly important for various media industries to become part of the business with VHS tapes, be it via VCR-only genres or by selling pre-recorded tapes. However, television broadcasters remained unable to take advantage of these options, partly because it was impractical to sell TV series on pre-recorded tapes. Yet, the television set found a new role as convergence medium in people's homes, largely via discourses of interactivity and associated ideas of control. Though television content has always been mixed and has drawn from other media, the technology was there to display one medium, broadcast television. This changed in the 1970s and 80s with different media forms becoming contingent on the set. This extension of options over how to use entertainment technology in the home may not have subverted existing power structures—though the video game industry became a new competitor for viewer attention—but gave viewers a different kind of control over the television set. Television as 'hub' of media convergence also significantly complicates gendered assumptions about the medium. As Chapter 6 explores, however, industry regained much of its power and control in the TV III era, ironically by purportedly giving more control to viewers. DVD and DVR promised viewers unprecedented control over the scheduling of television content. At the same time, DVD allowed rights holders to profit directly from the sale of TV series, allowing for an alternative revenue stream. It also limited possibilities to exchange content across geographical regions. Meanwhile, the DVR allowed broadcasters to collect more data on viewers, thus catering more specifically to audience tastes. The digital is premised on a deal between users, or viewers, and industry where the latter give increasingly precise data on viewing patterns and habits over to industry in exchange for cost-free or affordable access and productions designed to appeal to specific taste structures. Advertising remains an important factor in this economic model, but viewers can also pay to receive less of it, or none at all (as with DVDs). Even though financing models are changed, however, power relations do not shift. If anything, they become even more asymmetrical. Chapter 6 then moved on to discuss YouTube as a technology that heavily influenced how online television developed—despite its discursive linking to Web 2.0 and social media rather than television. The BBC iPlayer and Hulu developed as catch-up services to broadcast television. Limited to specific geographical regions, they signal how the international television industry intended to move its business online without significantly impacting on the national circumscription of television broadcasting.

Part II analysed Netflix more specifically and the relationships of power and control enabled by the concept of binge-watching. The concept of binge-watching implies autonomous scheduling and, therefore, a power relationship where the individual viewer exercises control. Yet, the way Netflix uses the concept of binge-watching to structure, brand and market itself suggests that the control given to viewers is shaped and controlled by Netflix. Chapter 8 discussed the way Netflix uses binge-watching to organise itself into Perks' model of insulated flow and entrance flow (2015). A particular focus is on the strategies used to establish entrance flow, largely through Netflix' recommendation algorithm. Binge-watching allows Netflix to create an organisational structure to nudge viewers towards specific decisions and explain how to watch it. This emphasis on the privileging of binge-watching heavily influences how other streamers organise potential viewer choices and interfaces, making Netflix' influence on the structures of streaming obvious. As explored in Chapter 9, then, binge-watching is central to the Netflix brand, which first positioned itself by exploiting a linkage between 'quality' television and binge-watching. Netflix' close association with binge-watching and its normalisation as a viewing practice (see Jenner 2019) may also serve to explain the way its competitors largely avoid using the term. The chapter then moved on to explore issues of 'quality' and cultural value through Netflix' comedy strand. The relationship between Netflix' sitcoms, opening credits and binge-watching is particularly important here. This is largely linked to the relationship of 'quality' TV and binge-watching, which is complicated when genres associated with more popular, formulaic narratives are produced for binge-watching. The complicated role of opening credits and their dissonance with Netflix sitcoms formulates this tension in a particularly obvious manner. Chapter 10 then developed a closer understanding of the Netflix brand via its marketing in 2013 through star Kevin Spacey and *auteur* figure Mitch Hurwitz. Since 2015, however, Netflix has moved its brand towards the concept of diversity by focussing on female-led sitcoms, racial and linguistic diversity or questioning heteronormativity. This may be linked to its broader transnational outlook, following a vast expansion project between 2014 and 2016. Nevertheless, Netflix' concept of diversity remains tied to an American definition of the term, linking in with nationally specific cultural, historical or economic conditions. More recently, Netflix has adopted a visibility politics that allows it to emphasise the visual signifiers of diversity more than focussing on cultural change.

The more global outlook is explored in depth in Part III on Netflix as transnational broadcaster. Netflix' combination of online distribution and binge-watching, meaning it is independent from geopolitical and cultural organisations of time, positions it differently as transnational broadcaster than satellite broadcasters. Yet, Netflix does not abandon notions of an ideological system of 'the nation' but integrates into national media systems. Chapter 12 explored this positioning in more detail by looking at how the binge model as a publication model is transnationally inclusive of a variety of national contexts. It then moved on to develop an understanding of how it negotiates transnationalism on a textual level and how it offers texts up for domestication via translation. The transnational streaming franchise is only set to grow in importance, not just due to the centrality of diegetic universes on Disney+, but Netflix is also set to extend this, most recently by publishing a reality show based on *Squid Game*. Amazon's recent forays into adapting different films and dramas for different cultural contexts (as with its *Modern Love* franchise) also speak to the centrality of this thinking. Chapter 13 carried this further by exploring how Netflix and other streamers organise transnational networks of meaning via the use of existing industry concepts of franchises and formats to construct what I have called here transnational streaming franchises. Chapter 14 developed a concept of a transnational 'Netflix audience' to understand how its audience is distinct from traditional mass media audiences. This has consequences for the way power and control are distributed between audience, national media systems and Netflix. Control over schedules is given to the audience in exchange for incredibly detailed data on individual viewing behaviour. Other streamers have adopted Netflix' secrecy on audience data, which largely makes sense considering that, as argued in the Introduction to the Second Edition, different streaming services often have diverging goals. Yet, national media policies control how Netflix operates: policy, national audiences' demand for domestic programmes or imports, national conventions for alterations of imported texts (such as translation) or national marketing campaigns, heavily influence how Netflix is shaped and perceived in different countries. As the example of Poland shows, Netflix' neoliberal impetus for growth has led it to offer significant control to various national media industries. For example, the early availability of Polish as translation language indicates that Netflix' 'grammar of transnationalism' can be (potentially) mitigated via the norms of national media industries, shaped by national official and unofficial regulations. Thus, 'the nation', as ideological construct, is unavoidable, be it through strict norms for (self-) censorship or less strict translation systems. On the other hand, the choice (over content and language) and control given to audiences also has the power to interrogate national media systems, as transnational audiences (albeit fragmented) organise across borders. Netflix' transnationalism shows ways in which it challenges and conforms to national media systems. The detailed data on viewing behaviour collected by

Netflix also influences what programming is developed based on the preferences of transnational, rather than national audiences. Yet, it is complicated to determine what potential effects this can have on national and transnational power structures.

Netflix and the Re-invention of Television explored different kinds of control that emerge in the analysis of Netflix. The regimes of control discussed here are mostly over the schedule of commercial television. Netflix' relationship with control is grounded in a specific history of television, its ancillary technologies, the symbolic power of these technologies within broader cultural discourses, real or imagined possibilities of communication and negotiation of power relations between audience and industry and its role as convergence medium. Following on from this history, it is hardly surprising that binge-watching takes on such a prominent position. This suggests that, even though binge-watching was an audience practice prior to Netflix, it is more closely linked with the discourses of ancillary technologies than emerging as a 'natural' way to watch television. Netflix' marketing has constructed a discourse around binge-watching that suggests that this is what the 'evolved audience' Spacey likes to invoke wants or needs. As much as the pre-history of Netflix may suggest this, different regimes of control in relation to television and its ancillary technologies and neoliberalism point to the discursively manufactured nature of these needs. Binge-watching is also highly relevant for Netflix to integrate itself into transnational markets, as it implies that Netflix does not have to abide by the national norms of time (for example, how long school is, when work commonly starts or ends, what a common bedtime is, etc.). The way Netflix contributes to the project of TV IV, thus, hinges on concepts of control. Binge-watching, and specifically Netflix' use of it, is of high importance in this, as is the re-thinking of the transnational possibilities of the internet and its relationship with television. These are decidedly different from the interactive possibilities of social media or other communications media, largely due to the positioning of the television audience.

The emphasis on Netflix and control limits the discussion in this book to largely exclude processes of democracy, nationalism and individuation of television. This is not to deny the importance of these areas in contemporary culture. In fact, the discussions in this book on the history of ancillary technologies, binge-watching and transnationalism and their framing through neoliberalism may contribute to these debates, even if they are not the focus here. As argued in the introduction, Netflix is not the only force in the reconception of television, but it is, nevertheless, a powerful one. For example, Netflix' use of binge-watching has mainstreamed the term to the extent that other streamers still avoid using it. Binge-watching and the way it has been used by Netflix as a structuring force, in marketing and branding is important to the way TV IV is reconceptualised. This highlights Netflix' importance to the developments of TV IV. As this suggests, Netflix is only one of the processes of TV IV.

Netflix and the Re-invention of Television describes some areas of the processes of TV IV where Netflix is significant. Yet, Netflix is only one piece of a broader puzzle that is in need of constant interrogation as the process of TV IV moves forward. As such, *Netflix and the Re-invention of Television* understands itself as a contribution to an ongoing debate about TV IV and Netflix' role within it. As Netflix' economic importance recedes, its influence may also change. However, its influence is already visible in the regimes of control streaming employs, in the function and importance of binge-watching and Netflix' role as transnational broadcaster. This contribution is of importance as it establishes how exactly Netflix needs to be understood as television and how it reconceptualises what television is. By establishing an increasingly direct system for the negotiation of power between viewers and commercial television and finding new ways to apply and interpret this data and continuously moving away from national television systems, Netflix plays an important part in reconceptualising television in a TV IV era.

Revisiting *Netflix and the Re-invention of Television* in 2023, and assessing the company's role in the streaming wars, I have come to understand it as a significant contribution in understanding what streaming is, and how it develops. Many of the infrastructures of streaming have been developed by Netflix and its role in conceptualising it cannot be underestimated, as the continued interest in the platform shows. As fast as technological and cultural realities shift in the TV IV era, Netflix remains an important element of this and is likely to remain so. Its approach to programming and diversity have moved it more and more to a more 'middlebrow' understanding of culture, which moves it more towards what is often understood as 'normality' within culture. Within the so-called streaming wars, this positions Netflix in interesting ways, especially in relation to Disney+ and its back catalogue.

Bibliography

Andrejevic, Mark, and Hye Jin Lee. 2014. "Second-Screen Theory: From the Democratic Surround to the Digital Enclosure." In Jennifer Holt and Kevin Sanson (ed.), *Connected Viewing: Selling, Streaming, & Sharing Media in the Digital Era*, 40–61. London: Routledge.

Androutsopoulos, Jannis, and Jessica Weidenhöffer. 2015. "Zuschauer-Engagement Auf Twitter: Handlungskategorien Der Rezeptionsbegleitenden Kommunikation Am Beispiel Von #tatort." *In Zeitschrift Für Angewandte Linguistik* 62 (1): 23–59.

Anstead, Nick, and Ben O'Loughlin. 2011. "The Emerging Viewertariat and BBC Question Time." *The International Journal of Press/politics* 16 (4): 440–62.

Carr, D. 2013. "With 'Alpha House,' Amazon Makes Bid for Living Room Screens and Beyond." In *The New York Times*. Available online http://www.nytimes.com/2013/11/04/business/media/with-alpha-house-amazon-makes-bid-for-living-room.html?smid=tw-nytmedia&seid=auto&_r=2&pagewanted=all&, Accessed on: 03.01.2015.

Harrington, Stephen, Axel Bruns, and Tim Highfield. 2013. "More than a Backchannel: Twitter and Television." *Participations* 10 (1): 405–409.

Jenner, Mareike. 2019. "Control Issues: Binge-Watching, Channel-Surfing and Cultural Value." *Participations* 16 (2): 298–317.

Perks, Lisa Glebatis. 2015. *Media Marathoning: Immersions in Morality*. Lanham, Maryland: Lexington Books.

Tussey, Ethan. 2014. "Connected Viewing on the Second Screen: The Limitations of the Living Room." In Jennifer Holt and Kevin Sanson (ed.), *Connected Viewing: Selling, Streaming, & Sharing Media in the Digital Era*, 202–16. London: Routledge.

TV

Squid Game (2021–), KR: Netflix

Index

M. Jenner, *Netflix and the Re-invention of Television*, https://doi.org/10.1007/978-3-031-39237-5

Printed by Printforce, the Netherlands